# DOS 6 for the Guru Wanna-Be

# The DOS Guru's Crib Sheet

## Using the *DIR* Command

The `DIR` command displays a list of files and subdirectories. Using the following options, you can tell DOS what kind of files or directories to display, and how to sort them.

### DIR *Attribute Options*

| Use | To List |
|---|---|
| `/AA` | Files with their archive attribute set |
| `/AD` | Directories only |
| `/AH` | Hidden files |
| `/AR` | Read-only files |
| `/AS` | System files |

### DIR *Sorting Options*

| Use | To |
|---|---|
| `/OD` | Sort by date (oldest to newest) |
| `/OE` | Sort by extension (a to z) |
| `/OG` | Display subdirectories first |
| `/ON` | Sort by name (a to z) |
| `/OS` | Sort by size (smallest to largest) |

## Customizing the Prompt

You can customize the appearance of the DOS command prompt by entering `PROMPT` and then any combination of metastrings. For example, `PROMPT $d$t` displays the date and then the time.

| Metastring | Use It To |
|---|---|
| `$p` | Display the current drive and directory |
| `$n` | Display the current drive only |
| `$d` | Display the current date |
| `$t` | Display the current time |
| `$v` | Display the DOS version number |
| `$g` | Display the greater-than sign (>) |
| `$l` | Display the less-than sign (<) |
| `$b` | Display the pipe symbol (\|) |
| `$q` | Display an equal sign (=) |
| `$$` | Display a dollar sign ($) |
| `$_` | Move the cursor to a new line |
| `$h` | Backspace (and delete) one character |
| `$e` | Set the cursor position and screen colors |

If you have the ANSI.SYS device driver installed in your CONFIG.SYS file, you can also use the `PROMPT` command to set text attributes and colors on your screen. The syntax is:

```
PROMPT $e[text-attribute;text-color;background-colorm
```

For example, `PROMPT $e[1;33;44m` gives you bold yellow text on a blue background.

| Value | Attribute |
|---|---|
| 0 | Turns off all text attributes |
| 1 | Makes screen characters bold |
| 2 | Makes screen characters normal |
| 4 | Displays characters underlined (on monochrome screens only) |
| 5 | Makes characters blink on and off |
| 7 | Reverses foreground and background colors |
| 8 | Hides characters |

| Color | Text | Background |
|---|---|---|
| Black | 30 | 40 |
| Red | 31 | 41 |
| Green | 32 | 42 |
| Yellow | 33 | 43 |
| Blue | 34 | 44 |
| Magenta | 35 | 45 |
| Cyan | 36 | 46 |
| White | 37 | 47 |

# DOSKEY Commands

The DOSKEY command lets you recall commands you've entered earlier, and then edit them. To install this useful guru tool, just enter DOSKEY.

## DOSKEY Command Recall Keys

| Press | To |
|---|---|
| Page Up | Recall the oldest command in the list |
| Page Down | Recall the newest command in the list |
| F7 | Display the entire command list |
| Alt+F7 | Delete all commands from the recall list |
| F8 | Have DOSKEY recall a command that begins with the letter or letters you've typed on the command line |
| F9 | Have DOSKEY prompt you for a command list number (you can see the numbers with the F7 key); type the number and press Enter to recall the command |

## DOSKEY Command-Line Editing Keys

| Press | To |
|---|---|
| Left arrow | Move the cursor one character to the left |
| Right arrow | Move the cursor one character to the right |
| Ctrl+left arrow | Move the cursor one word to the left |
| Ctrl+right arrow | Move the cursor one word to the right |
| Home | Move the cursor to the beginning of the line |
| End | Move the cursor to the end of the line |
| Delete | Delete the character over the cursor |
| Backspace | Delete the character to the left of the cursor |
| Ctrl+Home | Delete from the cursor to the beginning of the line |
| Ctrl+End | Delete from the cursor to the end of the line |
| Insert | Toggle DOSKEY between "insert" mode (your typing is inserted between existing letters on the command line) and "overstrike" mode (your typing replaces existing letters on the command line) |

# Switches for the *REPLACE* Command

The REPLACE command replaces files in one directory with files of the same name in another directory. For example, `REPLACE a:*.* c:\ /S /U` compares all the files on a disk in drive A: with matching filenames on drive C:, and then replace only the ones that have changed.

| Use | To |
|---|---|
| /A | Add missing files to the target directory |
| /P | Get prompted for confirmation before replacing a file |
| /R | Replace read-only files |
| /S | Replace matching files in subdirectories |
| /U | Replace only files that are older |
| /W | Have REPLACE wait before starting |

# DOS 6 for the Guru Wanna-Be

Paul McFedries

SAMS PUBLISHING

A Division of Prentice Hall Computer Publishing
11711 North College,
Carmel, Indiana 46032 USA

*To Daryl Sharp, a wise guru who showed me how to see what was in front of my face.*



FIRST EDITION



International Standard Book Number: 0-672-30349-3

Library of Congress Catalog Card Number: 92-83592

96 95 94 93 4 3 2 1

Interpretation of the printing code: the rightmost double-digit number is the year of the book's printing; the rightmost single-digit, the number of the book's printing. For example, a printing code of 93-1 shows that the first printing of the book occurred in 1993.



Composed in MCPdigital by Prentice Hall Computer Publishing

Printed in the United States of America

**Publisher**
*Richard K. Swadley*

**Acquisitions Manager**
*Jordan Gold*

**Acquisitions Editor**
*Gregg Bushyeager*

**Development Editor**
*Mark Taber*

**Senior Editor**
*Grant Fairchild*

**Editorial Coordinator**
*Rebecca S. Freeman*

**Editorial Assistant**
*Sharon Cox*

**Formatter**
*Bill Whitmer*

**Technical Reviewer**
*Bill Candow*

**Marketing Manager**
*Greg Wiegand*

**Director of Production and Manufacturing**
*Jeff Valler*

**Production Manager**
*Corinne Walls*

**Imprint Manager**
*Kelli Widdifield*

**Book Designer**
*Michele Laseau*

**Production Analyst**
*Mary Beth Wakefield*

**Proofreading/Indexing Coordinator**
*Joelynn Gifford*

**Graphics Image Specialists**
*Dennis Sheehan*
*Susan VandeWalle*

**Production**
*Christine Cook*
*Lisa Daughtery*
*Mitzi Gianakos*
*Howard Jones*
*Julie Pavey*
*Linda Quigley*
*Barbara Webster*
*Donna Winter*
*Alyssa Yesh*

**Indexer**
*Jeannie Clark*

# OVERVIEW

## Part I Guru File and Hard Disk Management



## Part II Batch Files: The DOS Guru's Best Friend



## Part III Guru Style: Customizing DOS



## Part IV
## Taking DOS to a Higher Plane of Existence

## Part V Guru Doo-Doo: Troubleshooting DOS

# Contents

## Guru File and Hard Disk Management

# Batch Files: The DOS Guru's Best Friend

## Guru Style: Customizing DOS



## Taking DOS to a Higher Plane of Existence

# Guru Doo-Doo: Troubleshooting DOS

# Acknowledgments

Many kudos and hurrahs go to the Sams' editorial gurus for their high-quality work. In particular, I'd like to thank Acquisitions Editor Gregg Bushyeager for his patience (especially when his author takes off on vacation just before he's about to start a book), Development Editor Mark Taber for his insightful comments, and Senior Editor Grant Fairchild and Technical Editor Jim McCarter for tactfully pointing out the error of my ways.

# About the Author

Paul McFedries' first clash with a computer came in high school in 1975. It was one of those classes that taught "programming" by making you fill in absurdly small boxes on computer cards. These were then sent out to some mysterious location each night where some nasty behemoth of a computer would spit out any cards with marks outside of the lines. This conflicted miserably with McFedries' natural messiness, so it took about a month to get the evil beast to do anything.

Despite this inauspicious beginning, McFedries stuck with computers, and, thanks to countless, ill-advised all-nighters hacking out programs, he is now a guru computer consultant and the author of 10 computer books. McFedries lives in Toronto, but he is open to offers of accommodation in a warmer clime. He has no cats and his favorite hobbies are taking naps and writing blurbs about himself.

# Introduction

So, you want to be a DOS guru? You want to join the computer equivalent of Phi Beta Kappa and become one of the electronically enlightened? Well, who can blame you? After all, just think of the benefits:

- Your friends and family will burst with pride at your newfound knowledge.
- Your colleagues will be in awe of your unparalleled expertise.
- Your boss will be mightily impressed with your heightened competence.

What's that? You were hoping for something more along the lines of fame and fortune. Hey, with DOS, *anything* can happen!

## Just What the Heck Is a DOS Guru, Anyway?

That's a good question. Does being a DOS guru mean memorizing reams of arcane information? No (unless you want to). Does it mean hours of grueling study? Uh, uh. Does it mean you have to wear a pocket protector and eat Doritos and pizza all day? *Definitely* not.

No, above all, being a DOS guru is a state of mind. It means realizing that DOS is, if nothing else, a series of challenges (to put the best face on things). The average user bumps up against DOS' notoriously cryptic commands and snaggled syntax, and just moans and complains about how "unfriendly" DOS is. The guru, on the other hand, refuses to be cowed. The guru knows that DOS, although it doesn't yield easily, *can* be tamed. All it takes is patience and a willing mind.

Why bother with DOS in this era of shells and fancy-shmancy graphical user interfaces? One word: *speed*. Once you're comfortable with DOS' intricacies (which doesn't take very long), *nothing* is as fast as the command line. Yes, gurus take advantage of the amazing new applications designed for Windows and the like, but when they need to do anything serious, they always return to DOS. And besides, no matter what anybody's using as an interface, DOS is still the underlying operating system. If things go wrong (and things *always* go wrong), the more comfortable you are in DOS, the better your chances of getting up and running again quickly. DOS rules!

# Who Should Read This Book?

Another good question. Being a DOS guru is, obviously, not for everyone. Most of the 60 million or so DOS users are happy in their ignorance, and they should stay that way. Some of us, though, need to know more. You should read this book if:

- You've used DOS for a while, but you'd like to know more about what's going on and you'd like to get beyond the basics. This book gives you a more comprehensive initiation into DOS' mysteries.
- You've never used DOS, but consider yourself a quick study and don't want to slog through a book for rank beginners. Although this book assumes a minimal level of knowledge (such as how to turn on your machine and how to enter commands), you should be able to pick up what you need as you go along.
- You want to become the Office DOS Guru and have others grovel at your desk, begging for scraps of DOS lore.
- You've read a beginning-level book or two, but the typical hold-the-hand-of-the-poor-sensitive-user approach is wearing thin.
- You're no dummy and you hate it when books treat you like one.

# How This Book Is Organized

This book is definitely not meant to be read from cover-to-cover. Although I won't object if you start at page 1 and work your way through, I encourage you to leap around from topic to topic as your needs or interests dictate. Above all, don't be afraid to experiment. Playing with DOS (as opposed to *working* with it) is, more than anything, the royal road to DOS guruhood.

To make it easier to approach things non-linearly, I've set the book up so that most chapters can stand alone. However, some topics, out of necessity, are built upon previously learned knowledge. Forthwith (I love using words like that, although I promise not to succumb to this urge too often), the following sections contain a brief overview of the book and some reading hints.

## Part I—Guru File and Hard Disk Management

This section includes chapters on working with files, directories, your hard disk, and floppy disks. These chapters can be read willy-nilly, but I'd highly recommend, in particular, Chapter 5, "Working with a Net: Backing Up Your Files," because it takes you through the all-important task of backing up your files.

## Part II—Batch Files: The DOS Guru's Best Friend

The three chapters in this section are probably the only ones in the book that should be read sequentially. Chapter 6, "Batch File Basics," starts you off with some batch file basics, and then Chapter 7, "Using Variables for Batch File Flexibility," and Chapter 8, "Making Smart Batch Files," build on that knowledge. Also, many chapters later in the book use batch file examples, so a skim through this material will help you later on.

## Part III—Guru Style: Customizing DOS

DOS doesn't have a ton of customization options, but the ones that it does have can be both fun and powerful. Again, some of the techniques from this section—particularly the DOSKEY macros discussed in Chapter 11, "Customizing the Command Line with DOSKEY"—are used later in the book.

## Part IV—Taking DOS to a Higher Plane of Existence

Things really kick into high gear with the six chapters in this section. The first three chapters deal with CONFIG.SYS and AUTOEXEC.BAT files, which is crucial information that no guru should miss. Also, Chapter 15, "Memory Management Made Easy," is a must for gurus who want to maximize their PC's scarce memory resources.

## Part V—Guru Doo-Doo: Troubleshooting DOS

This section is about DOS problems, but two of the five chapters concentrate on preventing problems. I'd recommend that you read Chapter 18, "The Guru's Survival Kit," early on so you'll be in a better position to recover from DOS dilemmas, should they strike.

You'll also find a number of appendices in the back of the book. These include "20 Tips and Tricks Every DOS Guru Should Know,". (Appendix A) and a glossary of guru terms (see Appendix B).

# Features of This Book

*DOS 6 for the Guru Wanna-Be* is designed so you can quickly get the information you need and then go show off to someone. If you ever need to type something, it appears like this:

```
type this
```

General commands (ones that you don't have to type right away) appear like this:

COMMAND *filename* [switches]

The stuff in italics is parameters or switches you fill in yourself, and anything in square brackets is optional.

Also, look for the following icons that will help you learn just what you need to know:

These boxes contain DOS tips and tricks designed to instill feelings of awe and admiration in your friends and colleagues.

This icon gives you in-depth technical information that'll help you understand what you're doing (a guru necessity). People around you will be *very* impressed that you know this stuff.

DOS gives all of us lots of ways to look like dunces. These icons help you avoid that ignominious fate.

DOS, being the imperfect beast that it is, has inspired a huge market for third-party programs and utilities. This icon tells you about some of these tools and what advantages they offer. See Appendix E, "Guru Tools Directory," for a list of the names and addresses of products featured in these boxes.

# Guru File and Hard Disk Management

# PART I

# Guru File Management

## Guru Stuff in This Chapter ➤

1

CHAPTER

- *Important information on filenames and wildcards*
- *Little known facts about the* COPY *command*
- *Safe methods for deleting files (and how to undelete them, just in case)*
- *All kinds of file management tips and tricks*
- *Strange but true tales of procrustean beds, kiwi fruit, and steroids*

Once you've used your computer for a while, you'll soon notice that your files seem to multiply like rabbits. Oh, it all starts innocently enough—DOS and whatever utilities came with your machine probably accounted for no more than a couple of hundred files. But things can get quickly out of hand once you start loading some of today's humongous programs. To give you an idea, my machine currently has a little more than four thousand files (that's right, four *thousand*), and I would say I only have an average number of programs.

Clearly then, the DOS guru wanna-be's first task should be to learn how to maintain some sort of control over all those files. This chapter gives you some file fundamentals that every DOS guru should know. Chapter 2, "Guru Directory Management," extends things a bit and gives you a few more advanced techniques in directory management.

**Guru Tip**

> Want to know how many files are on your computer? Well, you could just run a **DIR** command in all your directories and add up the numbers, but I'm assuming you have things to do over the next week or so. Instead, run the **CHKDSK** command. After chugging away for a few seconds, you'll see all kinds of bizarre information on your screen (see Chapter 19, "The Guru's Survival Kit," for the lowdown on this information), but the line you want will look something like this (your numbers will be different):
>
> ```
> 147464092 bytes in 4014 user files
> ```
>
> The number of user files is, approximately, the number of files on your computer.

# "I Can Name That File in 8.3 Characters!"

DOS, being the cryptic beast that it is, often forces us into some pretty uncomfortable straightjackets. Perhaps the worst of these is its procrustean filename conventions. (In case you're wondering, Procrustes was a robber in Greek mythology who forced his victims to fit into a bed by either stretching those who were too small or lopping off pieces of those who were too big. Nice fellow.)

DOS filenames generally consist of a *primary name* and an optional *extension* separated by a period. The primary name describes the contents of the file, and the extension usually tells you what type of file you're dealing with. Common extensions are TXT (text files), DOC (word processing documents), DBF (database files), WKS (worksheets), BAT (batch files), and EXE or COM (executable files). So, for example, you could guess that a file named RUTABAGA.TXT was a text file containing information about rutabagas.

This all sounds very reasonable until you run into the various restrictions DOS imposes on filenames. There are three important ones to remember:

- Primary names must be no longer than 8 characters.
- Extensions must be no longer than 3 characters.
- You can't use a space or any of the following characters:

```
+ = \ ¦ [ ] ; : , . < > ? /
```

Dunce

As if these restrictions weren't enough, DOS also has a number of reserved words that you can't use for filenames because DOS uses them internally: AUX, CLOCK$, COM1, COM2, COM3, CON, LPT1, LPT2, LPT3, NUL, and PRN.

This format (DOS gurus call it the 8.3 filename format) doesn't exactly lend itself to legibility. Look through anybody's computer, and you're bound to see files with cryptic names like 2QTRP&L.WK1 or INVTRY93.DBF. (Names like these make me think we ought to call it the "buy a vowel" filename format.)

Guru Trivia

Since the 8.3 format is so restrictive, why doesn't Microsoft change it? Well, because this new version of DOS would be completely incompatible with all the previous ones! The problem is that this format is used internally in several important DOS data structures. For example, the directory entry that DOS creates for each file is 32 bytes long, but only the first 11 bytes can be used for the filename and extension. Changing the filename format would render these directory entries (and all the DOS programs that use them) obsolete. All is not lost, however. If you have the horsepower, OS/2 gives you 254-character filenames *and* DOS compatibility. Microsoft's NT operating system also runs DOS applications, and it literally goes OS/2 one better by offering 255-character filenames.

# True Gurus Do It with Wildcards

The wildcard characters `?` and `*` are powerful little shortcuts that any DOS guru worth his or her salt should be able to wield like a surgeon's knife. The question mark is designed to substitute for a single character in a filename. Consider, for example, the command `dir foo?.txt`. This command tells DOS to display a directory listing for those files that meet the following criteria:

- The primary name begins with FOO.
- They have any character for the fourth letter (or even no character at all).
- The primary name is at least 3 characters long (the three given letters) but no more than 4 characters long (the three letters plus the wildcard).
- They end with the extension TXT.

Not bad for a punctuation mark! This command would find (if they exist) files named FOOD.TXT, FOOL.TXT, FOOT.TXT, and even FOO.TXT. It would *not* find files named FO.TXT (too short), FOOLISH.TXT (too long), or FOOD.DOC (the wrong extension).

Although the question mark substitutes for only a single character, you're free to use it more than once in a name to substitute for multiple characters. For example, the command `dir ?o?ato.doc` would find TOMATO.DOC and POTATO.DOC (but not POTATOE.DOC).

The star (also known as the asterisk) substitutes for a group of characters. For example, `*.DBF` would represent all files that have any old primary name combined with the DBF extension. One of the most common uses of this wildcard is the `*.*` combination (pronounced star-dot-star), which represents files that have any primary name and any extension—in other words, every file. This is handy, for example, if you want to copy all the files in the current directory to a floppy disk in drive A. You just type `copy *.* a:`, and DOS does the rest.

Most people just use the star to substitute for entire primary names or extensions. But gurus know that the star comes in quite handy when you need to substitute for a group of characters inside a name. For example, you might be tempted to use, say, `A???????.TXT` to represent all text files that begin with the letter *A*, but there's an easier way. Just use `A*.TXT`, instead.

**Guru Tip**

> Keep wildcards in mind when you name your files. If you use a similar structure for related files (for example, 3Q93RENT.WKS, 4Q93RENT.WKS, and 1Q94RENT.WKS), then it makes it easy to use ? or * to work with the files you need.

# Guru File Copying

The `COPY` command is the workhorse of most people's DOS command stable. Whether it's copying files to or from a floppy disk or duplicating files on your hard disk, `COPY` gets quite a workout compared to most other DOS commands. However, did you know the following:

- That when you're copying large files or more than one file, you should use `XCOPY` instead?
- That you also can use `COPY` to create small text files from scratch?
- That you can use `COPY` to combine two files into a single file?

## Real Gurus Use *XCOPY*

If you want to copy a large file (one that's greater than 64K) or if you have more than one file to copy, you can speed things up by using DOS' `XCOPY` command instead of `COPY`.

> Why is XCOPY faster? Well, COPY works by reading a file, copying it, and then repeating the process. XCOPY, however, reads in as much data as the available memory in your computer will allow and only then copies everything to the destination.

In its basic form, XCOPY works just like COPY. So, for example, to copy all the BAT files in the current directory to a directory called BATCH in drive D:, use the following command:

```
xcopy *.bat d:\batch
```

Besides being faster, XCOPY also contains a number of features not found in the puny COPY command. Think of it as COPY on steroids. (The X in XCOPY means that it's an extended COPY command.) For example, suppose you want to copy all the BAT files in the current directory and all the BAT files in any attached subdirectories to D:\BATCH. With COPY, you first have to create the appropriate directories on the floppy disk and then perform separate COPY commands for each directory—way too much work! With XCOPY, all you do is add a single switch:

```
xcopy *.bat d:\batch /s
```

The /S switch tells DOS to copy the current directory and all nonempty subdirectories, and to create the appropriate directories on the destination disk, as needed. Now that's easy!

> If you want XCOPY to copy empty subdirectories, include the /E switch, as well.

Another useful feature of XCOPY is the ability to copy files by date. This is handy for performing incremental backups of files that you modified on or after a specific date. For example, suppose you keep your word processing documents in a directory called \WP\DOCS, and you want to make a backup copy (to a disk in drive B:) of all the DOC files that have changed since March 15, 1993. No problem. Just enter the following command:

```
xcopy c:\wp\docs\*.doc b: /d:03-15-93
```

In this case, you use the `/D` switch, followed by a colon (:), followed by the date in `MM-DD-YY` format. Cool.

## Using *COPY* to Create a Text File

You normally use a text editor or your word processor to create text files, but these can sometimes feel like overkill if you're only creating a file that's a few lines long (such as a simple batch file). Instead, you can use the `COPY` command to handle these quick-and-dirty jobs. For example, suppose you want to create a file called SMALL.TXT. To get started, use a command called `CON`:

```
copy con small.txt
```

When you press Enter, the cursor moves to the next line and awaits your input. Type each line you want to include in the file (you need to press Enter after each line). When you're done, press F6 and Enter to tell DOS that you're finished.

> When you press F6, the characters `^Z` appear on-screen (you get the same thing if you hold down the Ctrl key and press Z). This is called the *end-of-file marker*, and it simply tells DOS (and any other program that might read the file) that this is where the file ends.

What's going on here? Well, `CON` is the DOS name for your computer's *console* (which normal people refer to as the keyboard). This command simply tells DOS to copy everything you type into a file called SMALL.TXT.

> The problem with **COPY CON** is that, once you've pressed Enter, whatever line you were working on becomes etched in stone (unless, of course, you load the file into a text editor later on). For this reason, be sure there are no mistakes in a line before you press Enter. If you do see an error, use the Backspace key to wipe it out.

## Using *COPY* to Combine Text Files

One little known use of the COPY command is to use the plus sign (+) to combine (or, to use the proper guru term, *concatenate*) two or more text files. Suppose, for example, that you're working on your kiwi fruit dissertation and you have it broken up into two files called KIWI1.TXT and KIWI2.TXT. To concatenate both files into a new file called KIWI.TXT, use the following command:

```
copy kiwi1.txt + kiwi2.txt kiwi.txt
```

Just so you know, the destination file (KIWI.TXT, in this case) isn't necessary. You could just use the following command:

```
copy kiwi1.txt + kiwi2.txt
```

and DOS would simply add KIWI2.TXT to the end of KIWI1.TXT.

Guru Tip

Need to add just one or two lines to an existing text file? Don't bother loading your text editor. Instead, you can combine the **COPY CON** and concatenation techniques. For example, to add lines to a file called NOTDONE.TXT, enter the following command:

```
copy notdone.txt + con
```

Enter your lines, and then press F6 and Enter. DOS appends the new lines to the end of the file.

If you use **COPY** to create a new file, DOS gives the new file the same date stamp as the old file. If you prefer the new file to have today's date, you can use a concatenation trick. If the file is called TODAY.TXT, enter the following command:

```
copy today.txt +,,
```

The two commas tell DOS that you're not actually concatenating anything to TODAY.TXT, but DOS goes ahead anyway and creates a new TODAY.TXT file (the same as the old one) and gives it today's date.

# Guru File Moving

For years, DOS gurus bemoaned the fact that DOS had no command that would move a file from one location to another. Instead, you first had to copy the file to the new destination and then delete it from the old one. This was a pain, so an entire cottage industry was created by computer geeks trying to find the best way to move a file using batch commands.

DOS 6 changes all that thanks to its new `MOVE` command. You use `MOVE` just like you use `COPY`. So, for example, to move a file called MOVEME.WKS from your \123\OLD directory to a directory called \123\NEW, use the following command:

```
move c:\123\old\moveme.wks c:\123\new
```

# Guru File Deleting

Deleting files is a straightforward—although potentially dangerous—business. You just use the `DEL` command (`ERASE` does the same thing, but because it's longer, most DOS gurus never use it) and specify the file or files you want to delete. To make things a little safer, you can use `DEL`'s `/P` switch. For example, suppose you want to delete a file called USELESS.DOC from the directory \WP\DOCS. All you do is enter the following command:

```
del c:\wp\docs\useless.doc /p
```

and DOS responds with the following message:

```
c:\wp\docs\useless.doc,    Delete (Y/N)?
```

Type `y` to proceed with the deletion (or type `n` to cancel). The `/P` isn't all that useful for deleting a single file, but it can save you from yourself if you're using wildcards to delete multiple files.

If you have a lot of files to delete, it can be a real pain to have to respond to every prompt produced by the `/P` switch. Here's a trick you can use instead. First, check the files you'll be deleting by running the `DIR` command on the file specification. If everything looks okay, type **`del`** and then press F3 to redisplay the file specification. Now you can press Enter knowing that your deletion will proceed safely.

# To Err Is Human, to Undelete Divine

There are, it has been said, two types of computer users: those who've accidentally deleted files and those who will. In the old days, a deleted file was gone for good, but now, if you have DOS 5 or 6, you can use the life-saving `UNDELETE` command to recover lost files.

To understand how it's possible to undelete a file, you need to understand what DOS does when you ask it to delete the file in the first place. When you issue a `DEL` (or `ERASE`) command, DOS doesn't actually do anything to the file's contents. Instead, it simply marks the file's storage location as being available for another file to use (by replacing the file's first letter with another character). But you need to act quickly before any other file uses that location. The longer you wait, the less likely it is that you'll be able to recover the file.

Use the following steps to undelete a file:

1. Change to the directory that contained the file.
2. Type `undelete` followed by the name of the file you want to recover and press Enter. For example, to recover a file named VITAL.DOC, enter

undelete vital.doc. DOS checks its records, displays the file information, and asks if you want to undelete the file:

```
Directory C:\WP\CRUCIAL
File Specifications: VITAL.DOC
.
.
.
Using the MS-DOS directory method.

  ?ITAL  DOC   10435  3-17-93 11:18a  ...A Undelete (Y/N)?
```

3. Type y. DOS asks you to enter the first letter of the filename.
4. Just type the first letter of the filename and DOS recovers the file.

> This section just showed you the simplest method for undeleting files. For true guru undeleting, take a look at Chapter 19, "An Ounce of Prevention: How to Avoid Trouble."

# Guru Review

This chapter gave you the scoop on some guru file management techniques:

- DOS filenames follow the 8.3 filename format—the primary name must be no more than 8 characters long, the extension must be no longer than 3 characters, and the two parts must be separated by a period.
- Use wildcards to work easily with multiple files. The question mark (?) substitutes for single characters, and the star (*) substitutes for multiple characters.
- If you're copying a single file bigger than 64K, or if you're copying several files, use the faster XCOPY command instead of COPY.
- If you need to create a small text file fast, use the COPY CON command.

- Use `COPY` in conjunction with the plus sign (+) to concatenate two or more text files.
- If you have DOS 6, you can use the new `MOVE` command to easily move files from one location to another.
- For safer deleting, use `DEL` with the `/P` switch to force DOS to confirm each file. If you do make a mistake, use the `UNDELETE` command right away to recover the lost file.

# Guru Directory Management

2

CHAPTER

## Guru Stuff in This Chapter ➤

- *A refresher course in directories*
- *Tips on the best way to set up your directories*
- *Exploiting the power of the* `DIR` *command*
- *How to quickly copy, rename, and delete directories*
- *Miscellaneous ramblings on the Yellow Pages, gazebos, and those weird dot things*

Computers are set up so that everything, I mean *everything*, happens inside one directory or another. There's no avoiding them, so it pays to become friendly with them. As a DOS guru, you need to know three things:

- How to set up your directories logically and efficiently (even if you're not all that logical and efficient yourself).
- How to navigate your directories quickly and easily.
- The best ways to maintain (i.e., copy, rename, and delete) your directories.

# First, a Review of the Basics

Think of all the businesses in your town and imagine trying to contact any of them if you had no centralized listing of their addresses or phone numbers. It would be, at the very least, a nightmare. Fortunately, some genius at the phone company came up with the idea of the Yellow Pages directory, which is just an index of business names, addresses, and phone numbers.

Computer directories perform a similar function. They're really just an index of all the files on a hard drive or floppy disk. Without them, it would be virtually impossible to find and work with your programs and data.

## The Root of the Matter: the Root Directory

Whenever a disk is formatted, DOS creates a primary directory called the *root directory*. You can't, try as you may, assign a name to this directory, nor can you delete it. If you need to refer to the root directory, simply use a single backslash (\). For example, the command `dir \` gives you a directory listing of the root directory on the current drive. (Of course, if you're currently in the root directory, a simple `DIR` command will suffice.)

## Branching Out with Subdirectories

The Yellow Pages wouldn't do us a whole lot of good if the businesses were just listed willy-nilly. An alphabetical listing would be better, but it wouldn't help if, say, you needed a list of gazebo manufacturers. The beauty of the Yellow Pages is that the entries are subdivided into various subjects, such as automobiles, dentists, and, yes, even gazebos.

Computer disks work the same way. Stuffing all your files into the root directory not only makes it hard to find what you need, but because a single directory can't have more than one file with the same name, you could run into problems with name collisions.

**Guru Trivia**

> Another reason it doesn't pay to load all your files into the root directory is that DOS, bless its heart, imposes physical limitations on the number of entries in the root. When you format a disk, DOS sets aside a section of the disk for the root directory and the size of this area is set in stone. The maximum number of files varies depending on the size and capacity of the disk, but, in practice, you're looking at a limit of between 112 and 512 files. That's not much.

The solution is to use *subdirectories* to store related files. So, for example, all your DOS files are probably stored together in a "DOS" subdirectory (designated, if it's on drive C:, as C:\DOS), and you could have separate subdirectories for your word processor, spreadsheet, database, and so on.

**Guru Tip**

> A subdirectory is also sometimes called a *child* directory (aw, how cute), and so, as you might expect, the root becomes the *parent* directory. Subdirectories can have children of their own (in which case the root becomes the *grandparent*), and these children can have children, ad infinitum.

This network of directories and subdirectories is called a *tree* with the root directory at the base (hence its name) and the subdirectories branching out from there. If you would like to get a visual representation of your own directory tree, change to the root directory (by typing `cd\` and pressing Enter) and then run DOS' `TREE` command. Figure 2.1 contains a listing produced by the `TREE` command.

**Figure 2.1.**
The output of the TREE command.

```
E:\>tree
Directory PATH listing
Volume Serial Number is 1992-A624
E:.
├───DOS
├───WP
│   └───DOCS
│       ├───BUSINESS
│       └───PERSONAL
├───123
│   ├───SALES
│   └───EXPENSES
└───DBASE
    ├───CLIENTS
    └───INVENTRY

E:\>
```

If your tree listing goes zipping off the screen, you can pause it by piping it through the **MORE** filter like so:

```
tree ¦ more
```

For more information on handy DOS procedures such as piping and filters, see Chapter 17, "The Fun Stuff II: Advanced DOS Techniques."

# Pathnames

You may not be able to assign a name to the root, but you can create names for any other directory. (Note, however, that you're stuck with the same restrictions on directory names that I outlined for filenames in the last chapter.) The directory name by itself, however, is not enough to distinguish it from the pack. In the Yellow Pages, for example, a "Leasing" section doesn't tell us much (leasing what—trains, planes, automobiles?). Similarly, a STUFF directory doesn't mean anything unless you know what "stuff" you're dealing with (databases, spreadsheets, Pac Man?).

To remedy this, you need to specify the directory's *pathname*, which is a list of names of the parents and grandparents of the directory. For example, \DBASE\STUFF is the pathname for a directory called STUFF, which is the child of the DBASE directory, which is a child of the root directory (designated by the leading \).

**Guru Tip**

> Does DOS just show you a simple C> prompt no matter which directory you're in? If so, you can replace this brain-dead prompt with one that tells you the current directory by entering the following command:
>
> `prompt $p$g`
>
> See Chapter 9, "Customizing the Prompt," for the scoop on this and other cool `PROMPT` commands.

# Directory Structure Tips

DOS gurus know that an efficient and logical directory tree can not only make their computers easier to use, but can speed things up as well. To that end, here are a few tips to get you on your way to directory guruhood:

## 1. Keep Your Root Directory as Clean as Possible

One of the telltale signs of a DOS guru's hard disk is a root directory that contains only a bare minimum of files. This ensures that you don't run into the file limitations inherent in all root directories (and it allows you to find the root's child directories easily). However, it's unavoidable to have at least a few files in the root directory, such as the DOS system files (IO.SYS and MSDOS.SYS), AUTOEXEC.BAT, and CONFIG.SYS. Also, some programs and utilities may have one or two files that need to be in the root.

## 2. Store Related Files Together

One of the best ways to organize your hard disk is to set up your directories so that related files are kept together. Depending on the programs you use, you could set up your directories according to the following guidelines:

- Create separate directories off the root for each major program you use.

- Set up a directory called UTIL and create subdirectories for all your utilities.
- If you have any games, create a GAMES directory with individual subdirectories for each game.
- Create a BATCH directory to store your batch files.

## 3. Keep Your Data Files and Program Files Separate

Once you've installed a program, create separate directories below the main program directory to store your data files. For example, you could create a DOCS subdirectory below your word processor directory, or a DATA subdirectory for your database. This makes it easy to find your files, and it makes backing up your data a snap.

## 4. Don't Overdo Your Subdirectories

Once people see the benefit of subdirectories, they tend to go to town with them. For example, it often makes sense to divide your word processor documents into BUSINESS and PERSONAL directories. You could keep going and further subdivide things by addressee, subject matter, month, and so on. The problem with all this is that it can take you forever just to type the darn pathname! For example, the following command would be a mouthful (fingerful?) for even the fastest typist:

```
cd \wp\docs\business\donald\building\march93
```

That's only a `CD` command. Imagine trying to type a `COPY` command that uses two such unwieldy pathnames. Yikes!

> Another good reason to avoid unnecessary subdirectories is that DOS places some internal limitations on the size of pathnames and command lines. A pathname is limited to 66 characters, and DOS command lines are limited to 127 characters.

## 5. Keep Directory Names Short

One of the most important rules that all DOS gurus follow is to keep typing to a minimum. It's not only faster, but it also reduces the likelihood of fumbling fingers making a mistake. (Fortunately, being a good typist is not a prerequisite for becoming a DOS expert.)

Most DOS gurus use the short forms for DOS commands (`REN` instead of `RENAME`, `MD` instead of `MKDIR`, and so on) and they try to keep their directory names as short as possible. Why use "LOTUS123" when "123" is just as good (and five characters shorter)?

# Guru *DIR*

Most beginning DOS users quickly learn to use the `DIR` command to display a directory listing. Also common knowledge are the `DIR` switches `/P` (which pauses the listing after each screenful) and `/W` (which produces a wide listing of filenames only). In this section, you'll graduate from these no-brainer basics to some truly useful `DIR` techniques.

## *DIR* Star (*) Stuff

The `DIR` command is a bit of a maverick when it comes to the star (`*`) wildcard. As you learned in Chapter 1, "Guru File Management," you normally use star to substitute for a group of characters. For example, `WORF.*` represents all files with the primary name WORF and any extension. With `DIR`, however, you can leave off the dot and the extension and DOS assumes you mean `.*`. So, for example, the command

```
dir worf
```

produces the identical listing as

```
dir worf.*
```

Similarly, if you don't enter anything for the primary name, `DIR` assumes you mean `*`. So the command

```
dir .dbf
```

is the same as

```
dir *.dbf
```

## Sort Yourself

The normal `DIR` listing is a real dog's breakfast with files and directories all mixed up and displayed in seemingly random order. DOS 5, though, introduced the cool `/O` switch for `DIR` that lets you select from several different sort orders for the listing. Table 2.1 summarizes the various options.

**Table 2.1. DIR sorting options.**

| *Use* | *To* |
|---|---|
| `/OD` | Sort by date (oldest to newest) |
| `/OE` | Sort by extension (a to z) |
| `/OG` | Display subdirectories first |
| `/ON` | Sort by name (a to z) |
| `/OS` | Sort by size (smallest to largest) |

**Guru Tip**

The DOS manual tells you to put a colon (`:`) after `/O`, but DOS gurus, always on the lookout for ways to save keystrokes, know that it isn't necessary.

Here are some points to keep in mind when using the sort feature:

- You can combine multiple sort options into a single command. For example, to display subdirectories first and sort by size, use `/OGS`.

- To reverse the sort order, precede the sort letter with a minus sign (`-`). For example, to sort the files from newest to oldest, use `/O-D`.
- If you have a favorite sort option, use the `DIRCMD` variable to make it the default. For example, to tell DOS to always sort by name, enter the following command:

```
set dircmd=/on
```

Guru Tip

> Include the **SET DIRCMD** command in your AUTOEXEC.BAT file so your favorite **DIR** options are always set as the default every time you boot your computer. See Chapter 13, "AUTOEXEC.BAT: Your Most Important Batch File," for the skinny on this crucial file.

# Displaying Files by Attribute

DOS 5 also introduced the `/A` switch for `DIR`, which allows you to display your files according to attributes. Files can have up to five different attributes: archive (when set, it means that the file has been modified since it was last backed up), directory, hidden (the file doesn't normally appear in a `DIR` listing), read-only (you can't make changes to the file), and system (files used internally by DOS). Table 2.2 summarizes the options available with the `/A` switch.

**Table 2.2. *DIR* attribute options.**

| *Use* | *To List* |
|---|---|
| /AA | Files with their archive attribute set |
| /AD | Directories only |
| /AH | Hidden files |
| /AR | Read-only files |
| /AS | System files |

As with the sort options, you can combine multiple attribute options in a single command, and you can use the minus sign (-) to reverse each option.

## Other *DIR* Options

As if all this wasn't enough, DOS 5 also introduced three more `DIR` switches:

- `/B` Gives a bare listing that shows only the file and subdirectory names
- `/L` Displays file and subdirectory names in lowercase
- `/S` Displays the contents of the subdirectories as well

**Guru Tip**

Have you lost a file somewhere on your hard disk? Don't go searching through all your directories. Just change to your root directory and run the `DIR` command on the filename with the `/S` switch. For example, to find a file called WHEREAMI.DOC, use the following command:

```
dir whereami.doc /s
```

Because you're running the command from the root, `DIR` searches every directory on your hard drive for a file that matches.

# What the Heck Are Those Dot Things?

A typical `DIR` listing looks something like this:

```
 Volume in drive C is NOTEBOOK
 Volume Serial Number is 1CD0-4752
 Directory of C:\DBASE\DATA

.            <DIR>      12-16-92   6:38p
..           <DIR>      12-16-92   6:38p
CUSTOMER DBF     193258 01-24-93   4:57p
INVOICES DBF      56152 01-25-93  11:21a
INVENTRY DBF       3482 12-30-92   4:57p
```

```
        5 file(s)      252892 bytes
                     28413952 bytes free
```

Have you ever wondered what those strange first two entries—the dot (.) and the double dot (..)—mean? Well, it turns out that they're just DOS shorthand. The dot represents the current directory, and the double dot represents the parent directory.

This wouldn't be big news except that you can use these symbols to save some time. Here are a few tips that take advantage of this notation:

- You can use the double dots to jump quickly to the parent directory. If you're in, say, C:\ANIMAL\MAMMAL\DOLPHIN, just use the following command to move up quickly to C:\ANIMAL\MAMMAL:

  ```
  cd..
  ```

  To move up two levels, use the command

  ```
  cd..\..
  ```

- The double dots also make it easy to move to a directory on the same level with the same parent. For example, suppose you're in C:\ANIMAL\MAMMAL\DOLPHIN and you want to switch to C:\ANIMAL\MAMMAL\BABOON. You can do it with this command:

  ```
  cd..\baboon
  ```

- You can often use the dot or double dots in place of the `*.*` notation. For example, to copy all the files in the current directory to drive A:, you normally use the command

  ```
  copy *.* a:
  ```

  However, the following command does the same thing:

  ```
  copy . a:
  ```

# Copying Directories

DOS doesn't have a specific command for copying directories, but XCOPY is more than equal to the task. Suppose, for example, that you want to copy a directory called GURU from drive C: to drive D:. Here's the command that does it:

```
xcopy c:\guru d:\guru
```

Pretty simple! However, DOS can't tell if `D:\GURU` is a file or directory, so the following message appears:

```
Does D:\GURU specify a file name
or directory name on the target
(F = file, D = directory)?
```

Press `d` for directory and then sit back and watch things happen. (Remember, as well, to use `XCOPY`'s `/S` parameter if you have any subdirectories that you also want copied.)

**Guru Tip**

> To prevent DOS from asking you if the destination is a file or directory, add a backslash to the end of the destination pathname. For example, use the command
>
> `xcopy c:\guru d:\guru\`
>
> instead of the one shown above.

# Renaming Directories

High on most gurus' list of DOS gripes at one time was the fact that you couldn't easily rename directories. You first had to copy the directory to the new name and delete the old one (which was no picnic either).

This is one gripe, however, that you can strike off your list. You can now use DOS 6's new `MOVE` command to rename directories in a flash. For example, if the GAMES directory on your office computer doesn't portray the right image, you can rename it to LEISURE with the following command:

```
move c:\games leisure
```

Note that you don't need to specify a drive for the new name, because you can only rename a directory to one on the same drive. The following command is illegal:

```
move c:\games d:\games
```

**Dunce**

> It's not a good idea to rename any directories created by your programs. They usually expect to find their files in a certain location, and if the name is even off by a single character, the program may do some weird stuff or the darn thing may not run at all! As a rule of thumb, only rename directories you've created yourself.

# Deleting Directories

Before DOS 6 came along, deleting directories with the `RD` (remove directory) command was a royal pain in the you-know-what. You first had to delete every file in the directory and only then could you run `RD`. If you had subdirectories, well, you just had to phone home to say you would be late for dinner.

But now, hallelujah, there is the very cool `DELTREE` command. This little baby wipes out a directory (and all its subdirectories) in nothing flat, and it's real easy to use. All you do is type `deltree` followed by the name of the directory (just make sure you're not in the directory itself). For example, to blow away the JUNK directory on drive C:, simply enter

```
deltree c:\junk
```

DOS asks you to confirm that you want to delete `junk` and all its subdirectories. Just press `y` and Enter. That's it—no muss, no fuss.

**Dunce**

> `DELTREE` is one of those potentially disastrous commands that you should approach with extreme caution. To be safe, you should probably run a `DIR` on the directory to make sure you're not going to consign anything important to oblivion.

# Guru Review

This chapter gave you all sorts of useful information on guru directory management. I covered a few directory basics just to refresh your memory about things like root directories, subdirectories, pathnames, and so on. I then moved on to more advanced stuff. Here are some highlights:

- DOS gurus maintain efficient directory structures by, among other things, keeping their root directories clean, storing related files together, and keeping data files and program files separate.
- With `DIR`, if you leave out the dot and extension in a file spec, DOS assumes you mean `.*`. Similarly, if you leave out the primary name, DOS assumes you mean `*`.
- If you have at least DOS 5, use the `/O` parameter to sort your listing by name, date, and so on. You can also use `/A` to list files with certain attributes.
- In a directory listing, the dot (`.`) stands for the current directory, and the double dots (`..`) stand for the parent directory. You can use these symbols to navigate your directories. For example, `cd..` takes you quickly to the parent.
- Use `XCOPY` to copy your directories. If you have DOS 6, use `MOVE` to rename your directories and `DELTREE` to delete them.

# Guru Hard Disk Management

3

CHAPTER

## Guru Stuff in This Chapter ➤

- *Saving space by deleting old DOS versions, unnecessary DOS files, and those annoying temporary files*
- *Improving hard drive performance by defragmenting your files*
- *Doubling your disk space with DoubleSpace*
- *Various reminiscences about first computers and springtimes of long ago*

My first computer was one of those old dual-floppy systems that didn't even have a hard drive (as impossible as that is to imagine these days). Since then, hard disk prices have plummeted and their capacities have increased to the point where disks capable of holding several hundred megabytes or more are now commonplace.

All that hard disk real estate is great, but it means that as a DOS guru, you have to take extra care to keep things in order. The directory management techniques you learned in the last chapter were a good start, but now you need to turn your attention to the big picture: your hard disk as a whole.

# A Hard Disk Spring Cleaning

When I was a kid, I always knew when spring had sprung because my mother would suddenly start cleaning everything in sight and throwing out anything she thought was junk. (That, I'm sure, was what happened to my old comic book and baseball card collections.)

Most computers could use a good spring cleaning themselves. By tossing any old files that you don't need, you'll not only save disk space, you'll improve your machine's performance as well.

## Get Rid of Your Old DOS Versions

When you install DOS 5 or 6, the setup program saves your old DOS version in a directory called OLD_DOS.1. If you've used your new version for a while and are satisfied that it won't blow up in your face, you may as well delete the old files and reclaim a megabyte or two of disk space.

The good news is that the DOS programmers have thoughtfully supplied you with a utility called DELOLDOS that does the job for you. Not only that, but DELOLDOS also performs the nifty trick of deleting itself when it's done.

To proceed, all you do is type `deloldos` and press Enter. DOS, ever cautious, displays a screen warning you that deleting your old DOS files will make it impossible to recover your previous DOS version. To continue, just press `y` (if you get cold feet, you can return to the safety of the DOS prompt simply by pressing any other key). DOS quickly deletes the files (as well as the OLD_DOS.1 directory) and displays a message telling you when it's done. Press Enter to return to DOS.

# Blow Away Those Unnecessary DOS Files

DOS, trying to be all things to all people, installs all sorts of bizarre files that most people never use. These beasts take up valuable hard disk turf, so you should chuck whatever you don't need. Use the following table as a guideline (the figures showing the number of bytes saved are only approximations; the actual numbers vary between DOS versions).

### Table 3.1. Unnecessary DOS files.

| *If* | *Delete* | *To Save* |
|---|---|---|
| You don't need foreign characters or international language support. | COUNTRY.SYS | 17,066 bytes |
| | KEYBOARD.SYS | 34,694 bytes |
| | KEYB.COM | 14,983 bytes |
| You don't use code page switching. | *.CPI | 7,142 bytes |
| | DISPLAY.SYS | 15,789 bytes |
| | GRAFTABL.COM | 11,205 bytes |
| | NLSFUNC.EXE | 7,036 bytes |
| | PRINTER.SYS | 18,804 bytes |
| You're not a programmer. | *.BAS | 112,076 bytes |
| | DEBUG.EXE | 15,715 bytes |
| | EXE2BIN.EXE | 8,424 bytes |
| | QBASIC.HLP | 130,810 bytes |
| You have an 8088 or 8086 computer. | EMM386.EXE | 114,782 bytes |
| | HIMEM.SYS | 13,984 bytes |
| | LOADFIX.COM | 1,131 bytes |
| You have an 80286 computer. | EMM386.EXE | 114,782 bytes |
| | LOADFIX.COM | 1,131 bytes |

*continues*

**Table 3.1. continued**

| *If* | *Delete* | *To Save* |
|---|---|---|
| You have your own text editor, and you're not interested in programming. | EDIT.COM<br>EDIT.HLP<br>EDLIN.EXE<br>QBASIC.EXE | 413 bytes<br>17,898 bytes<br>12,642 bytes<br>194,319 bytes |
| You don't have an EGA video adapter. | EGA.* | 63,755 bytes |
| You don't have a Hercules video adapter. | MSHERC.COM | 6,934 bytes |
| You don't have expanded or extended memory. | SMARTDRV.EXE<br>RAMDRIVE.SYS | 42,073 bytes<br>5,873 bytes |
| You've read or printed the documentation files. | *.TXT<br>PACKING.LST | 83,272 bytes<br>2,587 bytes |
| You'll never use the DOS Shell. | DOSSHELL.*<br>OSSWAP.EXE | 433,112 bytes<br>18,756 bytes |
| You don't plan to use DOS 6's disk compression. | DBLSPACE.* | 406,120 bytes |

Dunce

If you don't program in BASIC, you might be tempted to delete QBASIC.EXE along with the other files suggested in the table. You'll need to keep this file, however, if you plan to use **EDIT**.

If you end up deleting a file that you find you need later, don't sweat it, you can always copy the file from your original DOS disks. However, some of the files on the installation disks are stored in compressed format, and they won't work if you just copy them to your hard drive. (All compressed files end with an underscore character, for example, EMM386.EX_.) Instead, use the EXPAND utility (it comes on the installation disks) to decompress the file you need. For example, to decompress EMM386.EX_ from a disk in drive A:, use the following command:

```
expand a:\emm386.ex_ c:\dos\emm386.exe
```

## Watch Out for Temporary Files

Many word processors and text editors play it safe and create backup copies of the documents you're working on. These files usually have the same name as the document but with a BAK extension. Although this is admirable behavior, those BAK files can really start cluttering up your hard disk after a while.

As if this wasn't enough, many programs also create temporary files as they swap bits of program code in and out of memory. This is perfectly normal and these files are usually deleted when you exit the program. However, if the program crashes or a power failure hits, you can end up with dozens of these temporary files strewn around your hard disk. You'll recognize them because they tend to have bizarre names like ~A28463X3.TMP or _7483629.$$$.

You should periodically do a sweep of your hard disk to look for these rogues and then delete them. One easy way to look for these files is to use `DIR`'s `/S` parameter. Just change to your hard disk's root directory and issue the command

```
dir *.bak /s
```

This gives you a list of all the BAK files on your hard drive. Repeat the command for TMP and $$$ files, as well.

**Dunce**

> Before you start merrily expunging your system's temporary files, be sure you're not not in a DOS session under the DOS Shell, Windows, or any other program. Deleting temporary files while a program is running can trash your data in the blink of an eye.

# Defragmenting Your Files for Better Hard Disk Performance

If you have DOS 6, you can use the new `DEFRAG` command to defragment (*defrag* is the cool guru term) the files on your hard disk and greatly improve performance. (If you haven't yet stepped up to DOS 6, you can still defrag your files using third-party utilities. I'll tell you about these later on.) This section explains fragmentation and shows you how to use `DEFRAG`.

# What the Heck Is File Fragmentation?

*File fragmentation* is one of those terms that sounds scarier than it actually is. It simply means that a file is stored on your hard disk in scattered, noncontiguous (I love using words like that) bits.

This is a bummer because it means DOS, when it tries to open such a file, has to make several stops to collect the various pieces. If a lot of files are fragmented, even the fastest hard disk can be slowed to a crawl.

Why doesn't DOS just store files contiguously? Well, unfortunately, it just isn't smart enough. You see, DOS stores information in fixed-sized chunks called *clusters.* The size of each cluster depends on the disk, but 2,048 bytes is typical.

**Guru Trivia**

> Want to know the cluster size of your hard disk? All you do is run the **CHKDSK** command and look for the line that says something like the following:
>
> `2048 bytes in each allocation unit`
>
> What **CHKDSK** calls an "allocation unit," the rest of us call a cluster.

DOS keeps track of all the clusters on a disk by means of the *file allocation table* (or FAT for short). When DOS needs to store a file, it looks at the FAT to determine where the empty clusters are. When you delete a file, DOS alters the FAT to reflect that the file's clusters are now available.

To see how fragmentation occurs, look at an example. Suppose three files are stored on a disk—FIRST.TXT, SECOND.TXT, and THIRD.TXT—and they use up 4, 3, and 5 clusters, respectively. Figure 3.1 shows how they might look on the disk.

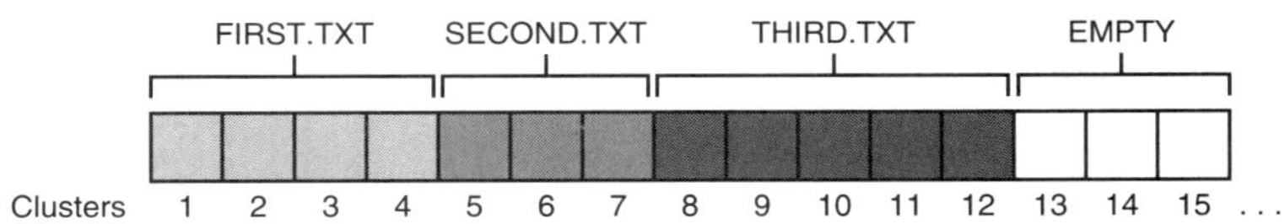


**Figure 3.1.** Three files before fragmentation.

If you now delete SECOND.TXT, clusters 5, 6, and 7 become available. But suppose the next file you save—call it FOURTH.TXT—takes up 5 clusters. What happens? Well, DOS starts at the beginning of the FAT and looks for the first available clusters. It finds 5, 6, and 7 are free, so it uses them for the first three clusters of FOURTH.TXT. DOS continues and finds that clusters 13 and 14 are free, so it uses them for the final two clusters of FOURTH.TXT. Figure 3.2 shows how things look now.

**Figure 3.2.** A fragmented file.

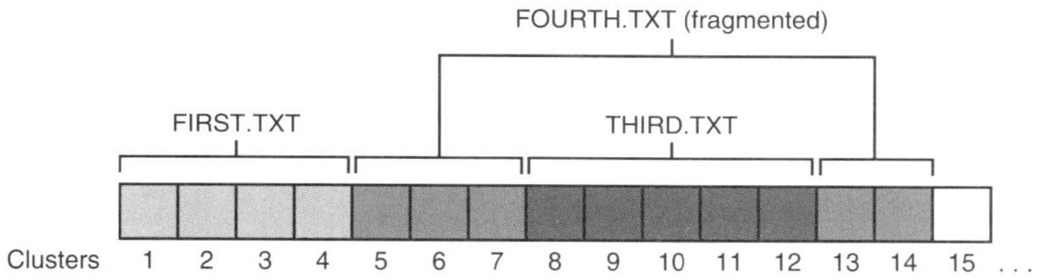


As you can see, FOURTH.TXT is stored noncontiguously—it is, in other words, fragmented. Although a file fragmented into two pieces is not that bad, it's possible for large files to get split up into dozens of blocks.

**Guru Tip**

> Fragmented files not only slow DOS down, but they're also harder to undelete. Why? Because deleting such a file frees up a whole bunch of small cluster blocks, and so increases the likelihood that some other file will usurp at least one of these small blocks.

## *DEFRAG* to the Rescue

DOS 6's `DEFRAG` utility works by physically rearranging the files on your hard disk so that each one has its clusters stored contiguously. Before using `DEFRAG`, though, you should do the following:

- ✦ As described above, delete any files from your hard disk that you don't need. Defragmenting junk files only slows down the whole process.

- Check for file allocation errors by running the command `chkdsk /f`. If CHKDSK finds any errors, you'll see a message that looks something like this:

  ```
  5 lost allocation units found in 2 chains.
  Convert lost chains to files?
  ```

  Press `n` to delete the errors.

- Shut down any memory-resident programs that may access the disk while DEFRAG is running. If you are not sure which programs to close, you should consider booting from a floppy disk to get a "plain-vanilla" DOS (Chapter 18, "The Guru's Survival Kit," tells you how to do this). Also, be sure you're not running in a DOS session under Windows, or that you haven't shelled out to DOS from another program.

**Guru Tip**

> If you have DOS 6, you can get a plain-vanilla boot by pressing F5 when you see the **Starting MS-DOS...** message. See Chapter 14, "Start It Your Way: DOS 6 Boot Options," for more details.

Without further ado, here are the steps to follow to use DEFRAG:

1. Type `defrag` and press Enter—you'll soon see a list of drives on your computer.
2. Use the Up or Down arrow keys to highlight the drive you want to optimize and then press Enter twice. DEFRAG reads the information from the disk and displays its recommended optimization method, as shown in Figure 3.3.
3. To accept DEFRAG's recommendation, just press Enter. DEFRAG then begins optimizing the disk. The Status area in the lower-left corner keeps you posted on the progress of the operation. The large area in the middle of the screen is a map of the drive you selected. Keep an eye on this area to watch DEFRAG moving files around.

**Figure 3.3.** DEFRAG recommends an optimization method.

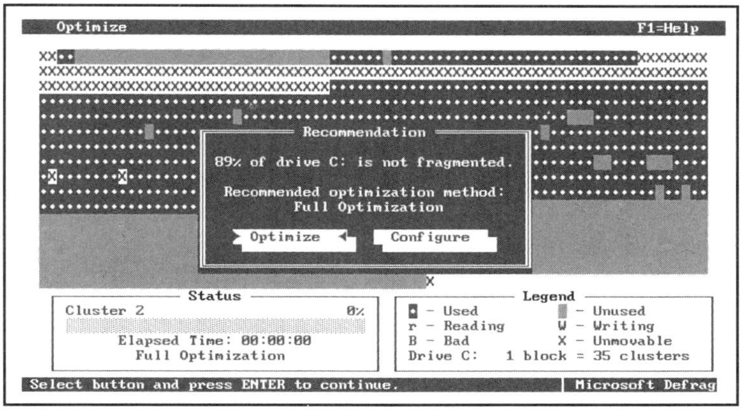


# Selecting a Different Optimization Method

You're usually safe in following DEFRAG's recommendation for an optimization method, but there may be times when you need to select a different method. DEFRAG gives you a choice of two optimization methods:

- **Full Optimization**: this method defragments all your files and, as it's doing so, rearranges the files on your hard disk so that there are no empty clusters between files.
- **Unfragment Files Only**: this method only defragments your files.

To select a different method, follow these steps:

1. In the recommendation window, press the Right arrow key once to highlight the Configure button and then press Enter. DEFRAG pulls down the Optimize menu.
2. Press o to select the Optimization Method command. This displays the Select Optimization Method dialog box.
3. Use the Up or Down arrow keys to move the cursor to the method you want, and then press the Spacebar.
4. Press Enter twice to return to the menu.
5. Press Alt+B to start the optimization.

Guru Tip

> How often should you defragment your hard disk? The answer really depends on how often you use your computer. If you use it every day, you should use the Unfragment Files Only method weekly and the Full Optimization method monthly. If your computer doesn't get heavy use, run **DEFRAG** every couple of months and follow the recommendation.

Guru Tools

> You can still defragment your files even if you don't have DOS 6. The Norton Utilities has a program called Speed Disk that does the job. (In fact, Speed Disk is a full-featured version of **DEFRAG** that gives you many more optimization and configuration options.) You can also check out PC Tools' Compress utility.

# Doubling Disk Space with DoubleSpace

Although hard disks have been getting bigger over the years, they haven't kept pace with the ever-fatter programs developers have been throwing at us. As a result, we have McFedries' "Bad News Law #17": No matter how huge your hard disk seems today, you'll wish it was twice as big six months from now.

But hey, why wait six months when you can double the size of your hard disk right now? If you have DOS 6, you can do just that with the gnarly new DoubleSpace disk compression utility.

## How Does Disk Compression Work?

Disk compression is based on a complex mathematical algorithm (called the Lempel-Ziv algorithm) that searches a file for redundant character strings and replaces them with small tokens. Let's look at a simple example. Consider the following phrase:

*It was the best of times, it was the worst of times, it was the age of wisdom, it was the age of foolishness*

To compress this quotation, the program starts at the beginning and looks for at least two consecutive characters that it has already seen. In this case, the first such match is the *t* at the end of the word *best* and the following space. This matches the *t* at the end of *It* and the space that follows. So now the program replaces the match with a token, as follows (I'll use a star to represent the tokens):

*It was the bes*of times, i* was the worst of times, i* was the age of wisdom, i* was the age of foolishness*

Not very impressive so far. But the program chugs along finding small redundancies (for example, the *es* in *times* matches the *es* seen earlier in *best*), and then it hits the jackpot: larger phrases such as *it was the*, *of times*, and *age of* are repeated and these can all be replaced by tokens. In the end, you end up with something that looks like this:

*It was the bes*of*im*, i*wor*age*wisdom*fool*hn*s*

It looks weird, but it's less than half the size of the original. To decompress such data, all the program has to do is translate the tokens back to their original form. It's all handled by a mathematical formula, and it's quite safe.

# Running DoubleSpace

What DoubleSpace does is complicated, but, fortunately, using the program isn't:

**Dunce**

> Be sure you haven't shelled out to DOS from within Windows or another program. If you have, quit Windows or the program before trying to run DoubleSpace.

1. Type `dblspace` and press Enter. The friendly DoubleSpace welcome screen appears.
2. Press Enter to continue. DoubleSpace asks if you want to run the Express Setup or the Custom Setup. Although the program recommends the Express Setup, DOS gurus always use the Custom Setup.

3. Press the Down arrow once to highlight the Custom Setup and then press Enter. DoubleSpace now gives you two options:

   **Compress an existing drive**: select this option if you want to maximize the amount of space on your hard drive. It takes longer, but it's worth the wait, especially if your drive is bursting at the seams.

   **Create a new empty compressed drive**: select this option if you still have plenty of free space on your hard drive and you just want to use the new compressed drive for archiving files.

4. Use the Up or Down arrow keys to highlight your choice and then press Enter. If you chose to compress an existing drive, skip to Step 6. Otherwise, DoubleSpace asks you to choose which drive's free space you want to convert into the compressed drive.
5. Select the drive and then press Enter. DoubleSpace displays the compression settings.
6. To change any of the settings, highlight them and press Enter to display the available options. Select the option you want and press Enter to return to the settings.
7. When you've got your settings set up the way you want, press Enter to continue. DoubleSpace tells you it's ready to go and provides you with an estimate of the time it will take to compress the drive.
8. Press `c` to start the compression. DoubleSpace restarts your computer to load its device driver, and then it starts compressing. When it's done (it may take quite a while depending on how many files it has to compress and the size of your hard disk), DoubleSpace defragments your new drive (if you compressed an existing drive) and then displays some compression statistics for you to drool over. When you're ready, press Enter to restart your computer.

> The *compression ratio* of a file is the ratio of the size of the compressed file to its uncompressed size. For example, a file that is 5,000 bytes compressed and 10,000 bytes uncompressed has a compression ratio

> of 2 to 1. You can check out the compression ratio of any file or group of files by using `DIR` with the `/C` switch. For example, to find out the compression ration of the files in your DOS directory, use the following command:
>
> ```
> dir c:\dos /c
> ```

Some files (especially text, database, and graphics files) compress more than the already compact EXE and HLP (Help system) files.

Guru Tools

> If you don't have DOS 6, you can still get the benefits of disk compression through products such as Stac Electronics' Stacker or SuperStor from AddStor Inc.

# Guru Review

This chapter showed you various methods or true guru hard disk management. Here's a quick review of the important stuff:

- If you've upgraded to DOS 5 or 6, delete your old DOS versions by using the `DELOLDOS` utility.
- You can save even more disk space by getting rid of any DOS files you'll never use and by periodically cleaning out any temporary files (those with extensions BAK, TMP, and $$$) created by your programs.
- Fragmented files (those stored in noncontiguous blocks) can slow down your hard disk. Use DOS 6's new `DEFRAG` program to defragment your files.
- Disk compression reduces the size of a file by replacing redundant characters with smaller tokens. You can effectively increase the size of your hard disk (sometimes as much as double) by using DOS 6's DoubleSpace utility.

# Floppy Disk Fun

4

CHAPTER

## Guru Stuff in This Chapter ➤

- *Floppy disks: what are they really like?*
- *A review of the 57 million disk types*
- *An advanced class in floppy formatting*
- *Disk copying made easy*
- *Oodles of tips and traps for floppy fanatics*

Occasionally, people will ask me, "So just what *is* a computer, anyway?" (As a DOS guru, you need to be prepared to handle questions like this. It's usually best to do two things: outwardly, just nod and smile; inwardly, say your favorite expletive ten times or so—try not to get these two mixed up.)

I usually answer with an analogy: a computer, I tell them, is like a house. The inside of the house is like a computer's hard disk, the various objects stored in the house are like files stored on the hard disk, and the different rooms in the house are like the hard disk's directories.

So how would floppy disks fit into all this? Well, the comedian George Carlin likes to talk about how people going on vacations tend to pack "smaller versions of their stuff." This is exactly what floppy disks are—if your hard disk contains all your "stuff" (your programs and data files), you can use floppy disks to store or transport just a few files (smaller versions of your stuff). This chapter takes a look at floppy disks from the guru's perspective.

# Floppy Disks: The Inside Story

It has always amazed me to think that you can stick a piece of plastic inside a slot in your computer and use it to read and write all the neat stuff you see on your screen. This minor miracle is a result of some pretty cool floppy disk technology that I'll take a quick look at in this section.

When you look at a typical floppy, what you're mostly seeing is a protective case. All the action is inside the case.

Pick up a disk and take a close look at it. If it's a 5.25-inch disk, look at the material you can see through the holes; if it's a 3.5-inch disk, slide the metal shutter to one side as far as it will go. The shiny plastic you can see inside the case is the actual disk: another piece of plastic (usually mylar) that has a special magnetic coating that allows it to store data (once it has been formatted, that is).

When you insert a disk in the appropriate drive, a special part (the *spindle*) grabs the disk firmly at the center, and two *read/write* heads position themselves on each side of the disk (most.disks nowadays use both sides to record information; this is what people mean when they say that a disk is "double-sided"). When you access a disk, a motor cranks up to speed (on 3.5-inch drives, you can actually hear the "click" of the disk's metal shutter when it is opened), and the spindle turns the disk to the appropriate area so the read/write heads can do their thing.

When the read/write heads access data on a floppy, they literally rest on the surface of disk. Removing a disk while this is happening is a real no-no, because you could easily cause the heads to go scraping over the surface of the disk, trashing all kinds of valuable data in the process. (This would be a lot like a needle scratching the surface of a record; remember records?) Fortunately, the drive light always tells you when things are safe. When the light is on, hands off the disk!

# Floppy Disk Types: So Many Choices, So Little Time

Some computer industry wag once said that the nice thing about "standards" is that there are so many of them. This applies only too well to floppy disks (over the years I've seen more "standards" than you can shake a stick at; although I'm not sure how you shake a stick at a standard).

## 5.25-Inch Disks

5.25-inch disks are the veterans of the PC wars. They've been around, in one form or another, since the days of the earliest PCs. Figure 4.1 highlights some features on the landscape of a 5.25-inch disk.

**Figure 4.1.**
The features of a 5.25-inch floppy disk.

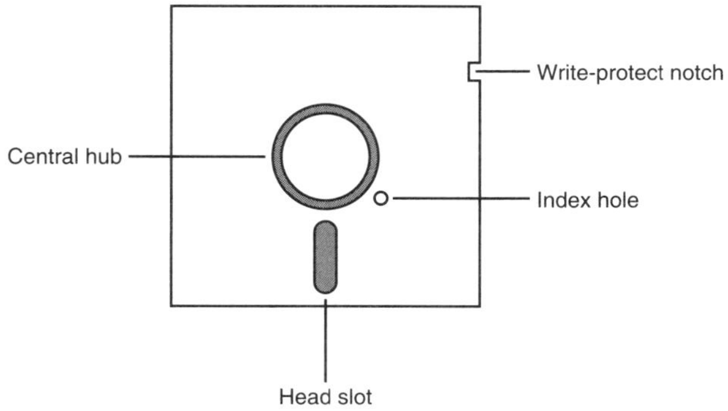

- **Central hub**—this is the hole that the spindle uses to grab and turn the disk.
- **Index hole**—if you turn the disk inside its case (carefully) and keep an eye on the index hole, you'll eventually see a small hole in the disk itself. The disk drive uses this hole to position the disk at the "beginning" (where DOS stores the disk's FAT).
- **Head slot**—this oval area is where the read/write heads do their reading and writing. The spindle turns the disk so that the appropriate area is visible through this hole.
- **Write-protect notch**—this notch tells DOS whether or not you can write or erase any information on the disk. If the notch is covered with tape (or if, in some cases, it's not there at all), the disk is said to be *write-protected*.

5.25-inch disks come in two capacities: double-density and high-density. (Actually, the term *double-density* is relatively meaningless in this day and age. It originates from the old days of computers—way back in the eighties—when there were such things as *single-density* disks. You'll often see double-density disks referred to as *low-density* or *regular-density*.) 5.25-inch double-density disks have a storage capacity of 360 kilobytes (of course, DOS gurus never use the word *kilobyte*; instead, we simply write "K"), and the high-density variety can store 1.2 megabytes (or, in guruspeak, "M" or *megs*).

**Guru Trivia**

The word *byte* gets bandied about a lot in computer circles, so I should be clear about what it means. A byte, put simply, is just a single character of information. So, for example, the phrase "This phrase is 28 bytes long" is, yes, 28 bytes long (you count the spaces, too). A kilobyte, then, is 1,024 bytes, and a megabyte is 1,024 kilobytes. What, I hear you asking, is this fetish for the number 1,024? Well, "kilo," as you may know, means "thousand" and it turns out that $2^{10}$ is 1,024, which is close enough. Why 2 to the power of 10? Well, internally, computers can only deal with 2 states: on or off. A circuit either has a high current (it's on) or a low current (it's off). Amazingly, *everything* inside your computer exists merely as a collection of on or off circuits.

## 3.5-Inch Disks

Although 3.5-inch disks are the relatively new kids on the floppy drive block, they're fast becoming the true "standard" (at least until the next one comes along). Figure 4.2 highlights the parts of a 3.5-inch disk that every guru should know.

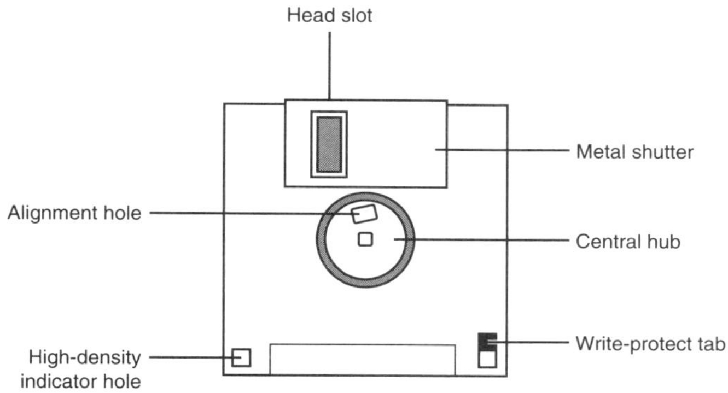


**Figure 4.2.** The features of a 3.5-inch floppy disk.

- **Central hub**—just like the 5.25-inch disks, the spindle uses this part to grab and turn the disk.
- **Alignment hole**—the spindle uses this hole to align the disk properly.
- **Metal shutter**—one of the problems with 5.25-inch disks is that the disk itself is exposed to the elements (such as your kid's grubby fingers) through the head slot. 3.5-inch disks add an extra level of protection by covering the head slot with a metal shutter. The drive opens this shutter automatically whenever the disk is accessed.
- **Head slot**—this is where the read/write heads operate. It works the same way as the 5.25-inch disk's head slot.
- **Write-protect tab**—this slidable tab controls whether or not information can be written to or erased from the disk. If you slide the tab toward the edge of the disk, the disk is write-protected.
- **High-density indicator hole**—this hole is present only on high-density disks, which gives you a quick way to determine the capacity of an unlabeled disk.

3.5-inch disks come in three capacities: double-density, high-density, and the new extended-density disks. Double-density disks store up to 720K, high-density disks store 1.44M, and the extended disks can pack a whollOping 2.88M of data.

**Guru Tip**

> As a DOS guru wanna-be, it is your responsibility to help shatter an old myth: that you can roll your own high-density disks simply by using a "disk notcher" to poke high-density indicator holes in low-density disks. Forget about it. It doesn't work. Oh sure, you might be able to use the disk two or three times without any ill effects, but, eventually, your data will get trashed and the disk will become useless (even as a low-density disk).

# Disk Dos and Don'ts

Here are a few pointers to keep in mind when working with disks:

- Don't touch the magnetic surface of a disk.
- Don't expose a disk to direct sunlight or temperature extremes.
- Don't place a disk near a strong magnetic or electronic source (such as a phone, modem, or even a magnetic paper clip holder).
- Don't fold, spindle, or mutilate a disk.
- Don't use a pen or pencil to write on a label attached to a 5.25-inch disk. Felt pens are okay, though.
- Don't cast these guru pearls before computer swine.

**Guru Tip**

> Non-gurus may try to tell you that airport x-ray machines and static electricity can mess up your disks. Don't believe them! These are just more urban fairy tales (like crocodiles in the sewers) that won't seem to go away.

- Place your 5.25-inch disks inside their protective pouches when not in use.
- Keep backup copies of important disks.

- Buy cheaper, no-name disks in bulk for everyday use.
- Buy top-quality disks for important needs (such as backing up your hard disk).
- Try to get out more.

# Formatting a Disk

You can't, of course, just stick any old piece of plastic in a disk drive and expect it to read and write information. Even official I-bought-it-at-the-local-Radio-Shack floppy disks need to be set up first, so information can be properly stored on the disk.

It's like the difference between a peg board and an ordinary piece of wood. Buying new disks (unless the box says they're "preformatted," in which case they're probably ridiculously expensive) is like buying a bunch of flat, featureless pieces of wood. You can try all day to stick pegs in 'em, but they'll just fall off. What you need to do is "format" the wood so that it has proper holes for the pegs. Then you're in business.

This peg-board analogy can also help explain the difference between double-density and high-density disks. Picture two peg-boards: one with large holes and one with smaller holes. The large-holed board is able to hold a certain number of pegs, but because the holes in the other board are smaller, it is able to hold even more pegs. So a double-density disk is like the board with large holes: it has less "pegs" (less *tracks per inch*, technically) on which to place data than a high-density (small-holed) disk. This also helps explain why you can't format double-density disks as high-density. All disks use a magnetic field to hold their data. High-density disks have to use a *lower* field strength than double-density disks because the data, like the pegboard with small holes, is closer together. If they didn't, the various magnetic bits would start moving around because of mutual attraction and repulsion. Not good! This is exactly what happens, though, when you format a double-density disk as high-density. The tracks are placed close together, but the disk's stronger magnetic field eventually trashes the data.

Why aren't all disks preformatted? Well, most disks can be used with both DOS and non-DOS computers, and different machines require different formats (think of peg boards with different shaped holes). The disk manufacturers simplify their lives by shipping their disks unformatted.

# The *FORMAT* Command Does the Job

When you need to format your disks, you can turn, appropriately enough, to the DOS `FORMAT` command. This one is a no-brainer. For example, to format a disk in drive A:, all you do is enter the following command:

```
format a:
```

DOS first prompts you to insert the disk, then, when it's done, it asks if you want to label the disk and if you want to format another.

**Dunce**

> Formatting a disk destroys any information the disk may contain. This isn't a problem for a fresh disk right out of the pack, but if you're reformatting a used disk, it can be disastrous. Always check the contents of used disks before reformatting them. If you accidentally format a disk, see the section "Recovering a Disk with *UNFORMAT*," later in this chapter.

**Guru Tools**

> Need to format a whole box of new disks? Using **FORMAT** for this takes forever, so you might consider picking up a copy of FormatQM. This neat little program formats disks on multiple drives, and it doesn't ask for a volume label. Its coolest trick, though, is that it doesn't need to ask for confirmation before formatting additional disks. As soon as it sees a new disk in a drive, it formats it automatically!

# Faster Floppy Formatting

When formatting a used disk, don't grow old waiting for DOS to do a complete format. Instead, use the `FORMAT` command's `/Q` switch to perform a quick format. For example, to quick format a used disk in drive B:, use the following command:

```
format b: /q
```

All this does is reset the disk's FAT and root directory, which takes only a few seconds. If you're sure a disk contains junk files that you won't need, you can get a super-quick format by using the `/U` switch as well. This tells DOS to perform an unconditional format (that is, it doesn't save any unformat information).

# "Look Ma, No Hands!" Formatting

One of the things that bugs me about using the `FORMAT` command on new disks is that, well, it's so much work! You have to answer when it prompts you to insert the disk (why the heck isn't it smart enough to know when we've already got a disk in there, for crying out loud?); you have to answer when it prompts you for a volume label; you have to answer when it prompts you to format another disk. Criminy!

If this bothers you, too, here's a secret way to exact revenge: to format a disk in drive A:, enter the following command:

```
format a: /autotest
```

When you use the undocumented `/AUTOTEST` switch (you need at least DOS 4.0), DOS simply dives right into the format, and when it's done, it just lands you back at the DOS prompt—no annoying volume label or `format another?` prompts!

If you really have your heart set on entering a volume label, use this command instead:

```
format a: /backup
```

The `/BACKUP` switch (another undocumented feature) also starts formatting right away, but it asks for a volume label when it's done.

Dunce

> If you plan to use either of these cool switches to show off to your friends, you need to keep three things in mind:
>
> - Because DOS doesn't prompt you to insert a disk, be sure you have a disk loaded before starting.
> - Be sure the disk you're using is the same capacity as the drive. See the section "The Disk Game: What's My Capacity?" later in this chapter for easy ways to determine the capacity of a disk.
> - You can't do a quick format (`/Q`) with either of these switches.

## Formatting a Low-Density Disk in a High-Density Drive

Many people have access to both high-density and low-density disk drives. For example, you may have a high-density drive at work and a low-density drive at home. Ideally, you want to use disks that both machines can read without complaint. The best way to do this is to format a low-density disk in a low-density drive. The high-density drive reads this disk with no problems.

However, you will often run into McFedries' "Bad News Law #22": when you need to format a low-density disk, the machine in front of you will only have a high-density drive. Fortunately, the wizards who created DOS finally added a way to overcome this (probably after it had happened to them a few times). The secret is to use the appropriate switches.

If you have DOS versions 3.0 to 3.3, you can use the `/4` switch to format a low-density 5.25-inch disk in a high-density drive. For example, to format a 360K disk in high-density drive A:, use the following command:

```
format a: /4
```

DOS versions 4.0 and later include the `/F` switch, which enables you to specify a format size. Table 4.1 summarizes a few of the available options (use the first two switches to format low-density disks in high-density drives).

**Table 4.1. Disk formatting options.**

| *Disk Type* | *Switch* |
|---|---|
| 5.25-inch double-density (360K) | `/F:360` |
| 3.5-inch double-density (720K) | `/F:720` |
| 5.25-inch high-density (1.2M) | `/F:1.2` |
| 3.5-inch high-density (1.44M) | `/F:1.44` |
| 3.5-inch extended-density (2.88M)* | `/F:2.88` |

*Requires DOS 5 or higher

**Dunce**

> Never try to format a disk in any capacity other than the one for which it was manufactured. In other words, don't try to cheat and format your double-density disks as high-density—you'll only end up with an unreadable disk.

# The Disk Game: What's My Capacity?

This happens to me a couple of times a week: I need to format an old disk before reusing it, but I don't know the capacity of the disk. (It's a good idea to always reformat your old disks. You start with a fresh playing field, and you also make sure there are no viruses lurking on the sidelines.)

Unfortunately, DOS always tries to format disks in the drive's capacity (for example, no matter what you stick in a high-density drive, DOS always tries to do a high-density format). This isn't disastrous because all you see is the following message:

```
Existing format differs from that specified.
This disk cannot be unformatted.
Proceed with Format (Y/N)?
```

At this point you can press n and Enter to abort the format, but it's a pain to have to do this. What you need is some way to determine the capacity of a disk beforehand. Here are a few ways to do this:

| *You'll Know the Disk Is* | *If You See* |
|---|---|
| 5.25-inch double-density | A reinforcing ring around the central hub |
| | DS/DD |
| | 40 TPI (tracks per inch) |
| 5.25-inch high density | No reinforcing ring |
| | HD |
| | 96 TPI |
| 3.5-inch double-density | No high-density indicator hole |
| | DS/DD |
| 3.5-inch high-density | The high-density indicator hole |
| | HD or 2HD |
| | 135 TPI |
| 3.5-inch extended-density | A high-density indicator hole |
| | ED or 2ED |

Guru Tip

Both the 3.5-inch high-density and extended-density disks have high-density indicator holes, but they are positioned a little differently—on high-density disks, the hole is even with the write-protect hole; on extended-density disks it's offset a little.

# Recovering a Disk with *UNFORMAT*

When you format a used floppy disk with DOS 5 or 6, DOS automatically saves a copy of the old disk structure. If you need to recover the old data, the `UNFORMAT` command uses this information to rebuild the disk.

**Guru Trivia**

> When you format a used disk (unless you use the `/U` switch), DOS always displays the following message:
>
> `Saving UNFORMAT info`

This means that DOS is saving an image of the disk's system area (the FAT and root directory). The disk's file area isn't touched, so it's possible to rebuild the disk simply by re-creating the system area. That's what `UNFORMAT` does: it looks for the saved image and uses that to rebuild the disk. For best results, though, always run `UNFORMAT` as soon as possible after formatting a disk. To unformat a disk in drive A:, use the following steps:

1. Place the disk you want to recover in drive A:.
2. Type `unformat a:` and press Enter. DOS reminds you to insert the disk.
3. You've done this, so just press Enter. DOS displays a warning about `UNFORMAT`, finds the image file, and asks if you're sure you want to continue.
4. Press `y` and DOS rebuilds the disk.

# Guru Disk Copying

Copying a floppy disk is one of those chores that only seems to come up now and then. For example, most software manuals tell you to make backup copies of the program's installation disks in case anything goes wrong. Nobody ever does this, of course, but it's nice to know the procedure, just in case. The DISKCOPY command is a rather mindless beast that at least gets the job done (most of the time, anyway). If you have two disk drives of the same capacity and you want to copy the disk in A: to the disk in B:, use the following command:

```
diskcopy a: b:
```

The more likely scenario is that you have only one drive or two drives with different capacities. In this case, to make a copy of, say, the disk in drive A:, enter the following:

```
diskcopy a: a:
```

DOS prompts you to enter the *source disk* (the one you want to copy), reads as much data as it can, and then asks for the *target disk* (the one getting the copy). Depending on the capacity of the disks, you may have to repeat the whole thing.

There are times, however, when XCOPY will do a better job. The following list contains some of the advantages of XCOPY:

- The source and target disks don't have to be the same size or capacity. Many machines nowadays ship with both 5.25-inch and 3.5-inch drives. DISKCOPY gags if you try to copy disks between these two drives; XCOPY eats it for breakfast.
- DISKCOPY makes a track-by-track copy of the source disk. This means that files that are fragmented on the source are also fragmented on the target. (Check out Chapter 3, "Guru Hard Disk Management," to learn why file fragmentation is such a bummer.) If the target disk is empty, XCOPY actually defragments the files as it copies them. The other problem with DISKCOPY's track-by-track method is that sectors marked as bad on the source are also marked as bad on the target (when in fact they may be perfectly fine).
- If the target disk has bad sectors, DISKCOPY bails out with the following message:

  ```
  TARGET diskette bad or incompatible
  ```

- XCOPY just works around the bad sectors.

# Guru Review

This chapter showed you the basics of working with floppy disks. Here's the short list of your new guru know-how:

- Floppy disks come in two basic flavors: 5.25-inch (with two capacities: 360K and 1.2M) and 3.5-inch (with three capacities: 720K, 1.44M, and 2.88M).
- To do a quick format on a used disk, use `FORMAT` with the `/Q` switch. For even faster formats, use the `/U` switch to do an unconditional format (i.e., one where no unformat information is saved).
- To avoid the `FORMAT` command's interminable prompts, use the undocumented `/AUTOTEST` switch when formatting new disks.
- You can format double-density disks in high-density drives by using the `/4` switch (if you have DOS 3.x) or the `/F` switch (if you have DOS 4.0 or later).
- If you accidentally format a disk and you have DOS 5.0 or later, immediately use the `UNFORMAT` command to recover the disk.
- When copying disks, use `XCOPY` instead of `DISKCOPY` if the disks have different capacities, if the source disk has bad sectors, or if you want the files on the target disk to be unfragmented.

# Working with a Net: Backing Up Your Files

5

CHAPTER

## Guru Stuff in This Chapter ➤

- *Advanced methods for both Microsoft Backup (DOS 6) and the* BACKUP *command*
- *Realistic backup strategies*
- *Restoring your data*
- *Lots of hints and suggestions for safe and (relatively) painless backups*

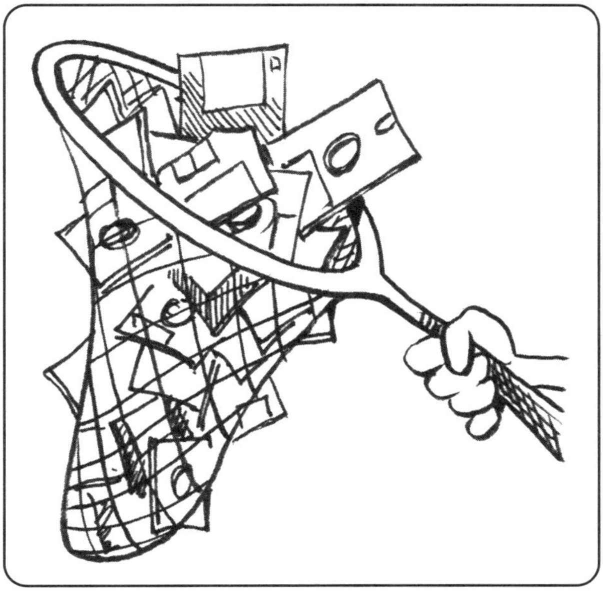

There's no shortage these days of books and magazine articles that list all the possible ways your hard disk can crash. You hear all kinds of war stories about hard disks bursting into flames, rogue programs running amok, lightning storm meltdowns, and, more and more often, vicious, disk-trashing viruses that give no quarter to your valuable data.

If you've read any of these stories, you're probably convinced that backing up your data is a good thing. To that end, this chapter takes you through the basics of using DOS to back up your hard disk. Once you've learned the basics, though, I'll show you a number of ways to make backups easier and faster.

# Backing Up with DOS 6 (Microsoft Backup)

Microsoft Backup, with its dialog boxes, buttons, and mouse support, is definitely a modern-day program. All these fancy-shmancy features mean that even the rawest novice can do a backup in no time flat. (Programs like this make me think they're trying to put us gurus out of business!) It's all very easy and civilized.

## Microsoft Backup: The Basics

Because Backup really is quite easy to use, I'll only skim over the basics in this section. With that out of the way, you can move on to more advanced topics.

Here are the basic steps required to use Microsoft Backup:

1. Start Microsoft Backup by typing `msbackup` and pressing Enter.

> If you're starting Microsoft Backup for the first time, you'll see a warning about a "disk compatibility test" not having been run. This test performs a small backup to verify that the program can back up and restore files properly and to make sure there are no hardware incompatibilities. To ensure safe backups, be sure you run this test (by first selecting the Configure button and then the Compatibility Test button) before using the program.

2. In the screen that appears, select the **B**ackup button to display the Backup dialog box.
3. Use the Bac**k**up From list to select the drive you want to back up and use the Se**l**ect Files button to pick out which files you want to include or exclude from the backup.
4. Use the Backup T**y**pe button to select one of the three backup types:

   **F**ull: backs up all the selected files. Each file's archive attribute is turned off.

   **I**ncremental: backs up only files that have changed since the last full or incremental backup. The selected files' archive attributes are turned off.

   **D**ifferential: backs up only files that have changed since the last full backup. The archive attributes are *not* turned off.
5. Use the B**a**ckup To button to select a destination for the files.
6. Select the **S**tart Backup button.
7. Follow the prompts on the screen for inserting disks.

# Using Backup's Setup Files

Setup files are one of the most powerful features of Microsoft Backup. Setup files "remember" things like the files you selected, the backup type, the floppy drive used for the backup, and whatever other options you've chosen. In the future, then, all you have to do is select the appropriate setup file, and Backup configures everything automatically.

To create a setup file, first get Microsoft Backup set up the way you want (file selections, backup type, and so on) and then select the Save Setup **A**s option from the **F**ile menu. In the dialog box that appears, use the File **N**ame box to enter an eight-character filename. If you also want to enter a description of the setup (it's probably a good idea), use the Des**c**ription box. Now just select the OK button and you're done.

**Guru Trivia**

> For each setup you save, Microsoft Backup creates two files to hold the option settings and the file selection. For example, if you have a setup named DBASE, the file DBASE.SET holds the option settings and the file DBASE.SLT holds the names of the selected files.

Anytime you need to use a setup file, just select the Setup File button in the Backup dialog box and open the one you want from the Setup File list that appears.

## Optimizing Microsoft Backup

As you can see in Figure 5.1, Microsoft Backup gives you a fairly impressive list of options (for a program that doesn't cost you anything extra). Most of these options have some effect on either the speed of the program or the security of the backed-up data.

When choosing your options, you need to keep in mind that you're dealing with a zero-sum game. You can make Backup perform faster, but usually at the cost of some security. Conversely, the more secure you make your data, the slower the program becomes. Which route you choose depends on how much patience you have and how good your nerves are.

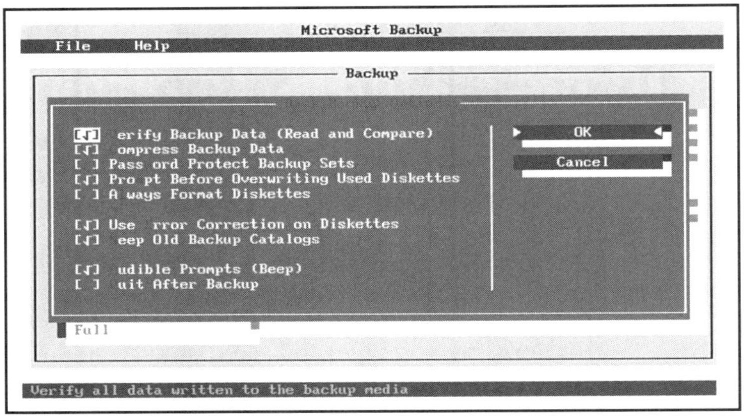


**Figure 5.1.** Microsoft Backup options.

## Optimizing for Speed

For the Type-A personalities in the crowd, here are some tips to make Microsoft Backup faster:

- Select the Compress Backup Data option. This saves time, not only by speeding up the program, but by shrinking the data so that it can fit on fewer disks.

The Compress Backup Data option speeds up Backup by switching to a sophisticated algorithm that tries to steal CPU cycles between the time it's reading data from the hard disk and writing it to the floppy. (You can tell this is going on when you see both the hard disk light and the floppy drive light on at the same time).

- Turn off the **V**erify Backup Data option. Data verification rereads the data written to the disk and compares it to the original files, which can really slow things down.

Turning off **V**erify Backup Data is less of a risk if you keep it on the first time you use a disk (or if you're using really old disks, which is never a good idea). The program alerts you if the disk contains any bad sectors.

- Be sure the A**l**ways Format Diskettes option is turned off. If you're backing up to used disks, this option really slows you down because it formats every disk you use.
- Turn off the Pro**m**pt Before Overwriting Used Diskettes option. Backup destroys any information on a previously used disk, and this option warns you if the disk contains any data. You don't need this convenience if you're recycling your backup disks.
- Use high-density disks (especially 1.44M, if possible). These disks not only hold more data (which means you need fewer disks), but files can be written to high-density disks faster than the low-density variety.
- Turn off the Use **E**rror Correction on Diskettes option. Error Correction writes information to a disk that lets you restore files from the disk if it gets damaged. These disk writes themselves take only a marginal amount of time, but they use up valuable disk space (13 percent of a 1.2M disk; 11 percent of a 1.44M disk).

## Optimizing for Data Security

For paranoid types, here are a few suggestions for maximizing the security of your data:

- ✦ Turn on the **V**erify Backup Data option. This is an option that leaves nothing to chance. Each hunk of data written to the floppy disk is reread and then carefully compared to the original. This lets Backup detect defective floppies and data transfer errors, but it basically doubles the backup time.
- ✦ Select the Use **E**rror Correction on Diskettes option. This option saves information on each backup disk that can be used to restore your files should the disk become damaged.
- ✦ Turn on the A**l**ways Format Diskettes option. For the truly paranoid, this option is a safeguard against writing data to a disk that was formatted on a drive with its heads out of alignment.
- ✦ Perform a compare immediately after each backup. This verifies that the data on the floppy is restorable.

# The *BACKUP* Command

The DOS BACKUP command has been around since Version 2.0. It may not be as pretty as DOS 6's Microsoft Backup, but it gets the job done. The topics in this section give you some background information on BACKUP, so you can use it to your best advantage.

## What *BACKUP* Does

If you run DIR on one of your backup disks, you may be surprised to see that none of your files are there! Instead, you'll see a listing that looks something like this:

```
Volume in drive A is BACKUP  001
Volume Serial Number is 123A-45B6
Directory of A:\
BACKUP   001   1212416 03-21-93  11:12a
CONTROL  001 1399 03-21-93  11:12a
```

```
2 file(s)    1213815 bytes
0 bytes free
```

(This is assuming you're looking at backup disk #1; backup disk #2 would have the files BACKUP.002 and CONTROL.002, and so on.) Just what's going on here?

Well, your files are there, but they've been combined into a single file on each disk (BACKUP.001, BACKUP.002, and so on). The CONTROL.001 file keeps track of which files are in BACKUP.001 (the filenames, their original directories, and so on). This may seem like a strange way of doing things, but it has a number of advantages:

- It maximizes the available disk space. `BACKUP` puts as much as it can on each disk and only leaves a little room for the CONTROL file (the size of this file varies depending on how many files it is tracking). As you can see in the preceding listing, backup disks always end up with 0 bytes free (unless, of course, there weren't enough files to fill the disk). This helps to keep both the number of disks you need and the time the whole thing takes to a minimum.
- It allows you to back up individual files that wouldn't normally fit on a single disk. Some humungous data files can be 2M or 3M in size. `BACKUP` parcels out pieces of such files so that they span 2 or 3 disks; the CONTROL files keep track of it all.
- DOS stores the original directory for each file, but not the original drive. This lets you restore the files to a different drive, if necessary. Also, if you're restoring files and the original directories no longer exist, DOS simply recreates them, no questions asked.

## *BACKUP* Switches

`BACKUP` comes with a number of switches that can give your backups greater flexibility:

| | |
|---|---|
| `/A` | Add backup files to a disk without deleting any files (BACKUP normally deletes the disk's root directory). |
| `/D:date` | Back up only those files that have been modified on or after `date` (use the MM-DD-YY format). |

`/F:[size]` Format the backup disk to the size you specify. If you have DOS 4.0 or 5.0, you only need to use this switch if you're using a double-density disk in a high-density drive. Otherwise, `BACKUP` formats disks automatically.

`/L:[name]` Create a text file that lists the date and time of the backup, the full pathname of each file backed up, and the disk where each file is located. The file created (in your root directory) is called BACKUP.LOG unless you specify a name.

`/M` Back up only files that have changed since your last backup.

`/S` Back up any subdirectories under the current directory.

`/T:time` Back up only those files that have been modified on or after `time`. You can't use this switch by itself—you have to use it in conjunction with the `/D` switch. Enter the time in HH:MM format.

**Guru Tip**

> The main disadvantage to **BACKUP** is that you can't use **DIR** to find a backed-up file. **RESTORE** (which I'll talk about later on) can help, but it's cumbersome. Instead, you should always use the **/L** switch to create a backup log. Because it's a simple text file, you can view it in **EDIT** or print it out and put it away for safekeeping.

# Backing Up Is Hard to Do

No one disputes that backing up is a necessary chore. After all, hard disk crashes do occur and one day it will happen to you. What I'd like to do, however, is inject a little sanity into all this backing up business. Most "experts" spout what seems to be the backup party line: "Do a full backup monthly and an incremental backup daily." This means that you back up everything on your hard disk once a month and only those files that have changed on a daily basis.

Well, I'm all for regular backups, but have you ever tried to do a "full" backup? It's ridiculous! If you have a nearly full 60M hard disk and you back up to 1.2M floppies, you'll need about 50 disks to do the job.

Even with the data compression in DOS 6's Microsoft Backup, you're probably still looking at 30 disks. Heaven help you if you have a 150M or 200M hard disk! Is it any wonder nobody can get serious about backing up their data? Sorry, I'd like to do a backup, but I have to shampoo my pit bull.

# Real-World Backups

DOS gurus take a "real-world" approach to backups:

- The problem with a full backup is that it includes all your program files. Presumably, however, you have these files on disk somewhere, so why include them in a backup? If worse comes to worse, you can always re-install your programs.
- If you're going to leave out your program files, however, you should seriously consider making backup copies of your program disks. You only have to do it once and you probably only have to do it for your most important programs. (See Chapter 4, "Floppy Disk Fun," for disk copying tips.)
- All of the energy you put into backing up should go toward protecting your data files because, unlike your programs, these are usually irreplaceable. To make life easier, create separate subdirectories to hold only your data. For example, if you use WordPerfect, create a subdirectory called \WP\DOCS to hold your documents. If you're using Microsoft Backup, you could then make a setup file that backs up the data from this directory. With `BACKUP`, use the following command:

  ```
  backup c:\wp\docs\*.* a:
  ```

- You will have less to back up if you delete the garbage files created by some programs. For example, many word processors create files with a BAK extension that don't need to be archived. Other candidates for the garbage bin include files with the extensions TMP and $$$.
- Take advantage of `BACKUP`'s `/M` switch and Microsoft Backup's Incremental backup type to do incremental backups. These tell DOS to look for only those files that you've modified since the last backup. Your strategy might look something like this:

1. Do an incremental backups of modified files every couple of days (although you might consider backing up really important stuff every day).
2. If you do most of your work in one or two programs, do a full backup of these program's data directories every week or two.
3. Back up all your data once a month or so.

- With BACKUP, use the /A switch to save disks when doing incremental backups. DOS normally deletes a disk's root directory before backing up, but /A tells DOS just to add any new files to an existing backup file.
- If, after all this, you still have a few dozen megabytes or more to back up, forget DOS altogether and invest in a tape drive. They are a little pricey (compared to DOS, anyway) but they can hold hundreds of megabytes and they do it all while you're doing lunch.

> If you plan to use a tape drive, or if you would like more speed and flexibility than you get with DOS's built-in backup facilities, you need to look at a third-party backup program. There are a lot to choose from out there, but three of the best are Fastback Plus, The Norton Backup (DOS 6's Microsoft Backup program is a scaled-down version of The Norton Backup), and Central Point Backup.

# Backup Dos and Don'ts

Here are a few more hints and suggestions to make backing up easier and safer:

- Run CHKDSK before a major backup to look for any problems. (See Chapter 18, "The Guru's Survival Kit," for the lowdown on using CHKDSK.)
- Set up a backup strategy and stick to it. Otherwise, you will fall victim to McFedries' "Bad News Law #8": hard disks only crash when they have priceless, irreplaceable data that isn't backed up.
- If you're using the BACKUP command, read Part II, "Batch Files: The DOS

Guru's Best Friend." A couple of simple batch files will help you automate your backup routine (especially if you're backing up files from a bunch of different directories).

- If you're using Microsoft Backup, use setup files to configure the program quickly.
- Have your pet spayed or neutered.
- Don't use 5.25-inch disks if you don't have to. With high-density 3.5-inch disks, you not only get a little more data on each disk, you also get the added safety of a sturdy case.
- Don't keep all your backup disks in one place. If a thief happens upon them, you'll be out of luck. Some folks go as far as keeping a copy in an offsite location such as a safety deposit box.
- Don't forget to print out a copy of your backup information and store it with your backup disks. If you're using `BACKUP`, add the `/L` switch to create BACKUP.LOG. With Microsoft Backup, print out a copy of the setup file data.
- Don't use low-priced, no-name disks for your backups. Stick with high-quality disks, and you'll sleep better at night.
- Don't be lazy. Back up your files now!

# Restoring Your Data

In the unhappy event that you need to use any of your backed-up files, you can't simply copy them from the appropriate backup disk because of the special format DOS uses to store them. Instead, you need to use either Microsoft Backup's Restore feature or the `RESTORE` command.

## Restoring with Microsoft Backup

Restoring files with Microsoft Backup is just as easy as backing them up. However, the options shown in Figure 5.2 let you gain total control over your restoration projects.

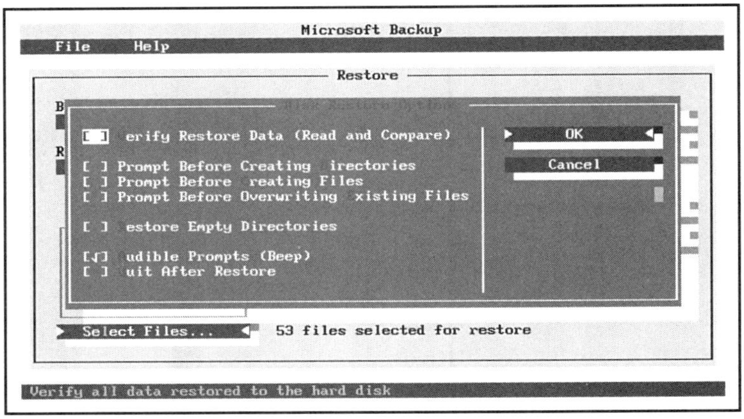


**Figure 5.2.** Microsoft Backup's restore options.

Here's a quick summary of some of the available options:

**V**erify Restore Data — Ensures that the data is written correctly to the hard disk. It's safe, but it really slows things down.

Prompt Before Creating **D**irectories — Alerts you before creating any new directories. This lets you skip directories you no longer need.

Prompt Before Creating **F**iles — Alerts you before restoring files not currently on your hard drive. This lets you skip old files that you don't want restored.

Prompt Before Overwriting **E**xisting Files — This option can help you avoid over writing files with older versions.

**R**estore Empty Directories — If you normally only back up data directories, this option lets you restore your entire directory structure in the event of a hard disk crash.

## The *RESTORE* Command's Switches

Like `BACKUP`, `RESTORE` also comes with a number of switches for added flexibility:

| Switch | Description |
|---|---|
| `/A:date` | Restore only those files date stamped on or after `date`. |
| `/B:date` | Restore only those files date stamped on or before `date`. |
| `/D` | Display a list of the files to be restored. Does not restore the files. |
| `/E:time` | Restore only those files time stamped at or earlier than `time`. |
| `/L:time` | Restore only those files time stamped at or later than `time`. |
| `/M` | Restore only files that have changed since the last time they were backed up. |
| `/N` | Restore only files that no longer exist on the target disk. |
| `/P` | Tell `RESTORE` to prompt you for permission to restore files that have changed since the last backup. |
| `/S` | Restore all subdirectories. |

> If you plan to use either `/E` or `/L`, be sure you also use one of the date switches (`/A` or `/B`) as well. Using, say, `/E` without a date means you'll get all files stamped at or before the time you specify, regardless of the date.

## Restoring Individual Files

If you accidentally delete a file (and `UNDELETE` won't bring it back), you can use `RESTORE` to get the file from your backup disks. This is much easier if you have a backup log. For example, suppose you want to restore a file called RESTORE.ME to your WP\DOCS directory. Look in the log to see which disk the file is on and enter the following command (assuming your backup disk is in drive A:):

```
restore a: c:\wp\docs\restore.me
```

DOS prompts you to enter backup disk 01. If your file is on disk 01, go ahead and insert it. Otherwise, just insert the appropriate disk. DOS, of course, gets all flustered and presents you with the following ominous-looking message:

```
WARNING! Disk is out of sequence
Replace disk or continue if OK
Press any key to continue...
```

At this point, you can laugh knowingly and press a key to restore the file. (Most DOS beginners sooner or later stumble upon the oldest DOS joke in the world. They see a message like the one above and say, "Gee, where's the 'any' key? Yuk, yuk." After you've heard this joke 57 times or so, you'll be sorely tempted to throttle the next person who says it. A few deep breaths should calm you down.)

If you don't have a backup log, you have to insert each backup disk in sequence until RESTORE finds the file you want.

# Guru Review

This chapter showed you how to protect your valuable data with both Microsoft Backup and the BACKUP command. Here are some things to think about:

- Use Microsoft Backup's setup files to easily switch between backup configurations.
- When optimizing Microsoft Backup, you have to choose between speed and security—you can't have both.
- Take full advantage of the BACKUP command's switches to get maximum control over your backups. You can use the switches for things like backing up modified files only, backing up files that have changed only after a certain date, and handling subdirectories.
- You should always use BACKUP's /L switch to create a backup log. This makes it easier to restore individual files.
- Set up a "real-world" backup strategy that includes backing up only your data files, performing frequent incremental backups, and deleting garbage and temporary files before backing up.

# Batch Files: The DOS Guru's Best Friend

# PART II

# Batch File Basics

## Guru Stuff in This Chapter ➤

# 6

CHAPTER

- *Batch file background information*
- *Using batch files to start your programs*
- *Using* ECHO *to give voice to your batch files*
- *Using* PAUSE *to temporarily halt a batch file*
- *Top-notch tips to get you started with batch files*

I once suffered through a course in assembly language programming back in my college days. (Assembly language is a low-level programming language that's only one step above the 1s and 0s of machine code; it is, in short, brutal.) The highlight of the course was hooking up a simple robotic arm to a PC and creating a program that controlled the arm from the keyboard. It wasn't exactly state-of-the-art robotics, but I got a real kick out of it.

This chapter is your equivalent of hooking up a robotic arm. The batch files you'll be working with will perform only very simple tasks; but, hey, it's still pretty cool stuff, and it's necessary work for the more powerful techniques to come in the next two chapters.

# Batch Files: Some Background

DOS uses a program called COMMAND.COM to handle anything you type at the prompt. COMMAND.COM has some DOS commands—such as `COPY`, `DIR`, and `DEL`—built right in (these are called *internal* commands).

For most anything else, including your software applications and the *external* DOS commands such as `FORMAT`, `UNDELETE`, and `BACKUP`, COMMAND.COM executes by calling a separate program. In both cases, DOS executes the command or program and returns to the prompt to wait for further orders.

If you tell COMMAND.COM to execute a batch file, however, things are a little different. COMMAND.COM goes into *batch mode*, where it takes all its input from the individual lines of a batch file. These lines are just commands that (in most cases) you otherwise have to type in yourself. COMMAND.COM repeats the following four-step procedure until it has processed each line in the batch file:

1. It reads a line from the batch file.
2. It closes the batch file.
3. It executes the command.
4. It reopens the batch file.

The main advantage of batch mode, of course, is that you can lump several commands together in a single batch file and tell DOS to execute them all simply by typing the name of the batch file. This is great for automating routine tasks such as program loading, backups, and formatting. And if you throw in any of the eight DOS commands that enhance batch files, you can do some really groovy guru stuff.

# Creating Batch Files

Before getting started with some concrete batch file examples, you need to know how to create the little beasts. Depending on the software you have loaded on your computer and which version of DOS you have, there are four different methods you can use to create batch files:

- Use the `COPY CON` command to create the file at the DOS prompt (refer to Chapter 1, "Guru File Management," for details). This is the fastest method, but you're out of luck if you want to make changes to the file. Only use this method for very short (2 or 3 lines) batch files.
- Use your word processor. If you use this method, be sure the file you create is a text-only file. Some word processors have a text mode that you can use. In others, you use the Save As command and select the "Text" or "ASCII" option. Although this method allows you to edit your files at will, it's probably over-kill for short batch programs.
- Use EDIT if you have DOS 5 or 6. EDIT is a handy little text editor that was introduced in DOS 5. Overall, this is probably the best method. You can quickly load the program, create or make changes to your batch file, exit the program, and then run the file.
- Use (ugh!) EDLIN. EDLIN is a program (it comes with all versions of DOS except DOS 6) that enables you to edit text files one line at a time. It's not very pretty, but it'll do if that's all you've got.

Once you've decided on a method for creating your batch files, the rest is easy. Just enter any DOS commands exactly as you would at the DOS prompt (with a couple of exceptions, as you'll see later) and include whatever batch instructions you need. When it comes time to name the file, you need to watch for two things:

- The primary name must follow the DOS naming conventions outlined in Chapter 1.
- The extension must be BAT.

**Guru Trivia**

> When naming your batch files, don't use the same name as a DOS command (for example, if you create a backup batch file, don't name it BACKUP.BAT). If you do, the batch file will never run! Here's why: when you enter something at the prompt, COMMAND.COM first checks to see if it's an internal DOS command. If it's not, it then checks for (in order) a COM, EXE, or BAT file with a matching name. Because all external DOS commands use COM or EXE extensions, COMMAND.COM never bothers to check if your batch file even exists!

# A Home for Your Batch Files

Once you start using batch files regularly, you'll probably wonder how you got along without them. In fact, many people find that once they get the hang of batch files (which is usually pretty quickly), the little munchkins seem to breed when you're not looking.

Things can get pretty confusing if you have BAT files scattered all over your hard disk. To remedy this, it makes sense to create a new directory (I call mine BATCH) to hold all your batch files.

To make this strategy effective, however, you have to tell DOS to look in the BATCH directory to find these files. You do this with the `PATH` command. This command has the following general form:

```
PATH dir1;dir2;...
```

where `dir1`, `dir2`, and so on are the names of directories. What this command effectively is telling DOS is "Whenever I enter run a command, if you can't find the appropriate file in the current directory, look for it in any of the directories listed in the `PATH` statement." In this case, you should at least enter the following:

```
path c:\;c:\dos;c:\batch
```

You might also want to include some of your program directories so you can run them from anywhere on your hard disk. You need to enter this command every time you start your computer. To have this command run automatically with each DOS session, refer to Chapter 13, "AUTOEXEC.BAT: Your Most Important Batch File."

Guru Tip

> If you already have an AUTOEXEC.BAT file, it probably includes a **PATH** statement. If it does, just add **c:\batch** to it (be sure, however, to separate each PATH directory with a semicolon).

# Using Batch Files to Start Programs

Starting programs on your computer is often an exercise in inefficiency. You have to first change to the program's directory, enter the command to start the program (including any switches or parameters required by the program), and then return to your original directory when you're done. What you need is a batch file robot to handle all this for you. For example, if you use WordPerfect, you could create a batch file called RUNWP.BAT with the following commands:

```
C:
CD\WP51
WP
CLS
CD\
```

The first two lines log on to the correct drive and change to the `\WP51` directory, and then the third line starts WordPerfect. Once you exit the program, the last two lines clear the screen and return you to the root directory. You can use this same basic setup for all of the programs you run regularly.

# *REM*: The Simplest Batch File Command

The first of the batch file-specific DOS commands is REM (which stands for "remark"). This simple little fellow tells DOS to ignore everything else on the current line. It's used by batch file mavens almost exclusively to add short comments to their files:

```
REM This batch file changes to the WordPerfect
REM directory and starts the program.
C:
CD\WP51
WP
CLS
CD\
```

Why would anyone want to do this? Well, it's probably not all that necessary with short, easy-to-understand batch files, but some of the more complex beasts that you'll be seeing in the next two chapters can appear incomprehensible at first glance. A few pithy REM statements can help clear things up (not only for other people, but even for you if you haven't looked at the file in a couple of months).

Dunce

It's best, however, not to get too crazy with your REM statements. Having too many slows a batch file to a crawl. You really only need a few REMs at the beginning to outline the purpose of the file and one or two to explain each of your more cryptic commands.

# *ECHO*: The Robot's Voice

When it's processing a batch file, DOS normally lets you know what's going on by displaying each command before executing it. This is fine, but it's often better to include more expansive descriptions, especially if other people will be using your batch files. The ECHO batch file command lets you do just that.

For example, here's a simple batch file that performs an incremental backup of files from two directories (\WP51\DOCS and \123\SHEETS) and courteously tells the user what's about to happen:

```
ECHO To let you get a good night's sleep, this batch
ECHO file is about to back up the WordPerfect files.
ECHO Please have a floppy disk handy...
BACKUP C:\WP51\DOCS\*.* A: /M /A
ECHO Hi, it's me again. Now to back up the 1-2-3 files... BACKUP
C:\123\SHEETS\*.* A: /M /A
```

The idea here is that when DOS stumbles upon the `ECHO` command, it simply displays the rest of the line on-screen. Sounds pretty simple, right? Well, here's what the first part of the file looks like when you run it:

```
C:\>ECHO To let you get a good night's sleep, this batch To let you get a
good night's sleep, this batch
C:\>ECHO file is about to back up the WordPerfect files.
file is about to back up the WordPerfect files.
C:\>ECHO Please have a floppy disk handy...
Please have a floppy disk handy...
C:\>BACKUP C:\WP51\DOCS\*.* A: /M /A
Insert last backup disk in drive A:
Press any key to continue...
```

Whoa, what a mess! The problem is that DOS is displaying the command and `ECHO`ing the line. Fortunately, DOS provides two solutions:

- To prevent DOS from displaying a command as it executes it, precede the command with the `@` symbol:

  ```
  @ECHO To let you get a good night's sleep, this batch
  ```

- To prevent DOS from displaying any commands, place the following at the beginning of the batch file:

  ```
  ECHO OFF
  ```

This tells DOS not to display anything unless you explicitly invoke the `ECHO` command.

**Guru Tip**

> DOS still displays the **ECHO OFF** command. To prevent this, add an **@** symbol so the command becomes **@ECHO OFF**. Most DOS gurus use this command instead of the individual **@** symbols.

Here's what the output looks like with the commands hidden:

```
To let you get a good night's sleep, this batch
file is about to back up the WordPerfect files.
Please have a floppy disk handy...
Insert last backup disk in drive A:
Press any key to continue...
```

Ah, that's better.

**Guru Tip**

> You might think that you can display a blank line simply by using ECHO by itself. That would be nice, but it doesn't work (DOS just tells you the current state of ECHO—on or off). Instead, use one of the following methods:

- If you're using DOS 5 or later, add a period (.) immediately after ECHO.
- For any DOS version, type ECHO then hold down Alt and press 255.

# The *PAUSE* That Refreshes

Sometimes you want to see something a batch file displays (such as a directory listing) before continuing. Or, you may want to alert users that something important is about to happen so they can chew over the possible ramifications (and bail out if they get cold feet). In both cases, you can use the PAUSE command to temporarily halt the execution of a batch file.

In Chapter 4, "Floppy Disk Fun," I showed you an undocumented FORMAT switch (/AUTOTEST) that formats a floppy without prompting you for the disk, volume label, or if you want to format another. This is pretty handy, but if you happen to forget to insert a disk, the entire format is abruptly aborted. Here's a batch file called MYFORMAT.BAT that formats a disk in drive A: with the /AUTOTEST switch, but uses PAUSE to make sure you've inserted the disk:

```
REM This batch file formats a disk in drive A using
REM the /AUTOTEST switch. PAUSE is used to prompt the
REM user to insert a disk.
@ECHO OFF
CLS
ECHO About to run FORMAT on drive A...
ECHO To cancel, press Ctrl+C or Ctrl+Break.
```

```
ECHO Otherwise, place a floppy disk in drive A and then
PAUSE
FORMAT A: /AUTOTEST
```

When you run this batch file, the following output is produced:

```
About to run FORMAT on drive A...
To cancel, press Ctrl+C or Ctrl+Break.
Otherwise, place a floppy disk in drive A and then
Press any key to continue . . .
```

Notice that the `PAUSE` command displays the following:

```
Press any key to continue...
```

To continue processing the rest of the batch file, all you do is press any key. If you don't want to continue, you can cancel simply by pressing Ctrl+C or Ctrl+Break. DOS asks you to confirm:

```
Terminate batch job (Y/N)?
```

Just press `y` to return to the prompt.

**Guru Tip**

> Pressing Ctrl+C or Ctrl+Break (they're the same thing) cancels any batch file. To cancel without the usual confirmation message, press Escape.

# Getting the User's Attention

The `PAUSE` command is designed to stop a batch file so the user can see something on-screen (such as a list of files) or perform some action (such as inserting a floppy disk). But it doesn't do a lot of good if the user doesn't notice the `PAUSE` prompt or is busy doing something else.

To give your `PAUSE`s the recognition they deserve, you can use the `ECHO` command to beep the computer's speaker. To demonstrate, create a batch file called BEEP.BAT by following these steps:

1. Type `copy con beep.bat` and press Enter.
2. Type `@ECHO OFF` and press Enter.

3. Type ECHO, press Alt+7, and then press Enter.
4. Press F6 and Enter to copy the file.

Now, if you run BEEP.BAT, you'll hear a short beep from your computer. Neat, huh? The secret is the Alt+7 character (which appears on-screen as ^G). This is simply the ASCII code for Control-G, the beep character.

To use this with PAUSE, press Alt+7 at the end of the ECHO command immediately preceding PAUSE in your batch file.

Guru Tip

> To add the beep character in EDIT, first press Ctrl+P to tell EDIT you want to add a control character, then press Alt+7. The character appears as a small dot.

# Guru Review

In this chapter, I presented you with some simple batch file basics to get you started:

- Batch files are really just collections of DOS commands. Their main advantage is that you can combine several commands in a single file and run them all simply by entering the name of the file at the DOS prompt.
- To keep your batch files in order, store them in their own directory and add the directory to your PATH statement.
- To run your programs from a batch file, simply include the appropriate commands to change to the program's directory, start the program, and return to your original directory.
- Use the REM batch command to add comments to your batch files. DOS ignores any line in a batch file that begins with REM.
- To output information to the screen from a batch file, use the ECHO command.

✦ To prevent DOS from cluttering up the screen with batch commands, include `@ECHO OFF` at the beginning of each batch file.

✦ Use `PAUSE` to temporarily halt a batch file. This is useful when you need time to digest some information displayed on-screen or if you want to confirm an action that's about to take place.

✦ To cancel a batch file, press Ctrl+C or Ctrl+Break, and then press `y` when DOS asks you if you're sure.

# Using Variables for Batch File Flexibility

## Guru Stuff in This Chapter ➤

7

CHAPTER

- *How variables add flexibility to your batch files*
- *Using replaceable parameters to enhance DOS*
- *Handling parameters with the* `SHIFT` *command*
- *A comprehensible explanation of the* `FOR` *command*
- *Umpteen batch file examples to get you up to speed quickly*

Most DOS commands require extra information such as a filename (for example, when you use `COPY` or `DEL`) or a directory path (like when you use `CD` or `MD`). These extra pieces of information—they're called variables or, to use the proper guru term, *parameters*—give you the flexibility to specify exactly how you want a command to work. You can add the same level of flexibility to your batch files and this chapter will show you how.

# How Variables Help

To see how variables work in a batch file, take a look at the following example, called PARAMS.BAT:

```
@ECHO OFF
ECHO.
ECHO The first parameter is %1
ECHO The second parameter is %2
ECHO The third parameter is %3
```

As you can see, this batch file doesn't do much except `ECHO` four lines to the screen (the first of which is just a blank line). Curiously, however, each `ECHO` command ends with a percent sign (`%`) and a number. Type in and save the PARAMS.BAT, and then to see what these unusual symbols mean, enter the following command at the DOS prompt:

```
params Tinkers Evers Chance
```

which produces the following output:

```
C:\BATCH>params Tinkers Evers Chance

The first parameter is Tinkers
The second parameter is Evers
The third parameter is Chance
```

The first line in the output:

```
The first parameter is Tinkers
```

is produced by the following `ECHO` command in PARAMS.BAT:

```
ECHO The first parameter is %1
```

When DOS sees the `%1` symbol in a batch file, it examines the original command and looks for the first word after the batch filename and then replaces `%1` with that word. In the example, the first word after `params` is `Tinkers`, so DOS uses that to replace `%1`. (This is why you'll often hear gurus call `%1` a *replaceable parameter*.) Only when it has done this does it proceed to `ECHO` the line to the screen. `%2` is similar except that, in this case, DOS looks for the second word after the batch filename (`Evers` in the example).

**Guru Tip**

> If your batch file command has more parameters than the batch file is looking for, the extras are ignored. For example, adding a fourth parameter to the **PARAMS** command line has no effect on the operation of the file.

Let's look at real-world example. First consider the following slightly useful, but highly inflexible batch file called NEWDIR.BAT:

```
@ECHO OFF
CLS
MD \GALLERIA
CD \GALLERIA
```

This batch file simply creates a new directory called GALLERIA and then changes to it. You'll be surprised how often you need to do something like this, so it makes sense to try to automate the whole procedure.

Unfortunately, this isn't the best way to go about it. I mean, you could set up a batch file each time you need to create and move to a directory, but I assume that you want to spend your remaining years on the planet in some more fruitful enterprise. Instead, you can use replaceable parameters to add instant flexibility to NEWDIR.BAT:

```
@ECHO OFF
CLS
MD %1
CD %1
```

Now, if you want to create and move to a new GALLERIA directory, enter the following command:

```
newdir \galleria
```

DOS replaces each `%1` in NEWDIR.BAT with `\galleria` (the first word after `newdir`), and so the batch file works as it did before. The difference, of course, is that you can now use it for other directories, as well. For example, to create a new MALL directory and move to it, use the following command:

```
newdir \mall
```

Guru Tip

> You can't use more than nine replaceable parameters in a batch file (%1 through %9).

Guru Tip

> Well, I lied slightly. There is a tenth replaceable parameter (%0), which holds the name of the batch file itself.

# Improving on DOS

Because a batch file's replaceable parameters work just like the parameters used in DOS commands, it's not hard to create batch files that mimic—and even improve upon—the standard DOS fare.

## Making *DEL* Safer

Probably 99.9 percent of all accidental deletions occur when you use wildcard characters to delete multiple files. A question mark in the wrong place, or a `*.*` in the wrong directory can lead to disaster.

It would help if you could see a list of all the files you were about to delete and then have the option of canceling the deletion if things weren't right. The easiest way to do this, of course, is to run a `DIR` using the same file specification as you'll use with `DEL`. But it's usually a pain typing two commands and making sure that you get the `?`s and `*`s in the right place each time. This is a situation that cries out for a batch file, and here it is (it's called SAFEDEL.BAT):

```
@ECHO OFF
CLS
ECHO %0 %1
ECHO.
ECHO Here's a list of the files that will be deleted:
```

```
DIR %1 /ON /W
ECHO.
ECHO To cancel the deletion, press Ctrl+C. Otherwise
PAUSE
DEL %1
```

**Dunce**

> This is as good a place as any to tell you to always leave spaces on either side of your replaceable parameters. A command such as `DIR%1` could replace, say, `DIR*.TXT`, which will produce an error.

You use SAFEDEL.BAT just like the `DEL` command. For example, to delete all the BAK files in the current directory, enter the following:

```
safedel *.bak
```

The following list is a quick summary of what happens:

- ✦ The command `ECHO %0 %1` simply redisplays the batch filename (`%0`) and the file specification (`%1`) for reference.
- ✦ The `DIR %1 /ON /W` command is used to get an alphabetical listing (in wide format so you can see more files) of everything that's about to be deleted.
- ✦ The batch file then `PAUSE`s so you can examine the files.
- ✦ If you decide to continue, the `DEL %1` command takes care of the job.

**Dunce**

> The percent sign (%) is a perfectly good character to use in a filename, but if you try to reference a file named, for example, PERCNT%.WKS, you'll run into problems. The reason is that when DOS processes batch files, it mindlessly deletes any single occurrences of % as part of its parameter replacement chores. So PERCNT%.WKS becomes PERCNT.WKS and things go haywire. To fix this, use double percent signs when referring to the file in a batch command (for example, PERCNT%%.WKS).

## Changing Directories and Drives in One Step

The CD command falls down on the job if you need to change to a directory on a different drive. You have to change to the drive first and then run CD. Tut, tut. Use CDD.BAT to do it all in one command:

```
@ECHO OFF
%1:
CD \%2
```

To change, for example, to the A: drive's BACKUP directory, simply use the following command:

```
cdd a backup
```

If you hate typing backslashes, you can avoid them altogether by adding a couple of extra CD commands:

```
@ECHO OFF
%1:
CD \%2
CD %3
CD %4
```

Now, to change to the \BACKUP\123\DATA directory on drive A:, enter the following:

```
cdd a backup 123 data
```

## Excluding Files from a Copy Command

The wildcard characters are used to include multiple files in a single DOS command. But what if you want to exclude certain files? For example, suppose you have a WP\DOCS directory that has files with various extensions—DOC, TXT, WP, and so on. What do you do if you want to copy all the files to drive B:, except those with the TXT extension? One solution is to use separate XCOPY commands for each extension you do need, but that's too much work (and besides, you might miss some). Instead, try this batch file (it's called DONTCOPY.BAT):

```
@ECHO OFF
CLS
ATTRIB +H %1
```

```
ECHO.
ECHO Copying all files to %2 except %1:
ECHO.
XCOPY *.* %2
ATTRIB -H %1
```

To use this batch file to copy all the files in the current directory to drive B:, except, for example, those with the extension TXT, use the following command:

```
dontcopy *.txt b:
```

The secret here is that DOS won't copy hidden files. So `DONTCOPY` uses the `ATTRIB` command to hide the files that you want to ignore. The first command, `ATTRIB +H %1`, does just that. So now all that's needed is an `XCOPY` command that copies everything that's not hidden (use `*.*` to do this) to the target (`%2`). When that's done, `DONTCOPY` uses another `ATTRIB` command to show the files.

Dunce

> To be safe, DONTCOPY.BAT should check to make sure that a destination parameter (**%2**) was entered. This is doable, but you need to use the batch file commands **IF** and **GOTO**. These commands are discussed in the next chapter.

Dunce

> You can use the same idea to exclude files with other DOS commands. For example, DOS won't delete or rename hidden files, so it wouldn't be hard to create the appropriate DONTDEL.BAT and DONTREN.BAT batch files. For more information on the **ATTRIB** command, see Chapter 16, "The Fun Stuff: Advanced DOS Commands."

# SHIFT: A Different Approach to Parameters

Although you won't be using it in this chapter, you should know that there's another way to handle parameters inside batch files—the `SHIFT` command. To see how it works, rewrite the PARAMS.BAT file to get PARAMS2.BAT:

```
@ECHO OFF
ECHO.
ECHO The first parameter is %1
SHIFT
ECHO The second parameter is %1
SHIFT
ECHO The third parameter is %1
```

If you enter the command

```
params Tinkers Evers Chance
```

you get the same output as before:

```
C:\BATCH>params Tinkers Evers Chance

The first parameter is Tinkers
The second parameter is Evers
The third parameter is Chance
```

How does this work? Well, each `SHIFT` command shuffles the parameters down one position. In particular, `%2` goes to `%1`, so the command

```
ECHO The second parameter is %1
```

really does display the second parameter. All the other parameters change as well, of course: `%3` goes to `%2`, `%1` goes to `%0`, and `%0` heads off to oblivion.

This sort of behavior is handy for two types of situations:

- Batch files that require more than 10 parameters. There aren't a whole lot of times when you'll need this many variables, but at least you know you can handle it when the need arises.
- Batch files that use a varying number of parameters. This is a much more common scenario and you'll see a couple of examples in Chapter 8, "Making Smart Batch Files."

Just so you know, I'm passing the buck on the `SHIFT` examples because, to use it properly, you need an `IF` command to test whether or not there are any more parameters left to shift. The `IF` command is discussed in Chapter 8.

# The Loopy *FOR* Command

Pound for pound, the `FOR` command is easily the most underutilized and misunderstood of all DOS commands. This is bad news because `FOR` is an extremely powerful weapon that shouldn't be left out of any DOS guru's arsenal. The problem, I think, is that `FOR` has a somewhat bizarre syntax that makes the command wildly unappealing at first glance. So before seeing what it looks like, I'll give you some background.

## Looping: The Basics

If you want to instruct someone on how to dress each day, you might begin with a simple step-by-step approach:

```
Step 1_Put on underwear.
Step 2_Put on socks.
Step 3_Put on pants.
Step 4_Put on shirt.
```

This is fine, but you can make things simpler by creating a list—underwear, socks, pants, shirt—and telling the person to put on everything in this list in the order they appear. Now, instead of a linear approach, you've got a primitive "loop" going—the person looks at the list, puts on the first item, looks at the list again, puts on the second item, and so on.

Now you can formalize our instructions into a single, pithy statement: for each item *X* in the following set (socks, underwear, pants, shirt) put on *X*.

Programmers often use loops like this to add generality to programs. Instead of writing a dozen different instructions, they can often write a single, generic instruction (something like `put on X`), loop through it a dozen times, and each time supply it with a different input (underwear, socks, and so on).

## Finally, the *FOR* Command

The `FOR` command is a batch file's way of looping through an instruction:

```
FOR %%variable IN (set) DO command
```

Looks like bad news, doesn't it? Well, see how it looks if you plug in the dressing instructions:

```
FOR %%X IN (underwear, socks, pants, shirt) DO put on %%X
```

Hmmm. That's a little more comprehensible, so now break down the `FOR` command for a closer look:

| | |
|---|---|
| `%%variable` | This is the variable that changes each time through the loop (`%%X` in the example). You can use any single character after the two percent signs (except 0 through 9). There are two percent signs because, as I explained earlier, DOS deletes single ones as it processes the batch file. |
| `IN (set)` | This is the list (it's called the *set*, officially) of choices for `%%X` (in the example, underwear, socks, and so on). You can use spaces, commas, or semicolons to separate the items in the set, and you have to enclose them in parentheses. |
| `DO command` | For each item in the set, the batch file performs whatever instruction is given by `command` (such as `put on X`). The variable `%%X` is normally found somewhere in `command`. |

# A Simple Batch File Example

Here's an example of the `FOR` command in a simple batch file that may help to clear things up:

```
@ECHO OFF
FOR %%B IN (Tinkers Evers Chance) DO ECHO %%B
```

This batch file (call it PARAMS3.BAT) produces the following output:

```
C:\BATCH>params3
Tinkers
Evers
Chance
```

All this does is loop through the three items in the set (`Tinkers`, `Evers`, and `Chance`) and substitutes each one for `%%B` in the command `ECHO %%B`. In other words, this `FOR` loop is equivalent to the following three `ECHO` commands:

```
ECHO Tinkers
ECHO Evers
ECHO Chance
```

# Different Sets for Different Folks

The set in a FOR command can hold more than simple strings such as Tinkers and Evers. The real power of FOR comes when you use file specifications, DOS command names, and even replaceable parameters as part of a set.

For example, have you ever copied a bunch of files into the wrong directory? It happens from time to time; and it's usually a mess to clean up, because these files get all mixed up with whatever was already in the directory. Before sticking the handiest object through your monitor, check out the following batch file (called CLEANUP.BAT):

```
@ECHO OFF
FOR %%F IN (*.*) DO DEL C:\WRONGDIR\%%F
```

This batch file assumes you copied all the files from the current directory into the WRONGDIR directory. In this case, the set is given by the *.* file specification. FOR ends up looping through every file in the current directory and, for each one, deleting it in the WRONGDIR directory.

To see how to use DOS command names in a set, you can redo the NEWDIR.BAT batch file created earlier. Here's NEWDIR2.BAT:

```
@ECHO OFF
CLS
FOR %%C IN (MD CD) DO %%C %1
```

As you can see, the set consists of the two DOS command names MD and CD. These are substituted each time through the loop for %%C, so this single FOR command is equivalent to the two commands in NEWDIR.BAT:

```
MD %1
CD %1
```

The FOR command is very powerful if you use replaceable parameters inside the set. The most common use for this potent combination is to create your own versions of DOS commands that accept multiple parameters. For example, here's a batch file (called SUPERDEL.BAT) that deletes up to nine file specifications at once:

```
@ECHO OFF
ECHO.
ECHO About to delete the following files:
ECHO %1 %2 %3 %4 %5 %6 %7 %8 %9
ECHO.
ECHO Press Ctrl+C to cancel. Otherwise,
PAUSE
FOR %%F IN (%1 %2 %3 %4 %5 %6 %7 %8 %9) DO DEL %%F
```

To use this file to delete, for example, all files in the current directory with the extensions BAK, TMP, and $$$, use the following command:

```
superdel *.bak *.tmp *.$$$
```

DOS must do two things to process the FOR command in SUPERDEL.BAT. First, it replaces the parameters inside the set so that the command looks like this:

```
FOR %%F IN (*.bak *.tmp *.$$$) DO DEL %%F
```

Then it loops through the set to delete each file specification. In the end, this is equivalent to the following three DEL commands:

```
DEL *.bak
DEL *.tmp
DEL *.$$$
```

Dunce

You can also use **FOR** at the DOS prompt. See Chapter 16, "The Fun Stuff: Advanced DOS Commands," for the scoop.

# Guru Review

This chapter lets you hit new heights of flexibility with your batch files. Here's the highlight film:

- You can run a batch file with parameters (just like in a DOS command) by including one or more replaceable parameters as part of the batch file commands.
- You can't use more than nine replaceable parameters in a batch file (%1 through %9).
- To handle more than nine parameters or an unknown number of parameters, use the SHIFT command.
- You can set up simple batch file loops by using the FOR command.

# Making Smart Batch Files

## Guru Stuff in This Chapter ➤

8

CHAPTER

- *Jumping around with the* `GOTO` *command*
- *Using the* `IF` *command to make decisions*
- *Getting feedback from other commands with* `ERRORLEVEL`
- *Using DOS 6's new* `CHOICE` *command to get user input*
- *More batch file examples than you can shake a stick at*

The stuff you learned in the last chapter—replaceable parameters and the SHIFT and FOR commands—are great for creating limber batch programs that can handle different inputs. But the batch files we've seen, well, let's be honest, they haven't been terribly bright. What you need now to reach true batch file guruhood is to learn how to construct batch files that can make decisions and alter their behavior based on those decisions. That's what this chapter is all about.

# Tell Your Batch Files Where to Go

Your basic batch file lives a simple, linear existence. The first command gets processed, then the second, the third, and so on to the end of the file. It's pretty boring, but that's all you need most of the time.

However, there are situations when this linear approach breaks down. For example, depending on a parameter or the result of a previous command, you might need to skip over a line or two. How do you do this? With the `GOTO` batch command:

```
...
... (the first batch commands)
...
GOTO NEXT
...
... (the batch commands that get skipped)
...
:NEXT
...
... (the rest of the batch commands)
...
```

Here, the `GOTO` command is telling the batch file to look for a line that begins with a colon and the word `NEXT` (this is called a *label*) and to ignore any commands in between.

Let's look at an example. Suppose your computer has two high-density disk drives and that one accepts 5.25-inch disks (drive A:, for example), and the other accepts 3.5-inch disks (drive B:). If you regularly format *double-density* disks in these drives, it can be a pain to remember the correct switches for each one.

One solution would be to set up two batch files that use the appropriate `FORMAT` command to format double-density disks in each drive. A much more elegant solution (and one that would allow me, finally, to get to the point) would be a single batch file (I'll call it DDFORMAT.BAT) that would accept the drive letter as a parameter. So the command `ddformat a` would automatically format a double-density disk in drive A:, and `ddformat b` would do the same for drive B:.

**Guru Trivia**

> Another good reason to create a single batch file instead of two is that it wastes less disk space. Here's why: the minimum amount of storage space that DOS allocates to a file is called a *cluster*. The size of a cluster depends on the disk, but 2,048 bytes is typical. This means that any small batch file that's really only, say, 50 bytes in size still occupies a full 2,048 bytes of disk real estate. The nearly 2,000 bytes of wasted space is called the *slack*. Because most batch files are smaller than a cluster, you're not going to eliminate slack problems, but you should keep it in mind when setting up your batch routines.

The tricky part is how to handle two different `FORMAT` statements in a single batch file. The old linear approach just won't cut it, but `GOTO` makes it easy:

```
REM A batch file to handle formatting double-density
REM disks in both a 5.25-inch high-density drive
REM (drive A) or a 3.5-inch high-density drive
REM (drive B).

@ECHO OFF
CLS
GOTO %1

:A
FORMAT A: /F:360
GOTO END

:B
FORMAT B: /F:720

:END
```

The command `GOTO %1` becomes `GOTO A` or `GOTO B` depending on the parameter you use in the command. If it's `A`, the batch file skips down to the `:A` label, formats the disk accordingly, and then skips to `:END` to avoid the second `FORMAT` statement. With the B parameter, the program skips past the first FORMAT to the :B label and then formats the disk in drive B:.

Another handy use of the GOTO command is for those times when you need to add copious comments to a batch file. As you know, you normally use REM to add batch file remarks. DOS doesn't try to execute these lines, but it still has to read them and this can really slow things down. Here's a way to use GOTO to get around this (literally!):

```
@ECHO OFF
GOTO START

You place your batch file comments here. Notice how
I'm not using the REM command at all. This not only
saves typing (a constant guru goal) but, hey, it
certainly looks a lot nicer, don't you think?

:START
...
... (Batch file commands)
...
```

As you can see, GOTO just leaps over the comments to end up at the :START label. DOS doesn't even know that the comments exist.

# Handling Forks in a Batch File's Road

We make decisions all the time. Some are complex and require intricate levels of logic to answer (Should I get married? Should I start a chinchilla farm?). Others are simpler and depend only on existing conditions (the proverbial fork in the road):

- If it's sunny, I'll go to the beach. Otherwise, I'll stay home and work.
- If this milk smells okay, I'll drink some. Otherwise, I'll feed it to the neighbor's cat.

No batch file (indeed, no software program yet developed) is sophisticated enough to tackle life's complex questions, but the simpler condition-based decisions are no problem. Here's a few examples of what a batch file might have to decide:

- If the `%2` equals `/Q`, jump to the Quick Format section. Otherwise, do a regular format.
- If the user forgets to enter a parameter, cancel the program. Otherwise, continue processing the batch file.
- If the file the user wants to move already exists in the new directory, display a warning. Otherwise, proceed with the move.
- If the last command failed, display an error message and cancel the program. Otherwise, continue.

# Using *IF* for Batch File Decision-Making

For these types of decisions, you need to use the `IF` batch command. `IF` has the following general form:

```
IF condition command
```

The *`condition`* is a test that evaluates to a yes or no answer ("Is it sunny?" "Did the user forget a parameter?"). The *`command`* is what gets done if the test produces a positive response ("Go to the beach," "Cancel the batch file"). The next few sections discuss the various ways you can use `IF` in your batch files.

## Testing Parameters with *IF*

One of the most common uses of the `IF` command is to check the parameters the user entered and proceed accordingly. For example, in the DDFORMAT.BAT batch file you saw earlier, the program formatted drive A: if `%1` was `A`, and it formatted drive B: if it was `B`. You can use `IF` to rewrite the batch file:

```
@ECHO OFF
CLS
IF "%1"=="A" FORMAT A: /F:360
IF "%1"=="B" FORMAT B: /F:720
```

In both `IF` statements, the *command* part is easy to spot—it's just the two `FORMAT` statements. The *condition* is a little trickier. Let's look at the first one: `"%1"=="A"`.

Remember that the condition is always a question with a yes or no answer. In this case, the question boils down to the following:

```
Is the first parameter (%1) equal to A?
```

(The double equal sign (==) looks weird, but it's just how you compare two strings of characters in a batch file.) If the answer is *yes*, the format proceeds. If it's *no*, the batch file moves on to the next `IF`, which checks to see if the parameter was `"B"`.

> Strictly speaking, you don't need to include the quotation marks ("). Using `%1==A` accomplishes the same thing. However, I prefer to use them for two reasons: first, it makes it clearer that the `IF` condition is comparing strings; second, as you'll see in the next section, the quotation marks allow you to check if the user forgot to enter a parameter at all.

> This batch file has a serious flaw that will prevent it from working under certain conditions. Specifically, if you use the lowercase `"a"` or `"b"` as a parameter, nothing happens because, to the `IF` command, `"a"` is different from `"A"`. The solution is to add extra `IF` commands to handle this:
>
> ```
> IF "%1"=="a" FORMAT A: /F:360
> ```

# Checking for Missing Parameters

Proper guru batch file techniques require you to not only check to see what a parameter is, but also whether or not one exists at all! This can be vital because a missing parameter can cause a batch file to crash and burn. For example, in Chapter 7, "Using Variables for Batch File Flexibility," I showed you a batch file called DONTCOPY.BAT designed to copy all files in the current directory to a new destination (given by the second parameter) except those you specified (given by the first parameter). Here's the listing to refresh your memory:

```
@ECHO OFF
CLS
ATTRIB +H %1
ECHO.
ECHO Copying all files to %2 except %1:
ECHO.
XCOPY *.* %2
ATTRIB -H %1
```

What happens if the user forgets to add the destination parameter (`%2`)? Well, the `XCOPY` command becomes `XCOPY *.*`, which terminates the batch file with the following error:

```
File cannot be copied onto itself
```

Bummer. The solution is to add an `IF` command that checks to see if `%2` exists:

```
@ECHO OFF
CLS
IF "%2"=="" GOTO ERROR
ATTRIB +H %1
ECHO.
ECHO Copying all files to %2 except %1:
ECHO.
XCOPY *.* %2
ATTRIB -H %1
GOTO END

:ERROR
ECHO You didn't enter a destination you naughty person!
ECHO Please try again (and pay attention this time)...

:END
```

The condition `"%2"==""` is literally comparing `%2` to nothing (`""`). If this proves to be true, the program jumps (using `GOTO`) to the `:ERROR` label and some sort of message is displayed to admonish the user. Notice, too, that if everything is okay (i.e., the user entered a second parameter), the batch file executes normally and jumps to the `:END` label to avoid displaying the error message.

**Guru Tip**

> Not everyone uses the straightforward `"%1"==""` format to check for missing parameters. You'll see bizarre constructions like `%1!==!` or `#%1==#`. They all work, but how obtuse can you get?

# Using the *SHIFT* Command

Now that you know a little about how `IF` works, I can show you how to use the `SHIFT` command introduced in the last chapter. You may recall that `SHIFT` operates by shuffling the batch file parameters down one position, so that `%1` becomes `%0`, `%2` becomes `%1`, and so on. The most common use for this apparently strange behavior is to process batch files with an unknown number of parameters. As an example, redo the SUPERDEL.BAT batch file from Chapter 7 so that it can delete any number of file specifications:

```
@ECHO OFF
IF "%1"=="" GOTO NO_FILES
:START
ECHO Now deleting %1 . . .
DEL %1
SHIFT
IF "%1"=="" GOTO DONE
GOTO START

:NO_FILES
ECHO You didn't enter a file spec!

:DONE
```

The first `IF` is familiar—it just looks for a missing parameter and, if that proves to be the case, leaps to `:NO_FILES` and displays a message. Otherwise, the program deletes the first file specification and then `SHIFT`s everything down. What was `%2` is now `%1`, and so you need the second `IF` to check the new `%1`. If it's blank, it means the user didn't enter any more file specs and the program jumps to `:DONE`. Otherwise, you loop back to `:START` and do it all again.

As you can see from SUPERDEL.BAT, it's okay to use **GOTO** to jump backward in a file and create a loop. This is often better than a **FOR** loop because instead of a single command, you can process any number of commands. However, you need to be careful or you might end up in the never-never land of an endless loop. Always include an **IF** command that will take you out of the loop once some condition has been met (such as running out of parameters).

# Using *IF* to Check Whether or Not a File Exists

Another variation of `IF` is the `IF EXIST` command that checks for the existence of a file. This is handy, for example, when you're using `COPY` or `MOVE`. You can check, first of all, whether or not the file you want to copy or move exists. Secondly, you can check to see if a file with the same name already exists in the target directory. (As you probably know, a file copied over by another of the same name is downright impossible to recover.) Here's a batch file called SAFEMOVE.BAT that uses DOS 6's new `MOVE` command to move a file, but first checks the file and then the target directory:

```
@ECHO OFF
CLS

IF EXIST %1 GOTO SO_FAR_SO_GOOD

ECHO The file %1, like, doesn't exist!
GOTO END

:SO_FAR_SO_GOOD
IF NOT EXIST %2 GOTO MOVE_IT

ECHO Whoa, the file %1 exists on the target directory!
ECHO Press Ctrl+C to bail out or, to keep going,
PAUSE

:MOVE_IT
MOVE %1 %2

:END
```

To explain what's happening, I'll use an example command:

```
safemove moveme.txt c:\wp\docs\moveme.txt
```

The first `IF` tests for the existence of `%1` (MOVEME.TXT, in the example). If there is such a file, the program skips to the `:SO_FAR_SO_GOOD` label. Otherwise, it tells the user that the file doesn't exist and then jumps down to `:END`.

The second `IF` is slightly different. In this case, I only want to continue if the MOVEME.TXT *doesn't* exist in the \WP\DOCS directory, so I add `NOT` to the condition. (You can include `NOT` in any `IF` condition.) If this proves true (i.e., that the file given by `%2` doesn't exist), the file skips to `:MOVE_IT` and performs the move. Otherwise, the user is warned and given an opportunity to cancel.

**Guru Tip**

Some batch files need to know if a directory exists (especially those, such as NEWDIR.BAT in Chapter 6, "Batch File Basics," that create new directories). Trying to plug a directory name into an `IF EXIST` condition won't work, but there's a trick that will. If you want to see if, say, the A:\BACKUP directory exists, use the following condition:

```
IF EXIST A:\BACKUP\NUL
```

It's a quirk of DOS that the NUL device "exists" in every directory and that DOS treats it as a file. So this condition will be true only if there's a directory called A:\BACKUP.

# Checking for Command Errors

McFedries' "Bad News Law #1" is really just the PC version of Murphy's Law: If anything can go wrong while using a program, it will. Good guru batch files (especially those that other people will be using) take this law to heart and always assume that *anything* can happen. So far, you've seen how `IF` can handle missing parameters and file problems, but there's lots more that can go haywire. For example, what if a batch file tries to use `XCOPY`, but there's not enough memory? Or what if the user presses Ctrl+C during a format or backup? It might seem impossible to check for these kinds of errors, but it's not only possible, it's really quite easy.

When certain DOS commands finish, they always file a "report" on the progress of the operation. This report, or *exit code* as gurus say, is really just a number that tells DOS how things went. For example, here's a list of the exit codes used by the `XCOPY` command:

| *Exit Code* | *What It Means* |
|---|---|
| 0 | Everything's OK; the files were copied. |
| 1 | Nothing happened because no files were found to copy. |
| 2 | The darned user pressed Ctrl+C to abort the copy. |
| 4 | The command failed because there wasn't enough memory or disk space, or because there was something wrong with the command's syntax. |
| 5 | The command failed because of a disk error. |

What does all this mean for your batch files? Well, you can use yet another variation of the `IF` command—`IF ERRORLEVEL`—to test for these exit codes. For example, here's a batch file called CHEKCOPY.BAT that uses some of `XCOPY`'s exit codes to check for errors:

```
@ECHO OFF
XCOPY %1 %2

IF ERRORLEVEL 4 GOTO ERROR
IF ERRORLEVEL 2 GOTO CTRL+C
IF ERRORLEVEL 1 GOTO NO_FILES
GOTO DONE

:ERROR
ECHO Bad news! The copy failed because there wasn't
ECHO enough memory or disk space or because there was
ECHO something wrong with your file specs . . .
GOTO DONE

:CTRL+C
ECHO Hey, what gives? You pressed Ctrl+C to abort . . .
GOTO DONE

:NO_FILES
ECHO Bad news! No files were found to copy . . .

:DONE
```

As you can see, the `ERRORLEVEL` conditions simply check for the individual exit codes and then use `GOTO` to jump to the appropriate label.

**Guru Trivia**

> How does a batch file know what a command's exit code was? Well, when DOS gets an exit code from a command, it stores it in a special data area set aside for exit code info. When DOS sees the `IF ERRORLEVEL` command in a batch file, it retrieves the exit code from the data area so it can be compared to whatever is in the IF condition.

One of the most important things to know about the `IF ERRORLEVEL` test is how it's interpreted by DOS. For example, consider the following `IF` command:

```
IF ERRORLEVEL 2 GOTO CTRL+C
```

DOS interprets this command as "If the exit code from the last command is *equal to or greater than* 2, then jump to the `:CTRL+C` label." This has two important consequences for your batch files:

- The test `IF ERRORLEVEL 0` doesn't tell you much because it's *always* true. If you simply want to find out if the command failed or not, use the test `IF NOT ERRORLEVEL 0`.
- To get the correct results, always test the highest `ERRORLEVEL` first and then work your way down.

Guru Tip

> Not all DOS commands produce exit codes. Some of the more common ones that do are **BACKUP**, **DISKCOPY**, **FORMAT**, **REPLACE**, **RESTORE**, and **XCOPY**. Your DOS manual lists the various exit codes for these commands.

# Do You Need to Get Input from the User [YN]?

One of the snappy new batch file features that you get with DOS 6 is the ability to ask the user questions and perform different actions based on the answer. This neat trick is handled by the `CHOICE` command. In its simplest form, you use `CHOICE` like this:

```
CHOICE Are you sure
```

When DOS processes this line, you see the following query on your screen:

```
Are you sure[Y,N]?
```

DOS then waits for the user to press either `Y` or `N` and then continues. The user's selection is stored in the `ERRORLEVEL`. The first choice (`Y`) would be `ERRORLEVEL 1` and the second choice (`N`) would be `ERRORLEVEL 2`. So all you need is one or more `IF ERRORLEVEL` tests to find out what the user selected.

Check out an example. Have you ever tried to change to a directory, only to have DOS give you an "Invalid directory" message because the directory doesn't exist? Here's a batch file called CCD.BAT that checks to see if the directory exists and asks if you want to create it if it doesn't:

```
@ECHO OFF
IF EXIST %1\NUL GOTO OK
```

```
ECHO The directory %1 doesn't exist.
CHOICE Do you want to create it
IF ERRORLEVEL 2 GOTO EXIT

MD %1
:OK
CD %1
:EXIT
```

If the directory exists, the program jumps to `:OK` and runs the `CD` command. Otherwise, you are asked if you want to create it. If they press `N` (`ERRORLEVEL 2`), the batch files skips to `:EXIT` and nothing is done. Otherwise, the directory is created with `MD`.

These simple yes/no questions are helpful, but that's not all `CHOICE` can do. For example, you can use the `/C` switch to specify the allowable keys in the prompt. For example, the command

```
CHOICE Red, Green, or Blue /C:RGB
```

produces the following prompt:

```
Red, Green, or Blue [R,G,B]?
```

Pressing `R`, `G`, or `B` produces, in this case, `ERRORLEVEL` codes of 1, 2, or 3, respectively. There are endless uses for this, but one of the most obvious is a simple menu system (MENU.BAT):

```
@ECHO OFF
CLS
ECHO 1. WordPerfect
ECHO 2. Lotus 1-2-3
ECHO.
CHOICE Which program do you want to run /C:12
IF ERRORLEVEL 2 GOTO LOTUS

CD\WP51
WP
GOTO END

:LOTUS
CD\123
123

:END
```

When you run this batch file, you see the following on your screen:

```
1. WordPerfect
2. Lotus 1-2-3

Which program do you want to run [1,2]?
```

**Guru Tip**

> Use the /N switch any time you don't want the choices and question mark to appear at the end of the prompt. This is useful for prompts that are instructions instead of questions (e.g., "Make your selection" or "Pick a number, any number").

# Guru Review

This chapter rounded out your batch file training by showing you how to create programs that leap around and make decisions. Here's a rehash of the really cool stuff:

- Use the `GOTO` command any time you need to vault over one or more commands. Don't forget to precede your labels with a colon (:).
- Use the basic `IF` command to check the parameters used when starting a batch file. If your batch file requires a parameter, be sure you test that one was entered before trying to process anything.
- `IF` normally tests if something is true. To check if something isn't true, use `IF NOT`, instead.
- The `IF EXIST` command checks to see if a specific file exists. This is a handy way to prevent errors or weird behavior in batch programs that manipulate files.
- Use the `IF ERRORLEVEL` command to check the results of certain DOS commands.
- DOS 6's new `CHOICE` command let's you get input from the user. You can keep it simple and ask basic yes/no questions, or you can "go to town" and set up elaborate menu systems.

# Guru Style: Customizing DOS

PART

# III

# Customizing the Prompt

9

CHAPTER

## Guru Stuff in This Chapter ➤

- ✦ PROMPT command basics
- ✦ *Using weird ASCII characters in your prompts*
- ✦ *Using* PROMPT *to position the cursor*
- ✦ *Using* PROMPT *to change the screen colors*
- ✦ *Lots of way-cool prompt ideas*

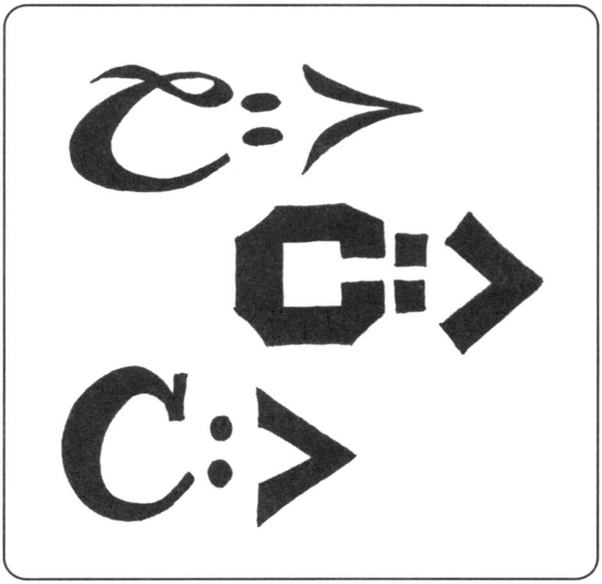

This may prove to be one of those chapters you wished you never read. Why? Well, after we get past the simple prompts that show you the basics, you'll be getting into all kinds of neat prompt special effects. Once you learn the ins and outs of creative prompting, you could easily spend hours playing with this stuff. Just don't forget to eat!

# Learning About *PROMPT*'s Metastrings

One of the first things most people learn about DOS is how to make the prompt show the current drive and directory. The proper command, of course, is:

```
prompt $p$g
```

What most people don't know (and what all gurus should know) is what this command actually means.

In the first place, DOS displays as the system prompt anything that comes after the `PROMPT` command. So, for example, if you enter the following command:

```
prompt What the @#*!$% do you want!
```

DOS uses the following prompt:

```
What the @#*!$% do you want!
```

However, not everything in a `PROMPT` command is taken so literally. The symbols `$p` and `$g` are called *metastrings* (or, sometimes, *metasymbols*), because they're strings (collections of characters) that represent other strings. Take `$p`, for example. When DOS sees this, it includes a string containing the current drive and directory as part of the prompt. Similarly, `$g` displays the one-character string > (the greater-than sign).

**Guru Tip**

In Version 6, DOS defaults to the **$P$G** prompt if you don't include a **PROMPT** command in your AUTOEXEC.BAT file. The only catch is that you have to install DOS in a directory called either DOS or MSDOS.

Have you ever wondered why DOS (prior to Version 6, anyway) didn't just show the current drive and directory by default? Well, the **$p** metastring provides the answer. When you include **$p** in your prompt, DOS has to read the drive and directory info after *every* command, and this can slow things down. To prove this for yourself, insert a floppy disk and change to it. Now enter the **VER** command and watch the drive light come on. Now enter the **PROMPT** command (no parameters) to clear the prompt and run **VER** again. No drive light this time!

Table 9.1 lists each of the `PROMPT` command's metastrings.

**Table 9.1. The *PROMPT* command's metastrings.**

<table>
<tr><th>Metastring</th><th>Use It To</th></tr>
<tr><td><code>$p</code></td><td>Display the current drive and directory</td></tr>
<tr><td><code>$n</code></td><td>Display the current drive only</td></tr>
<tr><td><code>$d</code></td><td>Display the current date</td></tr>
<tr><td><code>$t</code></td><td>Display the current time</td></tr>
<tr><td><code>$v</code></td><td>Display the DOS version number</td></tr>
<tr><td><code>$g</code></td><td>Display the greater-than sign (>)</td></tr>
<tr><td><code>$l</code></td><td>Display the less-than sign (<)</td></tr>
<tr><td><code>$b</code></td><td>Display the pipe symbol (|)</td></tr>
<tr><td><code>$q</code></td><td>Display an equal sign (=)</td></tr>
<tr><td><code>$$</code></td><td>Display a dollar sign ($)</td></tr>
<tr><td><code>$_</code></td><td>Move the cursor to a new line</td></tr>
<tr><td><code>$h</code></td><td>Backspace (and delete) one character</td></tr>
<tr><td><code>$e</code></td><td>Set the cursor position and screen colors</td></tr>
</table>

As an example, try entering the following command:

```
prompt $p$_$g
```

This command produces the following prompt:

```
C:\DOS
>
```

Three metastrings do all the work here. After `$p` displays the current drive and directory, the second metastring, `$_` (underline), moves the cursor down to the next line, which is where `$g`'s greater-than sign is displayed.

**Guru Tip**

> If you want to make any of the prompts from this chapter your regular prompt, be sure to include the appropriate command in your AUTOEXEC.BAT file. See Chapter 13, "AUTOEXEC.BAT: Your Most Important Batch File," for more information.

Many people like to show the date and time with their prompt. Here's a command that'll do the job:

```
prompt $d$_$t$_$p$g
```

And here's what you get:

```
Tue 03-30-1993
16:34:28.52
C:\DOS>
```

Remember that you can add your own text to a prompt. So, for example, you could liven up the last prompt by changing it to the following:

```
prompt Date: $d$_Time: $t$_Path: $p$_Yo!
```

This prompt looks like this:

```
Date: Tue 03-30-1993
Time: 16:34:28.52
Path: C:\DOS
Yo!
```

**Guru Tip**

> The `$t` metastring displays the time in hundredths of a second. I don't know too many people who plan their day to the nearest hundredth of a second, so this is a bit of overkill. You can use the backspace metastring `$h` to remove the hundredths digits (and the decimal point), like so:
>
> `$t$h$h$h.`

# Using ASCII Characters in Your Prompts

You don't need to restrict your prompt text to only the letters, numbers, and other characters that you see on your keyboard. Instead, you can use characters from the *extended ASCII character set*. This is a set of 128 special characters created for the IBM PC. You access these characters by holding down Alt and pressing the character's ASCII code. For example, the ASCII code for the cents sign (¢) is 155. So hold down Alt and press `155` to see this symbol at the DOS prompt.

**Dunce**

> To get the ASCII characters, be sure that you're using the numbers on the numeric keypad (and not the numbers above the letters) and that Num Lock is on.

The extended ASCII character set contains dozens of symbols that you can use in your prompts. Check out Appendix C to see a complete list of the IBM ASCII character set.

One thing you should note about the ASCII characters is that the first 32—they're called the *control characters*—are normally used to control certain aspects of hardware such as a printer or modem. If you want to use any of them in a prompt, you won't be able to display them at the command line (because DOS treats them literally). Instead, you need to fire up a text editor and create a batch file.

**Guru Tip**

> If you use **EDIT**, press Ctrl+P before trying to enter a control character. This tells **EDIT** not to treat the character literally.

One of the best uses for the extended ASCII characters is to create boxes like the one shown in Figure 9.1.

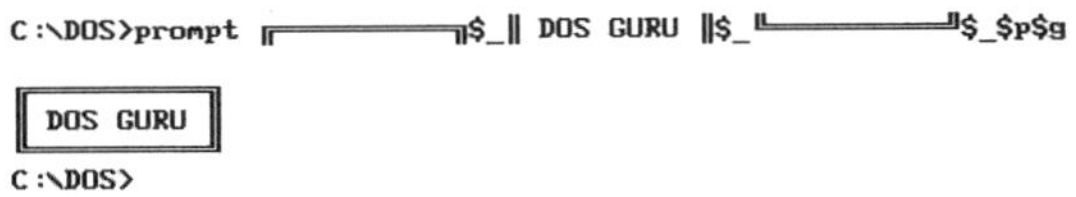


**Figure 9.1.** You can use the ASCII box-building characters to build boxes into your prompts.

As you can see, this prompt just uses a few of the so-called *box-building* ASCII characters.

**Guru Tip**

> These **PROMPT** commands can get pretty long, so you'll probably want to incorporate some of your favorites into batch files to save you having to type them at the DOS prompt every time.

**Guru Trivia**

> DOS, never one to make things easy, restricts your **PROMPT** command length in two ways. The first is DOS's normal restriction that no command be any longer than 127 characters. The second is the size of the *environment space*, a small chunk of memory that DOS uses to store, among other things, the current prompt definition. If your prompt gets too long, you may get an `Out of environment space` error message. If this happens and you have DOS 3.1 or later, add the following line to your CONFIG.SYS file (don't forget to reboot your computer when you're done):
>
> ```
> SHELL=C:\DOS\COMMAND.COM C:\DOS /E:1024 /P
> ```
>
> The **/E:1024** switch quadruples the size of the environment space to 1,024 bytes, which should be ample room. For more CONFIG.SYS fun, see Chapter 12, "CONFIG.SYS: What Every Guru Should Know."

# Using *PROMPT* to Position the Cursor

You've seen so far that the `$_` metastring lets you move the cursor to the next line. This positioning capability is useful but decidedly primitive. This section shows you several new metastrings that give you complete control over where you position the cursor on your screen.

Before beginning, your computer's CONFIG.SYS file requires a slight adjustment. In order to try any of the prompt techniques that I'll be showing you throughout the rest of this chapter, you need to add the following line to CONFIG.SYS:

```
DEVICE=C:\DOS\ANSI.SYS
```

When you've finished adding this line, reboot your computer to put the change into effect.

ANSI.SYS is a device driver for your display. If you want to do anything weird on-screen (such as moving the cursor around or changing colors) you need to have ANSI.SYS loaded.

You're now ready to try some `PROMPT` commands that move the cursor around on-screen. Each of these commands uses the `$e` metastring in the following general form:

```
$e[code
```

Here, `code` is a sequence of numbers and characters that define where you want the cursor to be positioned. These codes assume that the top-left corner of your screen is row 1, column 1, and the bottom-right corner of your screen is row 25, column 80. Table 9.2 summarizes the available codes.

When ANSI.SYS is loaded, it just sits around monitoring the action on your computer. It waits patiently until it detects an *escape sequence*, a specific series of characters that it recognizes as a command. (The `PROMPT` command's `$e` metastring is an example of an escape sequence.) ANSI.SYS then leaps into the fray and processes whatever codes follow the escape sequence.

**Table 9.2. Codes used with the $e metastring to position the cursor.**

| *Code* | *Use It To* |
|---|---|
| `$e[x;yH` | Move the cursor to row x and column y. Move the cursor to row 1, column 1 if you omit x and y. |
| `$e[xA` | Move the cursor up *x* rows. Move the cursor up 1 row if you omit *x*. |
| `$e[xB` | Move the cursor down *x* rows. Move the cursor down 1 row if you omit *x*. |
| `$e[xC` | Move the cursor to the right *x* columns. Move the cursor to the right 1 column if you omit *x*. |
| `$e[xD` | Move the cursor to the left *x* columns. Move the cursor to the left 1 column if you omit *x*. |
| `$e[2J` | Clear the screen and move the cursor to row 1, column 1. |
| `$e[K` | Clear all characters from the cursor to the end of the line. |
| `$e[s` | Save the current cursor position. |
| `$e[u` | Restore the cursor position saved with `$e[s`. |

As an example, enter the following command (note that `H` must be capitalized):

```
prompt $e[H$p$g
```

When you press Enter, the prompt moves to row 1, column 1. Try pressing Enter or running any DOS command (try `DIR`), and the prompt will always return to the top line of the screen. Now try the following command:

```
prompt $e[12;40H$p$g
```

When you press Enter this time, the prompt moves to the center of the screen.

There are many uses for this type of cursor flexibility, but one of the most common is to display information (such as the date and time) in one part of the screen and the DOS prompt in another. Here's a `PROMPT` command that will do just that:

```
prompt $e[s$e[1;40H$d$e[1;60H$t$e[u$p$g
```

Whew! That's a real mouthful! Let's take a close look at this to be sure you understand what's going on. The first part, `$e[s`, saves the current cursor position. The next part, `$e[1;40H$d`, places the cursor at row 1, column 40 and then displays the date. The next part, `$e[1;60H$t`, is similar. It places the cursor at row 1, column 60 and then displays the time. The metastring `$e[u` restores the cursor to its original position, and then the command ends with the standard `$p$g`. Easy as brain surgery.

# Using *PROMPT* to Change Screen Colors

Most DOS screens show either white characters on a black background or, as in many laptops, black characters on a white background. Dull as dishwater, in other words. If you're tired of looking at the same old screen, you can use the `PROMPT` command to really show your colors.

Here's how it works. Use the `$e` metastring string again, but this time it takes the following general format:

```
$e[x;x;...xm
```

The various `x` values control three things: certain text attributes (such as bold or blinking), the color of the screen characters, and the color of the background.

Guru Tip

> You'll need to issue a **CLS** command after setting the screen colors to put them into effect.

The values that control the text attributes are listed in Table 9.3.

**Table 9.3. Codes used with the $e metastring to set text attributes.**

| *Value* | *Result* |
|---|---|
| 0 | Turns off all text attributes. |
| 1 | Makes screen characters bold. |
| 2 | Makes screen characters normal. |
| 4 | Displays characters underlined (on monochrome screens only). |
| 5 | Makes characters blink on and off. |
| 7 | Reverses foreground and background colors. |
| 8 | Hides characters. |

As an example, consider the following `PROMPT` command:

```
prompt $e[1m$p$g
```

The `$e[1m` metastring sets the bold text attribute. Try this out and you'll be surprised how much easier it is to read the screen. (Table 9.4 lists the values that set the colors of the screen characters and background.)

**Table 9.4. Codes used with the $e metastring to set text and background colors.**

| *Color* | *Text* | *Background* |
|---|---|---|
| Black | 30 | 40 |
| Red | 31 | 41 |
| Green | 32 | 42 |
| Yellow | 33 | 43 |
| Blue | 34 | 44 |
| Magenta | 35 | 45 |
| Cyan | 36 | 46 |
| White | 37 | 47 |

With all these codes in hand, you can now set your display to any color you want. For example, if happiness for you is bold-yellow text on a red background, change your prompt to

```
prompt $e[1;33;41m$p$g
```

After you enter your new prompt, run the `CLS` command to get the full effect of your new colors.

**Guru Tip**

> To reset your colors to the DOS default, use the metastring `$e[m`.

# Guru Review

This chapter showed you how to customize the system prompt. Here's a fond look back at the more memorable stuff:

- ✦ You change the system prompt with the `PROMPT` command. Use the various metastrings to include things like the current drive and directory, the date, and the time.
- ✦ You can add text to your prompts and you can even use any of the characters in the extended ASCII character set.
- ✦ You can move the prompt to any position on the screen. Just use the `$e` metastring with the appropriate positioning codes.
- ✦ The `$e` metastring is also useful for changing the attributes of screen text (e.g., bold or blinking) as well as the colors of the text and the background.
- ✦ Before using `$e` in your `PROMPT` commands, be sure to load the ANSI.SYS device driver.

# Customizing the Keyboard

## Guru Stuff in This Chapter ➤

10

CHAPTER

- *Speeding up your keyboard*
- *Remapping keys*
- *Assigning DOS commands to keystrokes*
- *Tips and techniques to give you complete keyboard control*

On the surface, your keyboard seems like a pretty simple beast. If you press the *A* key, an *a* appears on your screen. If you hold down Shift and then press the *A* key, an *A* appears. (I take it you're with me so far.)

But (you knew there had to be a "but"), the keyboard is actually a fairly sophisticated piece of machinery. I'm not kidding. For example, if the mood strikes you, you can reassign the *A* key to display the word *Australopithecus* (no, I can't think of a reason why you would want to do this, but give me a minute). Or, more practically, you can assign DOS commands or even batch files to a single key or key combination. This chapter shows you how to do all these things and more.

# Giving Your Keyboard a Speed Boost

Before I show you how to set up your own custom keyboard configurations, I want to let you in on a little-known DOS secret that I guarantee will make you a hit around the office (if not at parties).

When you press and hold a letter on your keyboard, you should notice two things: first, once you press a key, there's a slight delay before the second letter appears, as though the keyboard has to think about what to do next; second, the subsequent letters appear at a constant rate. The secret is that you can change both the initial *delay* and the rate (called the *repeat rate*) at which the characters appear.

To see how this works, enter the following command (you need to be running at least DOS 4):

```
mode con rate=1 delay=4
```

> This **MODE** command doesn't work on older 83-key, XT-style keyboards.

Now hold down a key and watch what happens. The letters trickle out at a painfully slow speed.

This time I'll really rev things up. Enter the following command:

```
mode con rate=32 delay=1
```

Now, when you hold down a key, the letters really fly! This command can sure speed things up when you're editing text or using any program where you use your arrow keys to navigate the screen. You can enter any value between 1 and 32 for the rate (the default is 20 for AT-style keyboards and 21 for 101 key-enhanced keyboards) and between 1 and 4 for the delay (the default is 2).

**Guru Trivia**

> The numbers you plug in for the repeat rate and delay actually mean something. For the rate, the numbers represent, approximately, characters per second. (Actually, the range of values 1 to 32 corresponds to about 2 to 30 characters per second.) For the delay, the numbers represent quarters of a second.

**Guru Tip**

> Depending on the sensitivity of your keyboard and your skills (or, if you're like me, your lack of skills) as a typist, you may find yourself getting a lot of repeated letters with a delay setting of 1. If this is the case, try setting the delay to 2 or even 3.

# Your Keyboard: A Brief Primer

Okay, now I'm going to get into the stuff that'll give you complete control over your keyboard. (Ah, the power!). But first, you need a bit of painless background information about how your keyboard works.

Any time you press a key, a special circuit inside your keyboard sends out a code that tells DOS which character you pressed. For example, if you press *a*, the keyboard signifies the event by sending out a *97*. DOS recognizes this as the code for an *a* and arranges to have the letter displayed on your screen. Similarly, if you hold down Shift and press *a*, the keyboard sends out a *65* and DOS displays an *A*.

**Guru Tip**

> See Appendix D, "Keyboard Codes," for a complete list of keyboard codes.

# Hijacking Keyboard Codes

What if you could somehow intercept these codes before they get to DOS? Say, for example, you nabbed the 97 and replaced it with, 98. Well, because *98* is the code for *b*, DOS would display a *b* on your screen, instead of an *a*.

This sounds great in theory, but how can you possibly intercept these keyboard codes? Fortunately, DOS provides the solution: the ANSI.SYS device driver. When this program is loaded, all keyboard input goes through ANSI.SYS first. All you have to do is tell ANSI.SYS which codes to intercept and what to change them to. The best part is that you can do all this with some relatively simple `PROMPT` and `ECHO` commands that you can use at the command line or incorporate into a batch file.

To prepare for the rest of this chapter, you need to add the following line to your CONFIG.SYS file (if you haven't done so already):

```
DEVICE=C:\DOS\ANSI.SYS
```

(Be sure you reboot your computer to put this change into effect.)

# Using *PROMPT* to Customize Your Keyboard

If you read Chapter 9, "Customizing the Prompt," you saw how to use the `PROMPT` command's `$e` metastring to produce *escape sequences* that get the attention of ANSI.SYS. To reassign keys on your keyboard, use the `PROMPT` command and `$e` again. Here's the general format:

```
PROMPT $e[old_key;new_keyp
```

For example, the command

```
prompt $e[97;98p
```

reassigns keyboard code 97 (the letter *a*) with code 98 (the letter *b*). To restore the *a* key, use the same code twice, like so:

```
prompt $e[97;97p
```

> **Dunce**
>
> After entering any of these PROMPT commands, don't forget to reset your normal prompt.

Fortunately, you don't have to use these unfamiliar keyboard codes. Instead, you can just use the actual key names enclosed in quotation marks. So the previous example becomes the following:

```
prompt $e["a";"b"p
```

> **Dunce**
>
> To restore a letter, you have to use the keyboard codes. A command such as `prompt $e["a";"a"p` won't work, because once you've reassigned **a**, you can't use it in a command.

Replacing one letter with another isn't very useful. Here's a better example. If you rarely use the bracket keys—[ and ]—and would like to use the parentheses—( and )—without having to press Shift, replace the [ key with ( and the ] key with ). The following two PROMPT commands will do this:

```
prompt $e["[";"("p
prompt $e["]";")"p
```

> **Guru Tip**
>
> Keyboards go through a lot of abuse (coffee spills, lead-fingered users, various displays of violence), so over time you may end up with a key or two that no longer works. If you can't get a new keyboard any time soon, just reassign a seldom-used key to handle the missing character.

You're not restricted to substituting just a single character for another. For example, in the last two chapters you've been using the characters "$e[" a great deal. You can assign all three to, say, the tilde (~) with this command:

```
prompt $e["~";"$e["p
```

**Dunce**

> Many programs reset the keyboard on startup, so your new key combinations won't work. Before going crazy with keyboard substitutions, you should just try a couple and then load your favorite applications to see what happens.

# *ECHO*ing Escape Sequences

Although the `PROMPT` command does the job, it's a pain to have to remember to reset your prompt each time. You can avoid this by using the `ECHO` command to send an escape sequence to ANSI.SYS. For keyboard remapping, the general format is as follows:

```
ECHO ←[old_key;new_keyp
```

In this case, ← represents the Escape control character (ASCII 27). You can't enter control characters (the first 32 entries in the ASCII character set) at the command line, so you have to use a text editor and include the `ECHO` commands as part of a batch file (which is a good idea, anyway).

**Guru Tip**

> To produce the Escape character in Edit, press Ctrl+P and then press Alt+27 (be sure you use the numeric keypad) or, more simply, just press Escape.

# Assigning Commands to Keys

By far the most useful aspect of key reassignment is associating DOS commands with specific keys or key combinations. For example, suppose you want to assign the `DIR` command to, say, the F5 key. Because F5 isn't a character, you need to use its keyboard code, which happens to be 0;63 (a two-digit code such as this one is called an *extended code*). Your command then becomes the following:

```
ECHO ←[0;63;"dir"p
```

When you run this command in a batch file and press F5, the word *dir* appears on-screen. Press Enter to get your directory listing.

Although this is a neat trick, it's not as useful as it could be. It would be nice if you could press F5 and actually *run* the `DIR` command. Well, amazingly enough, you can, and all it takes is a small adjustment to the `ECHO` command:

```
ECHO ←[0;63;"dir";13p
```

The trick here is that `13` is the keyboard code for the Enter key. Now pressing F5 is equivalent to typing `dir` and pressing Enter, which means, of course, that you get your `DIR` listing.

**Guru Tip**

> Use keyboard reassignment for hard-to-type DOS commands like **CHKDSK** (you could use Alt+C, for example) or commands with a lot of parameters. Again, check out Appendix D for the appropriate keyboard codes.

**Dunce**

> Avoid reassigning keys that DOS uses, such as F1 or F3. Also, keep Ctrl+C unassigned so you can cancel DOS commands and batch files.

You can use this technique to run multiple commands and programs with a single keystroke. For example, the following command enables you to switch to the \123 directory and then run Lotus 1-2-3 by pressing F2 (keyboard code 0;60):

```
ECHO ←[0;60;"cd \123";13;"123";13p
```

# Quick *DIR* Commands

To demonstrate how you might use key reassignment, here's a batch file called KEYSET.BAT that sets each of the key combinations Alt+F1 through Alt+F10 to one of the `DIR` commands available in DOS 5 and 6:

```
@ECHO ←[0;104;"DIR /OGN /P";13p
@ECHO ←[0;105;"DIR /OGE /P";13p
@ECHO ←[0;106;"DIR /OGD /P";13p
@ECHO ←[0;107;"DIR /OGS /P";13p
@ECHO ←[0;108;"DIR /AA /P";13p
```

```
@ECHO ←[0;109;"DIR /AD /P";13p
@ECHO ←[0;110;"DIR /AH /P";13p
@ECHO ←[0;111;"DIR /AR /P";13p
@ECHO ←[0;112;"DIR /AS /P";13p
@ECHO ←[0;113;"DIR /OGN /W";13p
@PROMPT $e[s$e[H$e[30;46mAlt+F1=Name F2=Ext F3=Date F4=Size F5=Arch
F6=Dirs F7=Hid F8=R/O F9=Sys F10=Wide $e[m$e[u$p$g
```

The PROMPT command displays a line across the top of the screen to remind you what each key does. Be sure to enter this command on a single line. (If you're not sure what some of the stuff in the PROMPT command means, refer to Chapter 9 for the grisly details.)

When you need to reset these keys, use KEYRESET.BAT:

```
@ECHO ←[0;104;0;104p
@ECHO ←[0;105;0;105p
@ECHO ←[0;106;0;106p
@ECHO ←[0;107;0;107p
@ECHO ←[0;108;0;108p
@ECHO ←[0;109;0;109p
@ECHO ←[0;110;0;110p
@ECHO ←[0;111;0;111p
@ECHO ←[0;112;0;112p
@ECHO ←[0;113;0;113p
@PROMPT $p$g
```

# Guru Review

This chapter showed you various techniques for customizing your keyboard. Here's a quick review:

- Use the MODE CON command to give your keyboard a speed boost by reducing the delay and cranking up the repeat rate.
- Your keyboard sends out codes with each keypress to tell DOS what to display on-screen. You can use the ANSI.SYS device driver to intercept these codes and change them to something else.
- To remap keyboard codes, you can either use the PROMPT command's $e metastring or the ECHO command with the escape control character.
- The most promising use of keyboard remapping is to assign DOS commands to individual keys or key combos.

# Customizing the Command Line with DOSKEY

11

CHAPTER

## Guru Stuff in This Chapter ➤

- *Using DOSKEY to recall command lines*
- *Entering multiple commands on a single line*
- *Basic command-line editing techniques*
- *Creating DOSKEY macros*
- *Billions and billions of practical macro examples*

DOS 5 introduced a whole host of great new features, such as the improved `DIR` and `FORMAT` commands, the lifesaving `UNDELETE` and `UNFORMAT` utilities, and the ability to move DOS and other programs out of conventional memory. These are all useful guru tools, but the DOS 5 feature with the most day-to-day usefulness has got to be DOSKEY. Just check out what you can do with this little utility:

- Recall previously entered commands with just a few keystrokes.
- Enter multiple commands on a single line.
- Edit commands instead of retyping them.
- Create your own DOS commands with DOSKEY *macros.*

If you haven't used DOSKEY yet, I guarantee you'll be addicted to it within five minutes. The amount of time (not to mention the gray hairs) that you'll save will more than cover the few minutes it takes to learn. This chapter focuses on DOSKEY macros, but I'll begin with a quick introduction to the other DOSKEY features.

# Starting DOSKEY

Before you can use DOSKEY, you need to load it into memory. To do this, just enter the following command:

```
doskey
```

DOS reports `DOSKey installed` and you're in business.

# Recalling Command Lines

The simplest DOSKEY feature is command-recall. To see how this works, try entering the following commands:

```
cd\dos
dir
cd\
```

Now try pressing the up arrow key. You should see the `cd\` command. Press the up arrow again to see the `dir` command. DOSKEY keeps a list of the commands you enter and you use the up and down arrow keys to move through the list. To rerun a command, simply use the arrow keys to find it and then press Enter. Is technology great, or what?

**Guru Tip**

> If you don't want to enter any commands from the history buffer, press Esc to get a clean command line.

Table 11.1 lists the other command-recall keys you can use.

### Table 11.1. DOSKEY command-recall keys.

| *Press* | *To* |
|---|---|
| Page Up | Recall the oldest command in the list. |
| Page Down | Recall the newest command in the list. |
| F7 | Display the entire command list. |
| Alt+F7 | Delete all commands from the recall list. |
| F8 | Have DOSKEY recall a command that begins with the letter or letters you've typed on the command line. |
| F9 | Have DOSKEY prompt you for a command list number (you can see the numbers with the F7 key). Type the number and press Enter to recall the command. |

**Guru Tip**

> The memory buffer that DOSKEY uses to store commands is 512 bytes in size. This is enough to hold about 40 or 50 commands. If you need a larger buffer, start DOSKEY with the following command:
>
> ```
> doskey /bufsize=1024
> ```

# Entering Multiple Commands on a Single Line

Just as Superman could leap tall buildings in a single bound, DOSKEY can run multiple commands on a single line. To achieve this superhuman feat, press Ctrl+T between commands. For example, a common task is to change to a different drive and then run a directory listing. Normally, you would do this with two separate commands:

```
a:
dir
```

With DOSKEY, however, you can do it on one line, as follows:

1. Type `a:` (don't press Enter).
2. Press Ctrl+T. DOSKEY displays the carriage-return symbol: ¶.
3. Type `dir` and press Enter. DOS changes to drive A: and then runs the `DIR` command.

**Guru Tip**

> You can enter as many commands as you like on a single line, but just remember that the total length of the line can't be more than 127 characters.

# Command-Line Editing: Relief for Fumbling Fingers

Over the years, I've perfected (if that's the right word) my own four-fingered typing style (well, five-fingered, actually; I use my right thumb for the spacebar). But no matter how good I get as a typist, I still fumble certain words. For example, I *always* type "propmt" instead of "prompt." This can be a real problem because I like to try out different prompts. (If you haven't already done so, check out Chapter 9, "Customizing the Prompt," to get in on the fun.) Before DOSKEY came along, I'd type something like

```
propmt $e[s$e[1:40H$d$e[1;60H$t$e[u$p$g
```

and then end up pounding my head against the wall because I had to retype the whole thing.

With DOSKEY loaded, however, you can edit the command line. Instead of retyping commands, you can just use various keys to move the cursor to the offending letters and replace them. Ah, the promised land, at last. Table 11.2 summarizes DOSKEY's command-line editing keys.

### Table 11.2. DOSKEY command-line editing keys.

| *Press* | *To* |
|---|---|
| Left arrow | Move the cursor one character to the left. |
| Right arrow | Move the cursor one character to the right. |
| Ctrl+left arrow | Move the cursor one word to the left. |
| Ctrl+right arrow | Move the cursor one word to the right. |
| Home | Move the cursor to the beginning of the line. |
| End | Move the cursor to the end of the line. |
| Delete | Delete the character over the cursor. |
| Backspace | Delete the character to the left of the cursor. |
| Ctrl+Home | Delete from the cursor to the beginning of the line. |
| Ctrl+End | Delete from the cursor to the end of the line. |
| Insert | Toggle DOSKEY between "insert" mode (your typing is inserted between existing letters on the command line) and "overstrike" mode (your typing replaces existing letters on the command line). |

**Guru Tip**

By default, DOSKEY is in overstrike mode. If you prefer to use insert mode as the default, start DOSKEY with the command `DOSKEY /INSERT`.

# Learning About DOSKEY Macros

Perhaps the most powerful feature you get with DOSKEY is the ability to combine one or more DOS commands into a single easy-to-use command called a *macro*. If this sounds like a batch file, you're close. DOSKEY macros and batch files *are* similar, but they differ in some important ways:

**Macro Pros:**

- Macros are stored in memory and batch files are stored on a disk. This means that macros execute much faster than batch files.
- Batch files must have legal DOS filenames, but macro names can be longer than eight characters and can include the following symbols normally banned from DOS filenames:

  `* + [ ] : ; " , . ? /`

- You can use macros to replace DOS commands.

**Macro Cons:**

- Macros must be no longer than 127 characters, but batch files can be any length.
- There are no commands or symbols to suppress command echoing.
- There is no macro equivalent for the `GOTO` and `IF` batch file commands.
- You have to reenter macro definitions each time you start your computer. (However, you can automate this by using a macro library, a batch file that stores your macro definitions. I'll explain all this later in the chapter.)

In general, you should use macros as substitutes for complex DOS commands or to combine two or more DOS commands into a single command. You should use batch files for more sophisticated tasks.

# Creating DOSKEY Macros

To create a DOSKEY macro, enter a command that has the following form:

```
DOSKEY macroname=commands
```

Here, `macroname` is the name of the macro and `commands` is the list of DOS commands you want the macro to execute.

As an example, consider the following command:

```
dir /ogn /p
```

This displays a directory listing with the filenames in alphabetical order, the subdirectories grouped first, and a pause after every screenful. Instead of typing this command every time, you could define a macro called `SDIR`. Here's the command that'll do it:

```
doskey sdir=dir /ogn /p
```

Once you've defined a macro, you can use it like any other DOS command. For this example, just type `sdir` and press Enter, and DOS displays the sorted directory listing.

**Dunce**

> If you need to bail out of a macro, press Ctrl+C.

When you're defining a macro that contains more than one command, you need to be a little careful. For example, suppose you want to create a macro called CDD that changes to drive A: and then gives you a `DIR` listing. Your first instinct might be to enter the command

```
doskey cdd=a: ¶ dir
```

However, when DOS sees the command separator symbol, it assumes you're trying to run two commands: one to define the DOSKEY macro `CDD` and another to display a `DIR` listing. To avoid this confusion, use `$T` instead of Ctrl+T inside your macro definition. Here's the revised command:

```
doskey cdd=a: $T dir
```

**Guru Tip**

> To make the commands easier to read, I've included spaces before and after the `$T` symbol. If you prefer, you can leave these spaces out when defining your own macros.

Table 11.3 lists all the macro-definition symbols you can use.

**Table 11.3. DOSKEY macro-definition symbols.**

| *Use* | *To Replace* |
|---|---|
| `$B` | Pipe symbol (\|) |
| `$G` | Greater-than symbol (>) |
| `$L` | Less-than symbol (<) |
| `$T` | Command separator (¶) |
| `$$` | Dollar sign ($) |

**Guru Tip**

To delete a macro definition, use the following format:

```
DOSKEY macroname=
```

# Using Replaceable Parameters in Macros

In Chapter 7, "Using Variables for Batch File Flexibility," I showed you how to use replaceable parameters inside batch files. Macros, too, can use replaceable parameters. Instead of the symbols *%1* through *%9* that are available in a batch file, use the symbols *$1* through *$9* for macros.

For example, the CDD macro introduced in the last section is okay, but it lacks flexibility. Instead, change the macro to the following:

```
doskey cdd=cd $1 $T dir
```

If you now type, say, `cdd \wp`, DOSKEY replaces `$1` with `\wp` and runs the macro accordingly.

A neat macro trick is to use the `$*` replaceable parameter to represent everything that follows the macro name on the command line.

In Chapter 10, "Customizing the Keyboard," I showed you how to reprogram your keyboard by sending escape sequences to ANSI.SYS. The only way to get this to work at the DOS command line was to use the `PROMPT` command, which is a pain because you have to reset the prompt every time. DOSKEY gives us a way around this limitation. In a batch file, enter the following DOSKEY macro:

```
doskey esc=echo ←[$*
```

Here, ← is the Escape character (ASCII 27). Let's put this macro to work. Suppose, for example, you want to reassign the key combination Alt+F1 (keyboard code 0;104) to produce a `DIR` listing sorted by name. You can do it by entering the following command at the DOS prompt:

```
esc 0;104;"dir /on";13p
```

The `$*` replaceable parameter grabs everything after `esc` and dumps it at the end of the `ECHO` command.

# Macro Examples

To get you started, I'll show you a few of my favorite DOSKEY macros. Before I get going, though, you should probably think about increasing the size of your DOSKEY buffer. This buffer holds both the command history and your macro definitions, but the default buffer of 512 bytes is only enough to hold about 10 macros and 15 or so commands. A buffer of 1,024 bytes is probably a good size, although if you think you'll be defining a lot of macros, 2,048 bytes gives you all the room you need. To redefine the DOSKEY buffer with 1,024 bytes, enter the following command:

```
doskey /bufsize=1024 /reinstall
```

The `/REINSTALL` switch resets DOSKEY.

When you reinstall DOSKEY, DOS leaves the old copy in memory (taking up about 4K or so). Only use the `/REINSTALL` switch if you want to change the buffer size. If you want to clean out the command history, press Alt+F7 instead.

The first example uses the fact that DOS represents the current directory's parent with the double dot symbol (..). One way this comes in handy is to use the following command to change quickly to the parent directory:

```
cd..
```

This is pretty short as it is, but I prefer to use a macro called UP, that I define as follows:

```
doskey up=cd..
```

A similar macro is UP2, which I use any time I need to move up two directory levels:

```
doskey up2=cd.. $T cd..
```

So, for example, if you're in the WP\DOCS\BUSINESS subdirectory, entering the `UP2` command takes you to the WP directory.

Suppose you also have a subdirectory called WP\DOCS\PERSONAL and you want to move from the BUSINESS subdirectory over to PERSONAL. Normally, you have to use the following command:

```
cd \wp\docs\personal
```

However, both BUSINESS and PERSONAL have the same parent directory (DOCS), so you can create a macro called OVER as follows:

```
doskey over=cd..\$1
```

Once you've defined this macro, to move from BUSINESS to PERSONAL just enter the following command:

```
over personal
```

**Guru Tip**

> *To see a list of all your currently defined macros, use the command* `DOSKEY /M`.

Have you ever lost a file on your hard drive? You know it's there somewhere, but you can't remember where it is. It's happened to me more times than I've had hot dinners, so I use a macro called ? to help out. Here's the definition:

```
doskey ?=dir \$1 /s /b
```

The `/S` switch causes DOS to search all your subdirectories, and the `/B` switch displays only the filename, if one is found.

My final macro definition shows that you can use macros to replace existing DOS commands (this is called *command aliasing*). For example, the `DEL` command is safer if you use it with the `/P` switch (DOS asks you to confirm each deletion). You can actually create a macro called DEL with the following definition:

```
doskey del=del $1 /p
```

Macros take precedence over DOS commands, so whenever you use DEL, it's the macro that executes, not the DOS command. (If you need to run the DOS command, you can do so by preceding it with a space.)

**Guru Tip**

> If you're setting up a computer for a novice user, use macros to replace dangerous DOS commands such as **RECOVER** and **FDISK**. Instead of running the command, just display a message telling the users the peril they're in, like so:
>
> ```
> DOSKEY RECOVER=ECHO This command is for gurus only! $T
>
> ECHO Do not try this at home!
> ```

# Creating a Macro Library

One of the problems with macros is that your definitions are lost whenever you turn off your computer. The solution is to create a macro library—a batch file that contains all your macro definitions. Follow these steps to create a macro library:

1. Type `doskey /m > c:\batch\macros.bat` and press Enter (if you don't have a BATCH directory, substitute the directory where you keep your batch files). DOS redirects the output of the DOSKEY `/M` command into a batch file called MACROS.BAT.
2. Load the file MACROS.BAT into your text editor.
3. For each macro definition, add `DOSKEY` to the beginning of the line (be sure you leave a space between `DOSKEY` and the definition).

**Guru Tip**

An alternative method for creating a macro library is to use DOSKEY's **/H** switch instead. This switch lists all the DOSKEY commands and macros stored in memory. The following command redirects this output to the MACROS.BAT batch file:

```
doskey /h > c:\batch\macros.bat
```

Be sure you edit MACROS.BAT to remove any other DOS commands that were in the command buffer.

Now, whenever you need to load your DOSKEY macros, just run the MACROS.BAT batch file.

**Guru Tip**

You'll probably need to edit your macro library quite often to remove macros you never use and add new ones. To make this chore easier, here's another macro that loads the macro library into **EDIT** and then runs the batch file when you're done:

```
doskey editlib=edit c:\batch\macros.bat $t macros
```

# Guru Review

This chapter showed you how to use the powerful little DOSKEY utility. Here's a recap of the important stuff:

- Once DOSKEY is loaded, you can recall command lines by using the up and down arrow keys. Once the command you want to redo is displayed, just press Enter.
- To enter multiple commands on a single line, press Ctrl+T between each command. Remember, however, that you can't create command lines larger than 127 characters.
- DOSKEY command lines are editable. This means that you can use the left and right arrow keys to move to the offending letter or letters and delete at will.

- DOSKEY macros execute much faster than batch files, but they can't be any longer than 127 characters.
- Use DOSKEY macros to replace complex DOS commands or to combine two or more commands in a single line.
- Once you've defined a few macros, create a macro library batch file for easy macro loading.

# Taking DOS to a Higher Plane of Existence

# PART IV

# CONFIG.SYS: What Every Guru Should Know

12

CHAPTER

## Guru Stuff in This Chapter ➤

- *What is CONFIG.SYS?*
- *Controlling DOS with system parameters*
- *Controlling devices with device drivers*
- *A rundown of the DOS device drivers*
- *Untold numbers of CONFIG.SYS secrets for the curious guru wanna-be*

Most of us have a morning routine that we go through every day when we wake up. After our alarms stir us from our dreams (and after we've hit the snooze button four or five times), we get up and run through all the tasks that get us going: shaving, showering, getting dressed, eating, getting dressed, getting the kids off to school.

Your computer has its own morning rituals that it goes through each time you turn it on or reboot. After a few hardware checks (memory, disk drives, keyboard, and so on), your PC looks for and loads a couple of startup files that set up certain aspects of DOS and configure devices attached to your computer. One of these files—CONFIG.SYS—is the subject of this chapter. (The other is AUTOEXEC.BAT, and I'll get to it in the next chapter.)

# A CONFIG.SYS Caveat

CONFIG.SYS is a powerful file that can give you tremendous control over your PC. However, this power comes with a price: if you make any errors in CONFIG.SYS, your whole system could crash. You need to take three precautions anytime you work with CONFIG.SYS:

- Always double-, no triple-check your work to be sure you've entered everything correctly.
- If anything does go wrong and you have DOS 6, use the F5 and F8 keys to either bypass CONFIG.SYS entirely or single-step through the commands. Take a peek at Chapter 14, "Start It Your Way: DOS 6 Boot Options," to get the details.
- If you don't have DOS 6, keep a bootable floppy disk handy, just in case. If your system locks up because of a CONFIG.SYS error, you can get control back by booting from the floppy. (If you don't have a bootable disk, check out Chapter 18, "The Guru's Survival Kit," to see how it's done.)
- Store a backup copy of CONFIG.SYS either in a different directory or on a floppy disk. If something goes wrong, restore control by using F5 or F8 (if you have DOS 6), or by booting from a floppy and restoring the backup copy.

# About CONFIG.SYS

CONFIG.SYS (gurus pronounce it con-fig-sis) is a simple text file that resides in your hard disk's root directory (or, more exactly, it resides in the root directory of whatever disk your computer boots from). CONFIG.SYS has two reasons for living:

- To configure DOS by assigning values to variables known as *system parameters*.
- To configure devices attached to your computer (such as a network card or a mouse) by loading small programs called *device drivers*.

**Guru Tip**

> If you have DOS 6, you can also use CONFIG.SYS to define different start-up configurations. To get the nitty-gritty on this cool new feature, see Chapter 14.

CONFIG.SYS does all this by executing a series of commands, each of which has the following form:

```
command=value
```

These are just text statements, so you can make changes to CONFIG.SYS simply by loading it into a text editor—using either the DOS `EDIT` command or a word processor. This makes it easy to get comfortable with the inner workings of CONFIG.SYS, which, as a guru, is crucial for gaining maximum control over the way your computer operates.

**Dunce**

> If you're going to be editing CONFIG.SYS in a word processor, be absolutely sure that the file remains pure text when you save it. If you accidentally convert CONFIG.SYS to the word processor's file format, DOS may choke on it the next time you reboot and your whole system could lock up.

**Guru Tip**

> Because DOS only processes CONFIG.SYS at startup, you need to reboot to put any CONFIG.SYS changes into effect. The quickest way to do this is the "three-fingered salute"—Ctrl+Alt+Delete.

# Using DOS System Parameters in CONFIG.SYS

DOS determines how it interacts with your system by referring to certain internal *system parameters*. These variables control things such as which program processes your DOS commands and how DOS works with your software. This section takes a brief look at each of the system parameters.

**Guru Tip**

> If you have DOS 4 or later, you can add comments to your CONFIG.SYS file. Just begin a line with `REM` and DOS ignores everything else on the line.

## *BREAK*

You use Ctrl+Break (or Ctrl+C, which is the same thing) to put the brakes (sorry about that) on a DOS command, batch file, or DOSKEY macro. The `BREAK` parameter can have two values—`ON` or `OFF`—and these determine how DOS checks for Ctrl+Break.

When `BREAK` is `OFF` (the default value), DOS only looks for Ctrl+Breaks while it's reading characters from or writing them to devices such as your keyboard, the screen, a printer, or a communications port.

Setting `BREAK` to `ON`, however, activates "extended" Ctrl+Break checking. This means that DOS also looks for a Ctrl+Break when it's doing things like reading and writing disk files. This is useful for interrupting things like large `XCOPY` operations (which, when `BREAK` is `OFF`, you normally need a shotgun to stop).

The downside is that DOS runs marginally slower because of all the checking it has to do. To turn the BREAK parameter ON, include the following line in your CONFIG.SYS file:

```
BREAK=ON
```

## Recommendations

You may as well turn BREAK on. The advantages of extended Ctrl+Break checking far outweigh the infinitesimal performance decrease.

**Guru Tip**

> To check the current BREAK setting at the DOS prompt, enter the following command:
>
> `break`

# BUFFERS

Many programs use the same piece of data or programming code over and over. It wastes time if DOS has to repeatedly go back to the hard disk to retrieve this information. To speed things up, you can include the BUFFERS parameter in your CONFIG.SYS file. This tells DOS to set up a number of *disk buffers*—small chunks of memory—to hold recently used data or program code. This speeds things up because DOS checks those pieces before going to the hard disk. To set up, say, 30 such buffers (you can use any number between 1 and 99), add the following line to CONFIG.SYS:

```
BUFFERS=30
```

I know what you're thinking: "If I crank the BUFFERS value up to 99, my programs will run even faster." Alas, that's not the case because DOS can end up taking longer to search through the buffers than it would to retrieve the information from the disk.

Guru Trivia

> DOS uses the "LRU" method for buffer allocation. LRU (which stands for *least recently used*) means that if DOS can't locate the information it wants in memory, it finds the buffer that hasn't been accessed for the longest time (the "least recently used" buffer), flushes its data back to the disk, locates the new information, and stores it in the buffer.

## Recommendations

Should you use the BUFFERS parameter? Absolutely. How many buffers should you set up? The answer depends on a number of factors including the size of your hard disk, the programs you use, and whether you use any memory software management. Table 12.1 lists the recommended BUFFERS setting for different hard disk sizes.

### Table 12.1. Recommended *BUFFERS* values for different hard disk sizes.

| *Hard Disk Size* | BUFFERS *Value* |
|---|---|
| Less than 40M | 20 |
| 40M to 79M | 30 |
| 80M to 119M | 40 |
| More than 120M | 50 |

Here are a few other things to consider when setting up the BUFFERS parameter:

- Software programs often recommend BUFFERS settings. Use the highest value recommended by any of the programs you use most often.
- Another good reason to keep the number of buffers to a minimum is that they inhabit valuable memory. Each buffer uses about 532 bytes, so a BUFFERS setting of 40 hogs about 20K. You can circumvent this if you load DOS into the *high memory area* (see Chapter 15, "Memory Management Made Easy"), because DOS brings the buffers along with it (but only if you use a setting of 48 or less).

**Guru Tip**

> To see how much memory DOS has set aside for buffers, enter the following command (if you have DOS 6) and look for the BUFFERS line:
>
> ```
> mem /d /p
> ```
>
> If you're using DOS 5, use this command, instead:
>
> ```
> mem /d ¦ more
> ```

- ✦ If you use disk cache software such as DOS' SmartDrive (explained in Chapter 15), use a low BUFFERS setting (10 should do the job).

# FCBS

You use the FCBS parameter to limit the number of *file control blocks* (FCBs) that can be opened at any one time. What are file control blocks? Well, they're ancient data structures first implemented in DOS 1.0, but they're now virtually obsolete. The majority of today's programs use *file handles* instead of FCBs, and those are controlled by the FILES parameter discussed in the next section.

## Recommendations

Ignore the FCBS parameter unless you're using a program that needs it. The only possible use for FCBS is to save a tiny bit of memory. DOS still allocates four file control blocks for old time's sake, so you can save a whopping 176 bytes by including the following line in CONFIG.SYS:

```
FCBS=1
```

# FILES

The FILES parameter controls the maximum number of files that your programs can have open at once. Most programs only use a few files at a time, but disk-intensive beasts such as database managers and Microsoft Windows normally juggle a couple of dozen files or more. If FILES is set too low, DOS may refuse to open a file needed by the program, and it will crash with an error message such as `Too many files open` or `No free file handles`.

Guru Trivia

> DOS versions 2.0 and higher operate by assigning a *file handle* to each file opened by a program. These file handles are 16-bit values that are used instead of the filename in subsequent references to the file. They're actually pointers to an internal DOS table that tracks info about open files. The `FILES` setting determines the size of this table and, if it's full, DOS won't let a program open any more files.

## Recommendations

You can set `FILES` to any value between 8 (the default) and 255, but the setting you use really depends on your software. If you use Windows or dBASE (or any other database program), use `FILES=60`. Otherwise, either check the recommended values in your manuals or just use a setting of 30 or 40.

Guru Tip

> As with `BUFFERS`, a large `FILES` setting can be counterproductive because each entry in DOS' file table takes up about 50 bytes of memory. This means that cranking `FILES` up to 255 uses about 12K.

# *LASTDRIVE*

The `LASTDRIVE` parameter simply sets the highest drive letter that DOS will recognize. The default value is either one more than the highest letter your system currently uses, or E. So, for example, if your computer has two floppy drives (A: and B:) and a hard drive (C:), you won't be able to create new virtual drives (by using SUBST or DRIVER.SYS, for example) past the letter *E* unless you adjust the `LASTDRIVE` setting.

**Guru Tip**

> I'll show you how to create virtual drives with DRIVER.SYS later in this chapter. For SUBST, you have to wait until Chapter 16, "The Fun Stuff: Advanced DOS Commands."

## Recommendations

Unless you plan to create new virtual drives, you should just ignore `LASTDRIVE` because each extra letter past E takes up 88 bytes of memory. If you do need more drive letters, set `LASTDRIVE` to one more than you need. For example, if you need 12 drive letters (A: through L:), set `LASTDRIVE` to M by including the following line in CONFIG.SYS:

```
LASTDRIVE=M
```

**Guru Trivia**

> If you have device drivers in your CONFIG.SYS file (see below) that set up additional physical drives on your system (such as an extra floppy drive), DOS allocates the appropriate drive letters automatically. So, in this case, you don't have to worry about changing the `LASTDRIVE` setting.

## *SHELL*

You use the `SHELL` parameter to control the program that DOS uses as a command interpreter. The format of `SHELL` is slightly different from the other parameters:

```
SHELL=filename [path] switches
```

Here, `filename` is the name of the command interpreter (including the directory if the file isn't in the root directory), `path` is the directory that contains the file (you only enter this if, again, the file isn't in the root), and `switches` are extra options that control the way the command interpreter works. Here's a typical `SHELL` line:

```
SHELL=C:\DOS\COMMAND.COM C:\DOS /E:1024 /P
```

This tells DOS four things:

- To use COMMAND.COM as the interpreter.
- That COMMAND.COM is located in the C:\DOS directory.
- To start COMMAND.COM with an environment size of 1,024 bytes (as given by the `/E:1024` switch). The *environment* is the memory area where DOS stores things like the current prompt and the path. The default is only 256 bytes, which can cause problems if you have a long prompt or path.
- To make this command interpreter "permanent" (the `/P` switch). This is just a safeguard that prevents you from accidentally exiting the interpreter program. It also tells DOS to go ahead and process AUTOEXEC.BAT.

Guru Trivia

> Why do you have to specify COMMAND.COM's directory twice in a `SHELL` statement? Well, the first parameter (`C:\DOS\COMMAND.COM` in the previous example) tells DOS not only which program to use as the command interpreter, but also where to find it during the boot process. The second parameter (`C:\DOS` in the example) tells DOS where to find the program should it need to reload any part of the program overwritten by another program. (I explain this in more detail in Chapter 13, "AUTOEXEC.BAT, Your Most Important Batch File.")

# Recommendations

The `SHELL` parameter is a staple in most guru's CONFIG.SYS file. Here are some recommendations for its use:

- DOS normally expects to find COMMAND.COM in the root directory. Because one of the tenets of good directory management is to keep your root directory relatively clean, you can use `SHELL` to move COMMAND.COM out of the root and into another directory (usually DOS).
- Increasing the environment space is a good idea not only for long prompts and paths, but also because many programs (including Windows) like to store things inside the environment.

✦ Always use the /P switch when you use SHELL. This not only tells DOS to process AUTOEXEC.BAT, it prevents system lockup if you accidentally enter the EXIT command in the main interpreter.

**Guru Tools**

> Two of the most popular replacements for COMMAND.COM are JP Software's 4DOS and the Norton Utilities' NDOS. If you want to use either of these programs, you have to load them with a **SHELL** statement in your CONFIG.SYS file.

## STACKS

The STACKS parameter sets up the number and size of the *stacks* that DOS uses. A stack is a temporary storage location in memory where DOS can set aside whatever it's working on in order to handle signals generated by devices such as the keyboard or a disk drive.

**Guru Trivia**

> The signals generated by the devices attached to your computer are called *hardware interrupts*. This is a good name for them, because these buttinskis stop the normal flow of things and insist on being serviced. A special program called an *interrupt handler* is then dispatched to see what all the fuss is about. DOS can only handle one thing at a time, of course, so it has to store whatever data it was working with on the stack for safe keeping.

Problems occur when the stack area is too small. DOS won't be able to save the data and you'll get an `Internal stack overflow` message. When this happens, you can use STACKS to increase the available stack area. The general format of STACKS is as follows:

```
STACKS=n,s
```

Here, n is the number of stacks, and s is the size of each one. The default number of stacks is 0 on 8088 and 8086 machines and 9 on all others. If you're going to use a nonzero value for n, use any number between 8 and 64. The default size is 0 bytes on 8088 and 8086 computers and 128 bytes for 80286s and up. The range of nonzero values is 32 to 512 bytes.

## Recommendations

Most programs actually have their own stack space and only rely on DOS as a last resort. This means that you can often get away with using the following line in your CONFIG.SYS file (and save about 1K of memory in the process):

```
STACKS=0,0
```

> Some computers don't respond well to the `STACKS=0,0` setting. If you find your system behaves erratically or locks up, remove this line from your CONFIG.SYS file.

If you're getting stack errors, increase the number of stacks to 12 or 15. If the errors persist, increase the size of each stack to 256 bytes.

# *VERIFY*

When the `VERIFY` parameter is set to `ON`, DOS performs a series of checks to ensure that each disk write was performed correctly and that no data was copied to a bad sector.

## Recommendations

`VERIFY=ON` gives you slightly greater protection during disk writes, but at the cost of drastically slower performance overall. I recommend keeping `VERIFY OFF` until you really need it (such as during a backup or when you're writing to an old floppy disk). Happily, you can turn on verification from the command line by entering the following command:

```
verify on
```

# Using Device Drivers in CONFIG.SYS

Normally, DOS and the various devices attached to your computer—such as a mouse, network card, or memory board—can't "talk" to each other, because they all, in effect, speak different languages. To overcome this problem, the world's programming geniuses invented *device drivers*, small programs that translate information passed between DOS and your system's hardware.

## Installing Device Drivers

To install a device driver for DOS to use, you need to add one or more `DEVICE` statements to your CONFIG.SYS file. A `DEVICE` statement has the following general form:

```
DEVICE=filename [switches]
```

Here, `filename` is the name (including the drive and directory) of the device driver (it usually has a SYS extension) and `switches` are any optional parameters and switches required by the driver. For example, here's a `DEVICE` statement that loads a mouse driver:

```
DEVICE=C:\MOUSE\MOUSE.SYS
```

Guru Tip

> DOS 5 introduced **DEVICEHIGH**, a variation of **DEVICE** that enables you to load device drivers into upper memory. See Chapter 15, "Memory Management Made Easy," for the scoop.

## DOS Device Drivers

Most device drivers are supplied by the manufacturers of the device. However, DOS comes with a few of its own.

# ANSI.SYS

You use ANSI.SYS to control certain aspects of your computer's screen and keyboard. See Part III, "Guru Style: Customizing DOS," for various ways to take advantage of ANSI.SYS.

# DRIVER.SYS

DRIVER.SYS is a device driver that you can use to create a *logical drive* (i.e., a drive that doesn't physically exist, but can be referred to in commands). For example, suppose your system has a 5.25-inch drive (drive A:), a 3.5-inch drive (drive B:), and a hard disk (drive C:). You could use DRIVER.SYS to set up the 5.25-inch drive so that it's also drive D:.

Why on earth would you want to do this? Well, the most common use is for copying files between floppies of the same type. Let's say you want to copy some TXT files from one 5.25-inch disk to another. Normally, you have to copy all the files from the original disk to the hard drive, insert the new disk, and then copy the files back from the hard drive. However, if you use DRIVER.SYS to set up a logical drive D:, you could do the whole thing with the following command:

```
xcopy a:\*.txt d:\
```

DOS reads the files from A: and then prompts you to insert the disk in D:. Neat, huh?

**Guru Tip**

> If your computer has only one floppy drive (as is the case with most notebooks), don't use DRIVER.SYS to set up the drive as a logical drive B:. DOS does this automatically.

The general format for DRIVER.SYS is as follows:

```
DEVICE=C:\DOS\DRIVER.SYS [switches]
```

Table 12.2 lists some of the available switches for DRIVER.SYS.

**Table 12.2. Some DRIVER.SYS switches.**

| *Switch* | *Description* | |
|---|---|---|
| `/D:n` | Specifies the drive number (`n`) of the physical floppy drive. The first drive (drive A:) is 0, the second (usually drive B:) is 1, and so on. | |
| `/F:n` | Specifies the type of disk drive. `n` can take the following values: | |
| | 0 | 320K/360K, 5.25-inch |
| | 1 | 1.2M, 5.25-inch |
| | 2 | 720K, 3.5-inch |
| | 7 | 1.44M, 3.5-inch |
| | 9 | 2.88M, 3.5-inch |

So, for example, to create a new logical drive from a high-density, 5.25-inch drive A:, add the following line to CONFIG.SYS:

```
DEVICE=C:\DOS\DRIVER.SYS /D:0 /F:1
```

> Before you create any new logical drives with DRIVER.SYS, be sure you set up the **LASTDRIVE** parameter to handle the new letters.

# DBLSPACE.SYS

This driver is used by DoubleSpace—DOS 6's disk compression program—to move the file that gives you access to your compressed drives (DBLSPACE.BIN) out of conventional memory and into upper memory. This can save you about 50K in conventional memory. Here's the proper syntax:

```
DEVICE=C:\DOS\DBLSPACE.SYS /MOVE
```

## EMM386.EXE and HIMEM.SYS

These device drivers control the configuration of your computer's memory. You can use them to set up logical disks in RAM and greatly increase the available memory in your system. For the poop on these powerful programs, see Chapter 15.

# Guru Review

This chapter was designed to make you a CONFIG.SYS expert. Just to be sure everything has sunk in, here's a review:

- Take care when editing CONFIG.SYS because mistakes will often lock up your system.
- CONFIG.SYS is a pure text file, so you can use any text editor to make changes. If you use a word processor, be sure you save the file as text only.
- You use CONFIG.SYS to establish values for certain system parameters, including `BREAK`, `BUFFERS`, `FILES`, and `LASTDRIVE`.
- It's a good idea to include a `SHELL` command in CONFIG.SYS. This lets you move COMMAND.COM out of the root directory, change the environment size, and safeguard against accidentally exiting COMMAND.COM.
- If you use any devices such as a mouse or network card with your computer, you need to install the appropriate device drivers in CONFIG.SYS.

# AUTOEXEC.BAT: Your Most Important Batch File

**Guru Stuff in This Chapter ➤**

13

CHAPTER

- *About AUTOEXEC.BAT*
- *What to put in AUTOEXEC.BAT*
- *An introduction to the DOS environment*
- *How to use environment variables in batch files*
- *Lots of must-have AUTOEXEC.BAT information for gurus-in-training*

Chapter 12, "CONFIG.SYS: What Every Guru Should Know," gave you the lowdown on the first half of DOS' morning wakeup call: CONFIG.SYS. Once DOS is done with CONFIG.SYS, it turns its attention to AUTOEXEC.BAT—your computer's second configuration file. This chapter takes you on a tour of this all-important file. You'll learn what AUTOEXEC.BAT is all about and how to unlock its secrets.

# AUTOEXEC.BAT: Not Just Another Pretty Batch File

As you can tell from its name, AUTOEXEC.BAT (the proper guru pronunciation is otto-exec-dot-bat) is a batch file. But not just any batch file, no sir. Oh sure, it looks more or less like other batch files you've come across. It is, as you'll see, just a list of DOS commands. The difference, though, is that when you boot your computer, DOS (after handling its CONFIG.SYS chores) looks for AUTOEXEC.BAT in your boot drive's root directory. If it finds it there, DOS automatically executes it (which is, incidentally, how AUTOEXEC.BAT gets its name).

So what goes into an AUTOEXEC.BAT file? Well, because AUTOEXEC.BAT is a batch file and therefore can contain any DOS command, there are as many answers to that question as their are millionaires at Microsoft. But keep in mind that AUTOEXEC.BAT is a configuration file, so you use it to configure your computer. This means you should include four basic types of commands: memory-resident software, one-time-only programs, your initial application, and DOS environment statements.

## Memory-Resident Software

*Memory-resident* programs (also called *terminate-and-stay-resident* or *TSR* programs) are loaded into memory where they wait patiently to be called upon. These programs respond to a specific event such as pressing a certain key combination or a file deletion before they kick into action.

**Guru Tip**

For best results, always include the full pathname (the drive, directory, and filename) of your TSRs in AUTOEXEC.BAT. This not only ensures that DOS finds the programs, but they'll load faster, too.

Common DOS TSRs found in guru AUTOEXEC.BAT files are DOSKEY (see Chapter 11, "Customizing the Command Line with DOSKEY"), `UNDELETE`'s deletion tracking program (see Chapter 19, "An Ounce of Prevention: How to Avoid Trouble"), and DOS 6's VSAFE virus checker (see Chapter 19). Other possibilities are productivity enhancers such as Borland's SideKick, screen capture programs, and network utilities.

**Dunce**

TSRs use up memory, and loading too many can leave your regular applications starved for kilobytes. To help out, DOS versions 5 and 6 include a `LOADHIGH` command that you can use in AUTOEXEC.BAT to load TSRs into upper memory. Chapter 15, "Memory Management Made Easy," gives you the `LOADHIGH` lowdown.

# One-Time-Only Programs

Some programs only need to be run once a day. If you include these in your AUTOEXEC.BAT file, they run automatically every morning (which gives you one less thing to worry about).

DOS has a number of one-time-only utilities that you can include in your AUTOEXEC.BAT. For example, many people like to run `CHKDSK` each day to ensure that their hard disk is in order. One command that no guru's AUTOEXEC.BAT file should be without is `MIRROR` (see Chapter 19 for details). Another possibility is the `MODE` command that sets up your keyboard, monitor, printer, or serial port. If you have DOS 6, you could also include MSAV, the new utility that scans your hard disk for viruses.

**Guru Tip**

> You can even run other batch files in AUTOEXEC.BAT. Just use the CALL command followed by the name of the batch file. For example, if you have a batch file named MACROS.BAT that stores your DOSKEY macros, add the following line to AUTOEXEC.BAT (after loading DOSKEY):
>
> ```
> CALL macros
> ```
>
> Just so you know: CALL is not exclusive to AUTOEXEC.BAT. You can use it in any batch file.

# Your Initial Application

The last line in AUTOEXEC.BAT is (usually) the command to load whatever program you like to start your day with. So, for example, if you work in WordPerfect, simply add the following line at the end of AUTOEXEC.BAT:

```
WP
```

Here's a trick that a lot of gurus use to automate their daily incremental backups. Consider the following lines from an AUTOEXEC.BAT file:

```
CD\DBASE\DATA
DBASE
BACKUP *.DBF /M
```

The first two lines just change to the \DBASE\DATA directory and run the dBASE program. When dBASE is exited, however, DOS executes the last line, which performs an incremental backup of any DBF files that were modified.

# DOS Environment Statements

You can also include DOS environment statements in your AUTOEXEC.BAT file. These statements assign values to *environment variables* (which are similar to the system parameters you set up in CONFIG.SYS) used by DOS, batch files, and some programs. This is a crucial guru subject, so I'll take the rest of this chapter to examine it carefully.

# What Is the Environment?

The *environment* is a small buffer set up in memory to hold *environment variables,* settings used to control certain aspects of DOS or other programs. The environment normally contains the current settings for the `PATH` and `PROMPT`, as well as any variables set up by your programs.

You usually assign values to environment variables using the `SET` command, like so:

```
SET variablename=string
```

Here, `variablename` is, you guessed it, the name of the environment variable, and `string` is the string value being assigned. So, for example, if you want to create an environment variable called `NAME` and assign it the string value `Alphonse`, use the following command:

```
SET NAME=Alphonse
```

To see a listing of all the environment variables, enter the `SET` command by itself. You should see a list that looks something like this:

```
COMSPEC=C:\DOS\COMMAND.COM
PATH=C:\;C:\DOS;C:\BATCH
PROMPT=$P$G
TEMP=C:\TEMP
NAME=Alphonse
```

The next few sections look at the five most common DOS environment variables.

Guru Tip

> Once you're done with an environment variable, you can delete it with the following `SET` format:
>
> `SET variablename=`

## COMSPEC

The `COMSPEC` environment variable specifies the name and location of the command interpreter (usually COMMAND.COM). DOS normally sets this variable automatically, but you can control it yourself (as described in Chapter 12) with the `SHELL` system parameter.

> **Guru Trivia**
>
> DOS normally loads the command interpreter in two parts: a *resident* part that always stays in memory, and a *transient* part that sits at the top of conventional memory (the first 640K; see Chapter 15 for more memory information). When you use other programs, they'll often overwrite the transient part without even so much as a by-your-leave. This means that DOS has to reload the transient part, and to do that it must first locate the command interpreter on the hard disk. That's where `COMSPEC` enters the picture—it tells DOS exactly where to look for the interpreter file.

## DIRCMD

`DIRCMD` is an environment variable introduced in DOS 5 to allow you to preset your `DIR` switches. For example, suppose you always want `DIR` to display directories first, sort everything in alphabetical order by filename, and pause after each screenful. You can accomplish all this by adding the following line to your AUTOEXEC.BAT file:

```
SET DIRCMD=/OGN /P
```

Now each time you use `DIR`, DOS automatically includes these switches as part of the command.

> **Guru Tip**
>
> To override the `DIRCMD` presets, include the switch with a minus sign. For example, if you don't want a particular `DIR` command to pause after each screenful, you could override the preset by entering the following command:
>
> ```
> dir /-p
> ```

## PROMPT

Any time you issue a `PROMPT` command, the `PROMPT` environment variable is set automatically. DOS then uses this variable whenever it needs to display the prompt. If you don't enter a `PROMPT` command, or if you just enter `PROMPT` by itself, DOS deletes the `PROMPT` variable and just uses its default system prompt—

the current drive letter followed by a greater-than sign (>). (Chapter 9, "Customizing the Prompt," tells you all you would ever want to know about the PROMPT command.)

**Guru Tip**

> With DOS 6, if you don't enter a **PROMPT** command in AUTOEXEC.BAT, DOS sets the prompt to **$P$G**. (You don't have to use **SET PROMPT=** in order to create the **PROMPT** environment variable. The regular **PROMPT** command is all you need.)

## TEMP

The TEMP variable specifies where programs can place their temporary files. DOS in particular (or Windows, if you use it) often creates temporary files as part of its normal operations. For example, a pipe (a technique that sends the output from one DOS command to another; see Chapter 17) always creates a temporary file.

**Guru Tip**

> You should periodically check whatever directory you've specified in the **TEMP** variable to look for stray files that some program was unable or unwilling to delete. It's okay to delete these files as long as there are no programs running. Deleting a temporary file belonging to a running program could possibly trash valuable data.

**Dunce**

> Before setting the **TEMP** variable, be sure the directory you're going to use already exists.

## PATH

The PATH variable, as you might expect, contains the list of directories that you specified in your PATH statement. When you ask DOS to run a program or batch file, if it can't find the appropriate file in the current directory, it starts working its way through the PATH directories. If it still can't find it, you'll get a `Bad command or file name` message.

The search path can have a noticeable effect on the way your system operates. Here are a few tips to optimize your use of this important variable:

- If you plan on starting any programs from somewhere other than their home directories (for example, if you set up separate data subdirectories), be sure to include the home directory in your path.
- Since DOS plows through the PATH directories in order, you can usually speed things up a bit by rearranging the PATH. The first directories should always be C:\, C:\DOS, and then C:\BATCH (or whatever subdirectory you store your batch files in). Then add your program directories in order of importance.
- Remember that PATH, like any DOS command, has a 127-character limit. If you're bumping your head on this ceiling, try using shorter directory names. If this doesn't cut it, remove some directories altogether and just use batch files to start these programs. (The SUBST command can also help; see Chapter 16, "The Fun Stuff: Advanced DOS Commands," for details.)

**Guru Tip**

> As with **PROMPT**, you don't need to use **SET PATH=** to create the **PATH** variable. Just use the plain, old **PATH** command.

# Using Environment Variables in Batch Files

Although using environment variables in batch files is not strictly an AUTOEXEC.BAT topic, this seems like as good place as any to bring it up. The basic idea is simple: you can access environment variables in a batch file simply by bracketing the variable name with percent signs (%). For example, if you create an environment variable called NAME, as follows:

```
SET NAME=Alphonse
```

you can then use this in a batch file:

```
ECHO Hi! My name is %NAME%
```

Here's what you see when you run the program:

```
Hi! My name is Alphonse
```

On a more practical level, here's a batch file (PATHLIST.BAT) that uses the `PATH` environment variable to list each `PATH` directory:

```
@ECHO OFF
ECHO.
ECHO The current PATH directories are:
FOR %%D IN (%PATH%) DO ECHO %%D
ECHO.
```

You can also create your own environment variables inside batch files. For example, here's a batch file called REVERSE.BAT that uses `PROMPT` to change the screen colors to black text on a white background (refer to Chapter 10, "Customizing the Keyboard," for the gory details about setting screen colors with `PROMPT`):

```
@ECHO ON
SET OLDPROMPT=%PROMPT%
PROMPT $E[1;30;47m
PROMPT %OLDPROMPT%
SET OLDPROMPT=
CLS
```

The first `SET` statement saves the current `PROMPT` variable to a new variable called `OLDPROMPT`. Then `PROMPT` is executed twice—first to change the screen colors and then to restore the `PROMPT` variable to its old value. The last `SET` statement deletes `OLDPROMPT` because it's no longer needed.

# Guru Review

The chapter showed you the ins and outs of AUTOEXEC.BAT. Now it's time for a quick review before moving on:

- AUTOEXEC.BAT is a batch file, but because DOS executes it automatically during startup, you can use it to configure certain aspects of your system.
- Most AUTOEXEC.BAT files contain four kinds of commands: TSRs such as mouse drivers and DOSKEY, one-time-only programs such as CHKDSK and VSAFE, your initial application, and environment statements.
- The environment is a small memory buffer used to hold *environment variables*, settings that control some aspects of DOS and other programs.
- The five most common DOS environment variables are `COMSPEC` (the location of the command interpreter), `DIRCMD` (the `DIR` command presets), `PROMPT` (the current prompt string), `TEMP` (the storage location for temporary files), and `PATH` (the current path directory list).
- To use environment variables in batch files, surround the variable name with percent signs.

# Start It Your Way: DOS 6 Boot Options

14

CHAPTER

## Guru Stuff in This Chapter ➤

- *Bypassing CONFIG.SYS and AUTOEXEC.BAT*
- *Confirming CONFIG.SYS commands*
- *Defining a startup menu*
- *Setting up different CONFIG.SYS configurations*
- *Handling different configurations in AUTOEXEC.BAT*
- *Unexpurgated coverage of all the new DOS 6 boot commands*

In the not-so-good old days of computers, you just cranked on your system and started hacking away. Configuration didn't matter a whole lot because the machines—and the software running on them—just weren't all that complicated. It was a simple, innocent time, but I wouldn't go back even at gunpoint.

Why? Well, because now we have machines that can keep up with us. Now we have software that will do what we want it to do (instead of what it wants us to do). Now we have, in short, power. But we also have McFedries' "Bad News Law #3": the price of power is complexity. So we have to deal with the exacting memory requirements of our sophisticated software—innumerable device drivers for peripherals, expansion boards, programs, finicky graphical applications, and memory-hogging networks.

To accommodate all this complexity, we've had to stuff command after command into our CONFIG.SYS and AUTOEXEC.BAT files (or have rude installation programs do it for us). The result, usually, is bloated configuration files, interminable startup times, and inevitable compromises because we tried to keep all our programs happy. With the coming of DOS 6, however, we can leave all that behind us. Now we have a whole host of new booting options that will tame even the most complicated setup. This chapter shows you how it's done.

**Guru Tip**

> The term *booting*, of course, has nothing to do with punting your monitor across the room. It comes from the old phrase "pulling yourself up by your own bootstraps." In this case, it refers to the self-loading program stored permanently in your system's ROM BIOS that gets everything going when you turn on your PC.

# The Clean Boot: Bypassing CONFIG.SYS and AUTOEXEC.BAT

I don't know how many times I've had trouble with either software or hardware that has stumped the company's technical support staff. I usually end up on hold forever while the geek checks his "database" of problems or just asks the old-timer next to him (the guy that's been with the company for six months) if he can figure it out. Inevitably, he'll come back on the line and give me the tech support party line: "You probably have a memory conflict. Remove all your device drivers and TSRs from your startup files and try again." Thanks, pal.

Before DOS 6 came along, you had two ways to get a clean boot (a startup without device drivers and memory-resident programs):

- Use `REM` to neuter the appropriate CONFIG.SYS and AUTOEXEC.BAT commands.
- Have clean versions of CONFIG.SYS and AUTOEXEC.BAT on hand so you could just copy them to your root directory (after, of course, saving copies of your current configuration files).

DOS 6 eliminates this drudgery by letting you accomplish the same thing with only a single keystroke. Here's how it works. When you start or reboot your computer, you will eventually see the following message:

```
Starting MS-DOS...
```

This message appears for two seconds and then DOS starts processing CONFIG.SYS. In that two-second window, you can tell DOS to completely bypass both CONFIG.SYS and AUTOEXEC.BAT (and get a clean boot) by doing one of two things:

- Press the F5 key.
- Hold down the Shift key until you see the DOS prompt.

**Guru Tip**

> You can tell DOS to skip the two-second delay after displaying the `Starting MS-DOS...` message by including the following line in CONFIG.SYS:
>
> `SWITCHES=/F`
>
> Remember that you need to reboot once before this will work.

Although DOS doesn't process CONFIG.SYS and AUTOEXEC.BAT, it does set some environment variables to default values. Enter the `SET` command after a clean boot and you'll see something like this:

```
PATH=C:\DOS
PROMPT=$P$G
COMSPEC=C:\DOS\COMMAND.COM
```

**Dunce**

> If you plan to use any programs after a clean boot, you may need to adjust your **PATH** to make things run properly. Also, remember that no device drivers have been loaded, so things like your mouse won't work.

# Confirming CONFIG.SYS Commands

If you've ever made a typing error in CONFIG.SYS, or added a device driver your system didn't like, you know the ensuing frustration when your machine hangs and no amount of coaxing (verbal or otherwise) will get it to respond.

In the past, your only recourse (short of throwing the thing out the window) was to boot from a floppy in drive A: and then, once control was restored, edit the offending line. In other words, it was a pain in the you-know-what.

## Confirming Each CONFIG.SYS Command

I guess this must have happened one time too many to the DOS programmers, because they've finally come up with a simpler, more elegant solution. When you see the `Starting MS-DOS...` message, just tap the F8 key (you've got the usual two-second delay to do this) and DOS goes through each CONFIG.SYS command and asks whether or not you want to run it:

```
DOS=UMB [Y,N]?
```

If you do want to run the command, just press `y`. Otherwise, press `n`.

**Guru Tip**

> During the confirmation process, you can either press Esc to tell DOS to go ahead and run all of the remaining commands, or press F5 to skip all of the remaining commands.

When CONFIG.SYS is done, DOS next asks about AUTOEXEC.BAT:

```
Process AUTOEXEC.BAT [Y,N]?
```

This is an all-or-nothing deal—you don't get line-by-line confirmation here. Select `y` to run AUTOEXEC.BAT or `n` to skip it.

**Guru Tip**

> If other people use your computer, they might accidentally press F5 or F8 during startup and cause all kinds of havoc. To prevent this, you can temporarily disable the F5 and F8 keys by including the following command in your CONFIG.SYS file:
>
> ```
> SWITCHES=/N
> ```
>
> Don't forget to reboot to put this new setting into effect.

## Confirming Individual Commands

Rather than stepping through every CONFIG.SYS command, you can tell DOS to ask for confirmation only on selected commands. You do this simply by adding a question mark (?) just before the equal sign. For example, if you want DOS to ask for confirmation before setting `BREAK` to `ON`, use the following command:

```
BREAK?=ON
```

# Specifying a Different Startup Batch File

Normally, once DOS is done with CONFIG.SYS, it moves on to process AUTOEXEC.BAT. With DOS 6, however, the `SHELL` system parameter has a new `/K` switch that lets you specify another batch file to use in place of AUTOEXEC.BAT. There are two reasons why this is a good idea:

- ✦ You'll be learning later in this chapter how to create different startup configurations. As part of this, you could also construct a different startup batch file for each configuration.
- ✦ It's a great way to protect your startup batch file. There's nothing worse than bull-in-a-china-shop installation programs that modify your finely tuned AUTOEXEC.BAT file (sometimes without even telling you!). By including your startup commands in a different batch file, you can foil this rudeness.

Dunce

> The downside to having a different startup batch file is that it may cause problems for installation programs that legitimately need to alter AUTOEXEC.BAT. The best thing to do is keep an empty file named AUTOEXEC.BAT in your root directory. When you've finished installing a program, take a look at what changes it made to this file and, if necessary, incorporate them into your real startup file.

If, for example, you've created a batch file in your BATCH directory called STARTER.BAT, you can make it your startup batch file by including a command such as the following in CONFIG.SYS:

```
SHELL=C:\DOS\COMMAND.COM C:\DOS /P /K C:\BATCH\STARTER.BAT
```

# Setting Up Multiple Configurations

You may not know it, but the life of a typical configuration file is a hard one. Consider what they have to put up with:

- ✦ They have to take into account the bewildering variety of demands today's software packages place on a system. Some use expanded memory, others use extended memory, and others don't care about either. Some use a mouse, some don't. Some need CONFIG.SYS' `FILES` parameter set to 100, and other programs are happy with 20 or 30.

- Large hard disks and data compression technology let you cram more and more programs onto your machine. This means that a configuration file has to load TSRs and device drivers to cover any eventuality. But, if you don't need the mouse, why load the driver? If you don't plan to log on to your network, why load all that memory-hogging software? In some cases, you can start everything from a batch file when you need it. Other times, though, the driver has to be loaded in CONFIG.SYS.
- In these cost-cutting times, there may be two or more people using a single computer. McFedries "Bad News Law #16" says that if two people share a computer, they'll inevitably use completely different software that requires completely different system configurations.

Before DOS 6, you either had to make compromises in CONFIG.SYS and AUTOEXEC.BAT, or you had to create separate startup files for different purposes and then set up elaborate and confusing batch file schemes to shuffle these files around. It was a real mess, in other words.

Ah, but DOS 6 changes all that. Now you can create nice, neat menus in CONFIG.SYS and, depending on your menu choice, DOS executes a particular *configuration block*—a collection of CONFIG.SYS commands. And you can even tie things into AUTOEXEC.BAT and use simple `IF` and `GOTO` statements to run different commands. The next few sections take you through, step-by-step.

# Step 1: Defining CONFIG.SYS Startup Menus

The first thing you need to do is define a startup menu in CONFIG.SYS. This menu appears every time you start or reboot your machine, and your menu choice determines which configuration DOS will run. You define your menus with five new CONFIG.SYS commands: `MENUITEM`, `MENUDEFAULT`, `SUBMENU`, `MENUCOLOR`, and `NUMLOCK`.

## *MENUITEM*

This command defines the menu options. Here's the general format:

```
MENUITEM=block, [menutext]
```

Here, `block` is the name of a configuration block (which I'll define in the next section) and `menutext` is an optional description that will appear as the menu option. (If you leave out `menutext`, DOS uses `block`, instead.) For example, here's a menu definition for a computer with three users:

```
[MENU]
MENUITEM=Les, Les Nessman's stuff (hog reports, etc.)
MENUITEM=Herb, Herb Tarlek's stuff (sales leads, etc.)
MENUITEM=Big_guy, Mr. Carlson's stuff (bait, tackle, etc.)
```

Notice how the definition begins with `[MENU]` (this is called a *block header*). This tells DOS that you're defining a menu. Here's what you'll see when you reboot:

```
MS-DOS 6 Startup Menu
_____________________

   1. Les Nessman's stuff (hog reports, etc.)
   2. Herb Tarlek's stuff (sales leads, etc.)
   3. Mr. Carlson's stuff (bait, tackle, etc.)

Enter a choice: 1
```

To select an option, press the number or use the up or down arrow keys to highlight your selection and then press Enter. DOS processes the corresponding CONFIG.SYS configuration block (see the next section).

Guru Tip

> While the startup menu is displayed, you can also press F5 to bypass CONFIG.SYS and AUTOEXEC.BAT, or F8 to single-step through CONFIG.SYS.

Some notes about `MENUITEM`:

- The `block` parameter can be up to 70 characters long, but it can't include spaces or any of the following characters:

  `\ / , ; = [ ]`

- The `menutext` parameter also can be up to 70 characters long, but it can include any characters that strike your fancy.
- You can't have more than nine `MENUITEM` commands in a menu block. (If you need more than nine items, use the `SUBMENU` command, as explained below.)

## MENUDEFAULT

This command defines a default choice for the startup menu. The general format is:

```
MENUDEFAULT=block, [timeout]
```

In this case, `block` is a block name used in a `MENUITEM` command, and `timeout` is an optional number of seconds that DOS waits before selecting the default choice automatically. Consider the following menu definition:

```
[MENU]
MENUITEM=Squab
MENUITEM=Rutabaga
MENUITEM=Kiwi_fruit
MENUDEFAULT=Rutabaga, 15
```

When DOS executes this menu, you will see the following:

```
MS-DOS 6 Startup Menu
_____________________

   1. Squab
   2. Rutabaga
   3. Kiwi_fruit

Enter a choice: 2        Time remaining: 15
```

DOS displays the number of the default choice in the `Enter a choice` prompt, and uses `Time remaining` to count down the timeout value.

**Guru Tip**

> To stop the countdown and keep the menu on screen, just press any key.

Some `MENUDEFAULT` notes:

- ✦ If you don't enter a value for `timeout`, DOS waits patiently until you press Enter.
- ✦ You can enter a timeout value between 0 and 90 seconds. If you enter 0, DOS selects the default choice automatically.

## SUBMENU

This command displays a menu option that, when selected, produces another menu of choices. The general format is just like `MENUITEM`:

```
SUBMENU=block, [menutext]
```

In this case, though, `block` refers to another block of menu commands. Here's an example menu definition:

```
[MENU]
MENUITEM=DOS, Run DOS configuration
MENUITEM=WINDOWS, Run Windows configuration
MENUITEM=NET, Load network drivers
SUBMENU=PROGRAMS, Display program configuration menu

[PROGRAMS]
MENUITEM=Run Lotus 1-2-3 configuration
MENUITEM=Run dBASE configuration
MENUITEM=Run WordPerfect configuration
```

Here, the `SUBMENU` command in `[MENU]` points to the `[PROGRAMS]` block. If you select option 4, `Display program configuration menu`, you get the `[PROGRAMS]` menu on-screen. You then select the option you want from the new menu.

> You can include submenus inside submenus to get even more choices. One handy use for this is to include a **SUBMENU** command that points back to the main menu:
>
> ```
> SUBMENU MENU, Return to main menu
> ```
>
> This gives you an out if you select the wrong option. The number of submenus is practically unlimited. The only restriction you face is that CONFIG.SYS can't get any bigger than 64K!

## MENUCOLOR

This command defines the text and background colors for the startup menu. Here's the general format:

```
MENUCOLOR=x, [y]
```

Here, x is the text color and y is the optional background color. Table 14.1 lists the available values for both parameters.

**Table 14.1. Available color values for the *MENUCOLOR* command.**

| *Value* | *Color* | *Value* | *Color* |
|---|---|---|---|
| 0 | Black | 8 | Gray |
| 1 | Blue | 9 | Bright blue |
| 2 | Green | 10 | Bright green |
| 3 | Cyan | 11 | Bright cyan |
| 4 | Red | 12 | Bright red |
| 5 | Magenta | 13 | Bright magenta |
| 6 | Brown | 14 | Yellow |
| 7 | White | 15 | Bright white |

> Be sure to specify different values for the text and background, or you won't see a thing on-screen.

## NUMLOCK

This command turns NumLock on or off. Because you can select startup menu options by either pressing a number or using the up or down arrow keys, this command lets you toggle NumLock to the appropriate setting for your keyboard. For example, to make sure NumLock is always on when the startup menu is displayed, include the following command in the `[MENU]` block:

```
NUMLOCK=ON
```

## Step 2: Defining CONFIG.SYS Configuration Blocks

Once you have your menu definition in place, you need to set up *configuration blocks* for each menu item. A configuration block is just a collection of CONFIG.SYS commands. When you select an option from the startup menu, DOS runs only the commands in the corresponding block.

A configuration block always begins with a *block header*, the name of the block enclosed in square brackets. You then place each block command below the header. Here's an example:

```
[MENU]
MENUITEM=EXTENDED, Extended memory configuration
MENUITEM=EXPANDED, Expanded memory configuration

[COMMON]
DEVICE=C:\DOS\HIMEM.SYS
DOS=HIGH
FILES=30
BUFFERS=15

[EXTENDED]
DEVICE=C:\DOS\EMM386.EXE NOEMS

[EXPANDED]
DEVICE=C:\DOS\EMM386.EXE 1024
```

`[COMMON]` is a special configuration block. DOS executes all the commands in this block, no matter which startup option you choose. This file contains two other configuration blocks: `[EXTENDED]`, which loads EMM386 with the NOEMS (no expanded memory) parameter, and `[EXPANDED]`, which loads EMM386 with 1M of expanded memory.

**Guru Tip**

> You can have more than one `[COMMON]` block and DOS executes the commands for all of them. It's a good idea to include a `[COMMON]` block at the end of CONFIG.SYS. This way, if any installation programs append commands to CONFIG.SYS, DOS definitely runs them.

DOS 6 has added two new CONFIG.SYS commands that you can use inside configuration blocks: `SET` and `INCLUDE`.

## SET

This command works just like SET in AUTOEXEC.BAT (see Chapter 13, "AUTOEXEC.BAT: Your Most Important Batch File," for the SET scoop). This means you can use it to establish values for environment variables such as PATH, PROMPT, and TEMP (see the example, below).

> If you set up environment variables in CONFIG.SYS, be sure to remove any corresponding commands from AUTOEXEC.BAT.

## INCLUDE

This command lets you include the contents of one configuration block inside another. Here's the general format:

```
INCLUDE=block
```

For example, the following CONFIG.SYS file presents the user with three configuration choices: DOS, Windows, and Windows for Workgroups. In the [WFW] block, the INCLUDE command tells DOS to also run all of the [WIN] block commands.

```
[MENU]
MENUITEM=DOS, Load DOS configuration
MENUITEM=WIN, Load Windows configuration
MENUITEM=WFW, Load Windows for Workgroups configuration

[COMMON]
DEVICE=C:\DOS\HIMEM.SYS
DOS=HIGH
BUFFERS=15

[DOS]
FILES=25
SET PATH=C:\;C:\DOS;C:\BATCH
SET TEMP=C:\DOS
DEVICE=C:\DOS\EMM386.EXE 1024

[WIN]
FILES=60
```

```
SET PATH=C:\;C:\DOS;C:\WINDOWS
SET TEMP=C:\WINDOWS\TEMP
DEVICE=C:\WINDOWS\MOUSE.SYS
DEVICE=C:\DOS\EMM386.EXE

[WFW]
INCLUDE=WINDOWS
LASTDRIVE=G
DEVICE=C:\WINDOWS\PROTMAN.DOS
DEVICE=C:\WINDOWS\WORKGRP.SYS

[COMMON]
```

## Step 3: Setting Up the Configurations in AUTOEXEC.BAT

The final step in setting up your boot options is to modify AUTOEXEC.BAT to handle your different CONFIG.SYS configurations. When you select a startup menu option, DOS places the name of the corresponding configuration block in an environment variable name `CONFIG`. So, in AUTOEXEC.BAT, all you need is a `GOTO %CONFIG%` command to send control to an appropriately named label. Here's an example AUTOEXEC.BAT file that uses the last CONFIG.SYS example:

```
@ECHO OFF
C:\DOS\SMARTDRV.EXE

GOTO %CONFIG%

:DOS
DOSKEY
SET DIRCMD=/OGN /P
PROMPT DOS Configuration$_$P$G
GOTO END

:WIN
PROMPT Windows Configuration$_$P$G
WIN
GOTO END

:WFW
PROMPT Windows for Workgroups Configuration$_$P$G
C:\WINDOWS\NET START
WIN

:END
```

SMARTDRV, because it's needed by all configurations, is loaded first. Then the GOTO %CONFIG% command sends DOS to one of three labels: DOS, WIN, or WFW (notice how the labels have the same names as the configuration blocks). The appropriate commands are executed, and then another GOTO sends DOS to the END label to avoid processing the other commands.

A slightly different AUTOEXEC.BAT strategy would be to use IF commands to check the CONFIG variable. In this case, the proper syntax is as follows:

```
IF "%CONFIG%"==value command
```

Here, value would be a block name, and command would be whatever you want DOS to do.

These new boot options are a welcome addition to DOS. However, there are tools available that give you greater flexibility. One of the best is BootSys. This program lets you define up to 20 main menu items, has shortcut keys for the menu, and even lets you use variables and branching in CONFIG.SYS.

# Guru Review

This chapter gave you the lowdown on the cool new boot options introduced in DOS 6. Here's the *Reader's Digest* condensed version:

- To get a clean boot, don't mess around with REMs and stripped down CONFIG.SYS and AUTOEXEC.BAT files. Just press F5 or hold down Shift when you see the `Starting MS-DOS...` message.
- If a CONFIG.SYS command is giving your computer gas, press F8 when you see `Starting MS-DOS...`, and DOS will single-step through each CONFIG.SYS line.
- DOS 6 lets you easily define different startup configurations for your system. The first step is to create a startup menu of configuration choices. You're limited to nine options on the main menu, but you can use submenus to get even more choices.

- Once you have a startup menu in place, you need to define corresponding configuration blocks for each item. When you select a startup menu option, DOS only executes the commands in its configuration block.
- If you have any commands that you want to run for all configurations, add a `[COMMON]` block to CONFIG.SYS.
- When you're done with CONFIG.SYS, add a `GOTO %CONFIG%` command in AUTOEXEC.BAT and arrange your labels accordingly.

# 15

CHAPTER

# Memory Management Made Easy

## Guru Stuff in This Chapter ➤

- *Memory basics to get you started*
- *The difference between expanded and extended memory*
- *Techniques for maximizing memory*
- *Using DOS 6's new MemMaker program*
- *A seemingly infinite number of strategies for managing your computer's memory*

Entire books can be (and have been) written about the relationship between DOS and memory. What it all boils down to, though, is quite simple: the more memory you have, the happier DOS (and most of your programs) will be. However, not all of us can afford to throw 64 megabytes of memory at our problems. We have to make do with less, and that, in essence, is what this chapter is all about. I'll show you some ways to fight back if a lack of memory is slowing DOS to a crawl.

# Memory 101

Your computer's memory is arguably its most important component, yet few people seem to understand just what it is or what it does. This is good because it means that you, as a DOS guru, will be able to leap into the breach and impress the heck out of everyone with your new-found memory savvy. To that end, I'll start off with a brief, guru-style explanation of some basic memory concepts.

## Memory Can Be Beautiful . . .

Your computer's *random access memory* (*RAM*, for short) is just an innocuous collection of chips on the system's main circuit board. But although they may not look like much, those chips can do some pretty cool things.

Their basic purpose in life, of course, is to be used as a work area for your programs and your data. These things normally slumber peacefully on your hard disk, but when you need them, DOS rouses everyone from their spacious beds and herds the program code and data into the cramped confines of memory. From there, different bits of code and data are swapped in and out of memory, as needed. Why not just work with everything from the hard disk itself? One word: *speed*. Even the highest of high-tech hard drives is a tortoise compared to the blazing memory chips.

## The Basic Problem

This all sounds well and good, but a fundamental problem underlies everything. Most hard disks can store dozens or even hundreds of megabytes of data, but the memory capacity of a typical computer is limited to a measly few megabytes or so.

Picture it this way: think of your computer as, say, a carpenter's workshop divided into two areas: a storage space for your tools and materials (the hard disk) and a work area where you actually use these things (memory). The problem is that your computer's "workspace" is much smaller than its "storage space." For a carpenter, a small work space limits the number of tools and the amount of wood that can be used at any one time. For a computer, it limits the number of programs and data files that you can load.

## The "640K Barrier"

The basic restriction placed on your computer's work space is the so-called "640K barrier." This means that the maximum amount of memory that DOS can use to run your programs and data files is 640K (this area is also called *conventional memory*).

Why 640K? Why not 650K or 6,400K? Well, 640K was the maximum amount of memory available to programs on the original IBM PC. To see how they came up with that number, you need to look at two things: the physical characteristics of the IBM PC's microprocessor and a decision made by its engineers.

First off, microprocessors work with memory chips via *address lines*, which are (more or less) physical connections between the processor and the individual memory locations (each of which stores a single byte of data). Each address line carries a single bit of a memory address, and so the total amount of memory (gurus call this the *address space*) that any microprocessor can work with is limited by the number of address lines. If you had only a single address line, for example, you could address only two memory locations (addresses 1 and 0; see the following sidebar for details), two lines could address four locations, and so on.

**Guru Trivia**

> Each address line can only ever take on one of two states: high current or low current (on or off). These two states are represented inside the processor by 1 and 0, respectively. Computers have to store all their data using this binary number system. In the simplest case (one address line), you have two memory locations. If you send a low current through the line, you get the byte stored at location 0. A high current refers to memory

location 1. In a two-line situation (call them lines A and B) you have four possibilities: both lines low (memory location 00), line A low and line B high (01), line A high and line B low (10), and both lines high (11).

The IBM PC used Intel's 8088 microprocessor, which has 20 address lines. This may seem like a lot (it sure did back then), but it only gives you an address space of 1,048,576 bytes (2 to the power of 20), or a mere one megabyte. For comparison purposes, Table 15.1 shows the address lines and address space for more recent microprocessors (a "GB," by the way, is a *gigabyte*, which is 1,024M or—take a deep breath—1,073,741,824 bytes).

**Table 15.1. Address spaces for different microprocessors.**

| *Microprocessor* | *Address Lines* | *Address Space* |
|---|---|---|
| 80286 | 24 | 16M |
| 80386SX | 24 | 16M |
| 80386DX | 32 | 4GB |
| 80486 | 32 | 4GB |
| Pentium | 32 | 4GB |

So, I hear you asking, if the 8088 can address 1M, why am I restricted to 640K? Well, the IBM PC engineers, in their not so infinite wisdom, decided to reserve the last 384K of the address space for hardware uses (video buffers, ROM BIOS, and so on). This is called the *upper memory area*. Subtracting 384K from 1M (1,024K) leaves us with 640K.

The bad news about all this is that, for compatibility reasons, you're stuck with the 640K barrier for the forseeable future. The good news, though, is that there are ways to overcome its limitations. In particular, the world's computer geniuses came up with three notable solutions: *expanded memory*, *extended memory*, and *upper memory blocks*.

# Expanded Versus Extended Memory

One sure way to tell a computer guru from a mere user is that the guru has at least a vague idea of expanded memory and extended memory. These concepts are almost universally confused and misunderstood, so I'll take a minute to see if I can knock some sense into them.

Return for a moment to the idea of a computer as a workshop. As a carpenter, you can increase your work space in two ways: you can *expand* the total area by erecting a separate building, or you can *extend* the existing work space itself with an addition.

This is the principal difference between expanded memory and extended memory. Expanded memory usually comes in the form of a separate piece of equipment (called a *memory board*) that you have to install. You get extended memory, on the other hand, just by plugging memory chips directly into your computer's main circuit board (provided you have an 80286 or better computer).

**Guru Tip**

> You need an 80286 or better for extended memory because, as you'll recall, only these machines have enough address lines to access memory beyond 1M (which is, by definition, extended memory).

How does this extra memory help? Well, your applications still have to stay within the 640K region, but there are small programs (called *memory managers*) that shuffle bits of program code and data files between the 640K area and the expanded or extended memory.

For example, suppose you're in your workshop and you need to use a lathe, but you haven't got the room. No problem. Your assistant (the memory manager) knows that the lathe is either outside in the tool shed (expanded memory) or in an adjacent area (extended memory). He makes room by grabbing something you don't need for now (a band saw, for instance), takes it to the expanded or extended memory area, exchanges it for the lathe, and then brings the lathe to your workshop.

**Guru Trivia**

> An expanded memory manager operates by establishing a 64K chunk of upper memory called a *page frame*. For programs that can use expanded memory, it swaps data from the expanded memory board into the page frame one 16K page at a time, and then makes this data available to the program. This technique is called *bank switching*.

Which type of memory is better: expanded or extended? The answer to that question depends on what type of software you use. Some programs (such as Lotus 1-2-3 Version 3 or AutoCAD) require expanded memory. However, most programs nowadays prefer to see extended memory on your system.

## Upper Memory Blocks

The upper memory area (the memory between the first 640K area and 1M) is never completely filled in. It always contains gaps not used by the BIOS or video buffers. These gaps are called *upper memory blocks* (or UMBs, for short). If you have an 80386 or higher computer, you can use a program called a *386 memory manager* to send TSRs and device drivers over the 640K barrier so that they reside not in conventional memory, but in the UMBs.

## DOS to the Rescue

Before DOS 5 came along, you could have gobs of extra memory on your computer and *still* have problems running some memory-intensive programs (or, even if you could get them up and running, they would be so slow that it wouldn't be worth it). Starting with Version 5, however, you're now in a new era of DOS memory management. For the rest of this chapter, I'll show you how to take advantage of DOS' memory-related commands to maximize the available memory on your computer.

**Guru Tip**

> If you're running DOS 6, you have a cool new utility called MemMaker that automatically optimizes your memory for you. If you like, you can skim the next few sections so you know what's going on and then skip to the "Using MemMaker" section.

# A Benchmark: the *MEM* Command

To measure your progress, you need to have some way of measuring how much memory you have available at any time. DOS' `MEM` command can do the job. For a quick and dirty listing, just run `MEM` without any parameters. For something more detailed, use the `/C` switch, like so (the `/P` switch, introduced in DOS 6, just pauses the output):

```
mem /c /p
```

If you're running DOS 6, you'll see a report that looks something like this (for modules using memory below 1M):

```
Name            Total      =    Conventional   +  Upper Memory
--------    ------------      ------------      ------------
MSDOS        57597   (56K)     57597   (56K)         0     (0K)
ANSI          4128    (4K)      4128    (4K)         0     (0K)
DBLSPACE     52304   (51K)     52304   (51K)         0     (0K)
COMMAND       4992    (5K)      4992    (5K)         0     (0K)
DOSKEY        4144    (4K)      4144    (4K)         0     (0K)
Free        532224 (520K)    532224 (520K)          0     (0K)

Memory Summary:

Type of Memory        Total       =      Used       +      Free
--------------   --------------   --------------   --------------
Conventional     655360   (640K)    123136   (120K)   532224   (520K)
Upper                 0     (0K)         0     (0K)        0     (0K)
Adaptor RAM/ROM  393216   (384K)    393216   (384K)        0     (0K)
Extended (XMS)  3145728 (3072K)   3145728 (3072K)         0     (0K)
Expanded (EMS)        0     (0K)         0     (0K)        0     (0K)
--------------   ----------------   --------------   --------------
Total memory    4194304 (4096K)   3662080 (3577K)   532224   (520K)

Total under 1 MB 655360   (640K)    123136   (121K)   532224   (520K)

Largest executable program size         532000    (520K)
Largest free upper memory block              0      (0K)
The high memory area is available.
```

The report from the `MEM` command contains a ton of information, but you can break it down into five areas:

- **Modules using memory below 1M.** This is a listing of programs (modules) currently in memory—including both conventional memory and upper memory. The last line (`Free`) tells you how much free memory you have in both areas. Your goal is to maximize these values.

**Guru Tip**

> If you're running DOS 6, use the command `MEM /F` for a quickie report on your system's free memory.

- **Memory Summary.** This is a summary of the total memory (used plus free) for each of the five major memory areas: conventional, upper, adapter RAM/ROM, extended, and expanded.
- **Largest executable program size.** This value tells you the largest program you can run in the current setup. Increasing this number means you can load larger programs and more data.
- **Largest free upper memory block.** To get this number, MEM scans upper memory and looks for the largest gap. This is important because you can't load a TSR or device driver into upper memory if there is no block large enough to accommodate it.

**Guru Tip**

> `MEM` reports a value of 0 for the largest UMB if no 386 memory manager is loaded.

- **The high memory area is available.** The high memory area (HMA) is a 64K segment of extended memory on 80286 or better computers (provided they have more than 1 megabyte of total memory). As you'll see in the next section, you can transfer much of DOS itself out of conventional memory and into the HMA.

# Thanks for the Memory: Loading DOS High

**Dunce**

> The next two sections require you to make adjustments to your CONFIG.SYS and AUTOEXEC.BAT files. There's a chance that some of these changes could cause your system to hang. If that happens, reboot your computer and, if you have DOS 6, press F5 to get a clean boot. If you have DOS 5, keep a bootable disk nearby just in case. See Chapter 18, "The Guru's Survival Kit," to learn how to create a bootable disk.

One of the biggest memory hogs on your system is DOS itself. As you saw earlier, DOS 6 uses up about 61K of precious memory (counting both the MSDOS and COMMAND modules). Fortunately, DOS versions 5 and 6 are capable of reducing the amount of conventional memory they use. The secret is that DOS loads as much of itself as it can into a region called the *high memory area* (HMA). This is a 64K area (approximately) that is available on any 80286 or better computer with extended memory. To load DOS into the HMA, include the following two lines in your CONFIG.SYS file:

```
DEVICE=C:\DOS\HIMEM.SYS
DOS=HIGH
```

**Guru Tip**

> For best results, place these lines at the beginning of your CONFIG.SYS file.

HIMEM.SYS is DOS's extended memory manager. Loading it from CONFIG.SYS makes your computer's extended memory (if you have any) available to other programs. HIMEM.SYS also takes control of the high memory area. By setting the DOS system parameter to `HIGH`, you're telling HIMEM.SYS that you want to usurp the entire HMA for DOS.

Once you've added these lines, reboot your computer and run the `MEM /C` command again. Here's part of the report from my system:

```
Memory Summary:

Type of Memory          Total       =       Used       +       Free
--------------    --------------    --------------    --------------
Conventional      655360   (640K)     76976   (75K)    578384   (565K)
Upper                  0     (0K)         0    (0K)         0     (0K)
Adaptor RAM/ROM   393216   (384K)    393216 (384K)          0     (0K)
Extended (XMS)   3145728  (3072K)     65536   (64K)   3080192  (3008K)
Expanded (EMS)         0     (0K)         0    (0K)         0     (0K)
--------------    --------------    --------------    --------------
Total memory     4194304  (4096K)    535728 (523K)    3658576  (3573K)

Total under 1 MB 655360   (640K)      76976   (75K)    578384   (565K)

Largest executable program size         578160    (565K)
Largest free upper memory block              0      (0K)
MS-DOS is resident in the high memory area.
```

With Version 6, DOS' presence in conventional memory is reduced to a mere 16K (again, counting both the MSDOS and COMMAND modules), a savings of around 45K! On my system, this brings my largest executable program size up to 565K. Notice, too, that the presence of HIMEM.SYS also makes your extended memory available to programs that need it.

**Dunce**

> If you have any problems loading DOS into the HMA, you may need to add the `/MACHINE` switch with HIMEM.SYS. For example, if you have an IBM PS/2, the CONFIG.SYS line would change to `DEVICE=C:\DOS\HIMEM.SYS /MACHINE:PS2`. See the DOS manual for a list of the available values.

# Maximizing Your Available Memory

Loading DOS into the HMA saved a lot of memory, but, provided you have an 80386 computer or better, there's still more you can do. Specifically, you can load your TSRs and device drivers into upper memory.

The secret is EMM386—DOS' 386 memory manager utility. To use it, you need to do four things:

1. In your CONFIG.SYS file, add the following line below the HIMEM.SYS line you added in the last section:

   ```
   DEVICE=C:\DOS\EMM386.EXE NOEMS
   ```

Guru Tip

> If you run programs that need expanded memory, change the **NOEMS** parameter to **RAM**. This gives you access to both expanded memory and upper memory.

2. Add the line `DOS=HIGH`.
3. For each of your device drivers, change the command `DEVICE` to `DEVICEHIGH`.

Dunce

> Don't use the **DEVICEHIGH** command for either HIMEM.SYS or EMM386.EXE.

4. Edit your AUTOEXEC.BAT file to include the word `LOADHIGH` at the beginning of each line that runs a memory-resident program (such as DOSKEY, VSAFE, or SideKick).

Dunce

> The SmartDrive disk cache automatically loads itself high so, if you use it, you don't have to add **LOADHIGH**.

When you've completed these steps, reboot your computer to put the changes into effect and run `MEM` again. Here's part of my listing:

```
Memory Summary:

Type of Memory        Total       =      Used       +      Free
--------------   --------------   --------------   --------------
Conventional      655360  (640K)    20320   (20K)    635040  (620K)
Upper             142464  (139K)    59840   (58K)     82624   (81K)
Adaptor RAM/ROM   250752  (245K)   250752  (242K)         0    (0K)
Extended (XMS)   3145728 (3072K)   364544  (356K)   2781184 (2716K)
Expanded (EMS)         0    (0K)        0    (0K)         0    (0K)
```

```
--------------   -------------   -------------   -------------
Total memory      4194304 (4096K)   695456    (679)   3498848 (3471K)

Total under 1 MB  797824   (779K)    80160    (78K)    717664   (701K)

Largest executable program size          635024    (620K)
Largest free upper memory block           82496     (81K)
MS-DOS is resident in the high memory area.
```

EMM386 has moved my device drivers (ANSI.SYS and DBLSPACE.SYS) and my TSR (DOSKEY) out of conventional memory and into UMBs. The result is a whopping 620K of free memory! As a bonus, I still have 81K in upper memory that I can use for any other resident software I need to load.

# Using MemMaker

If you have DOS 6, you can use the new MemMaker utility to automatically optimize your computer's memory. Aside from being easier, there are a few other advantages to using MemMaker:

- MemMaker analyzes your setup and determines the optimal positions for TSRs and device drivers in upper memory.
- MemMaker looks for possible conflicts in the upper memory area.
- MemMaker scopes out as much as 80K more memory in UMBs.

To run MemMaker, enter the following command:

```
memmaker
```

## Real Gurus Use the Custom Setup

Once MemMaker is loaded, follow the screen instructions and, when the program asks if you want to run the Express or Custom setup, choose Custom. After first asking if you need access to expanded memory, MemMaker presents a list of advanced options.

## Specify which drivers and TSRs to include in optimization?

MemMaker normally does the politically correct thing and includes *all* device drivers and TSRs in the optimization process. Leave this option on `No` and only change it if MemMaker chokes on a particular program.

## Scan the upper memory area aggressively?

MemMaker tries to look for UMBs in an upper memory region used by some computers during startup. If your computer won't start properly after running MemMaker, reboot (be sure to hold down F5 to bypass your configuration files), load MemMaker, and change this option to `No`.

## Optimize upper memory for use with Windows?

Leave this option on `No` if you don't use Windows or if you rarely run DOS applications from within Windows. This gives your DOS programs more conventional memory.

## Use monochrome region (B000-B7FF) for running programs?

One of the video buffers in the upper memory area is set aside for monochrome displays. If you have a CGA, EGA, or VGA display, your system probably doesn't use this area. Select `Yes` to free up this 32K block (it runs from 704K to 736K or, in hexadecimal notation, B000 to B7FF).

> Don't select **Yes** in this option if you have a SuperVGA display. If you're not sure, you can use the MSD program to check it out. See Chapter 18 for the scoop on MSD.

### Keep current EMM386 memory exclusions and inclusions?

You can use EMM386's `X` and `I` switches to exclude and include upper memory areas as UMBs. You can select `Yes` to preserve these switches, but Microsoft recommends that you let MemMaker decide everything.

### Move Extended BIOS Data Area from conventional to upper memory?

Select `Yes` here to save 1K by moving the Extended BIOS Data Area into upper memory.

Once you've made your selections, press Enter and follow the instructions on-screen.

## Using SmartDrive

Earlier in this chapter I used the analogy of a carpenter's workshop to describe the difference between a hard disk and memory. When you start a program, portions of the code are retrieved from the hard disk (the storage area) and are loaded into memory (the work space). As you work with different parts of the program, different chunks of code are swapped between memory and the hard drive. This is analogous to a carpenter swapping different tools and materials between the work area and the storage area.

For example, suppose the carpenter is using a screwdriver and wants to switch to a drill. Well, he or she could return the screwdriver to the storage area and grab the drill at the same time. However, suppose there's a possibility that the carpenter may need the screwdriver again soon. Wouldn't it make sense to keep it handy, just in case? For these situations, he or she could establish a temporary storage area for tools and materials that may be needed in the short term.

The computer equivalent to this temporary storage location is a chunk of memory called a *disk cache*, and it's monitored by a disk cache program. Portions of your applications and their data files are stored in the cache and, if they're needed again, they're retrieved from memory instead of the hard disk. Because memory is a whole lot faster than a hard drive, this results in a noticeable speed boost.

DOS comes with its own disk caching program called SmartDrive. To use it, add the following line to the beginning of your AUTOEXEC.BAT file:

```
C:\DOS\SMARTDRV.EXE
```

**Dunce**

> If you're running DOS 6, you can only set up a SmartDrive cache if you have extended memory. The new version of SmartDrive won't cache in expanded memory.

# More Memory Maximization Magic

With today's humongoid programs, every last byte of conventional memory is as precious as gold. Forthwith, here are a few more tips to help you maximize that all-important first 640K:

- If you use DOS 6's new DoubleSpace disk compression utility, include the following line in CONFIG.SYS:

  ```
  DEVICE=C:\DOS\DBLSPACE.SYS /MOVE
  ```

  This moves the 50K DBLSPACE.BIN file out of conventional memory and into upper memory.

- If you use SmartDrive, reduce the `BUFFERS` setting in CONFIG.SYS down to 10 or so. In any case, load DOS high if you can because DOS brings the buffer area with it into the high memory area (but only if `BUFFERS` is less than 48). This is important because each buffer hogs about 532 bytes of RAM.

- Try running CONFIG.SYS with the following command:

  ```
  STACKS=0,0
  ```

  On most machines, this saves about 1K.

- To save a further 176 bytes, include the following command in CONFIG.SYS:

  ```
  FCBS=1
  ```

- Don't set `LASTDRIVE` higher than you need to. Each `LASTDRIVE` letter past *E* takes up about 88 bytes of RAM.
- Use MSD, the Microsoft Diagnostics program that comes with DOS 6, to see if your system uses the upper memory region from C000h to C5FFh. (To learn how to use MSD, refer to Chapter 18, "The Guru's Survival Kit.") If it doesn't, you can get another 24K of free upper memory by changing your CONFIG.SYS file so that it contains the following line:

  ```
  DEVICE=C:\DOS\EMM386.EXE I=C000-C5FF
  ```

- On some systems, you can grab even more upper memory by including the `HIGHSCAN` parameter with EMM386.

Guru Tools

> DOS versions 5 and 6 brought memory management to the masses, but there are companies out there that have been specializing in this field for years. The two most notable are Quarterdeck, with QEMM-386, and Qualitas, with 386MAX. Both programs offer state-of-the-art features that squeeze even more RAM from your system than MemMaker.

# Guru Review

Well, that wasn't so bad was it? Here's a summary of some of the mondo memory stuff you went through in this chapter:

- Thanks to the architecture of the original IBM PC and some strange decision making by its engineers, the rest of us have had to put up with the 640K barrier ever since.
- Over the years, countless unsung programmers struggled to break the 640K barrier, and they came up with three solutions of interest: expanded memory, extended memory, and upper memory blocks.

- Starting with DOS 5, you could take advantage of these solutions by loading DOS into the high memory area and moving TSRs and device drivers in upper memory.
- DOS 6 takes DOS memory management to new heights with the MemMaker program that automatically configures TSRs and device drivers in upper memory.
- Use SmartDrive to greatly improve the performance of your computer.

# The Fun Stuff: Advanced DOS Commands

16

CHAPTER

## Guru Stuff In This Chapter ➤

- ✦ *Using* SUBST *to create virtual drives*
- ✦ *Using* REPLACE *to copy files*
- ✦ *Command line looping with* FOR
- ✦ *Setting file attributes with* *ATTRIB*
- ✦ *Other commands and lots of examples for the mechanically inclined DOS guru*

Lift up the hood of a car and within five minutes you'll have a bunch of guys standing around gazing at the car's innards. The composition of these groups is always the same: one or two guys, who actually know what they're doing, work on the car, while the rest shuffle their feet and nod sagely.

This is the principle difference between a *DOS dabbler* and a *true guru*. The dilettante is content merely to start programs and shuffle around a file or two, while the guru is comfortable wielding all of DOS' tools. To that end, this chapter looks at some powerful DOS commands that will be welcome additions to your toolkit.

# SUBST

In Chapter 12, "CONFIG.SYS: What Every Guru Should Know," you learned how to use the DRIVER.SYS device driver to create *virtual drives*—drives that don't physically exist, but ones you can refer to anyway. The `SUBST` command does the same thing, except that you use it to substitute (hence its name) a drive designation for a directory path.

**Guru Tip**

> Versions of DOS prior to Version 6 also came with an **ASSIGN** command that performed much the same function as **SUBST**. However, this command has been deleted from DOS 6, and Microsoft recommends that you always use **SUBST** instead of **ASSIGN**.

## Using *SUBST* to Manage Long Pathnames

Suppose you regularly use a directory called C:\PLANTS\EDIBLE\RUTABAGA. That's quite a mouthful for even the fastest typists, but, to ease the burden, you can use the following command:

```
subst d: c:\plants\edible\rutabaga
```

Now, instead of struggling with C:\PLANTS\EDIBLE\RUTABAGA, you can just use D:. For example, the following command gives you a listing of the DOC files in this directory:

```
dir d:\*.doc
```

**Dunce**

> Before you start **SUBST**ituting drives for directories willy-nilly, be sure you bump up the number of drive letters DOS can use by adding a **LASTDRIVE** statement to your CONFIG.SYS file (see Chapter 12 for the **LASTDRIVE** lowdown).

To remove the substitution, use SUBST with the /D switch, as follows:

```
subst d: /d
```

**Guru Tip**

> To see a list of your substitutions, run the **SUBST** command by itself.

# The Shortest *PATH*

SUBST can help if you find your PATH statement is bumping its head on DOS' 127-character command-line ceiling. For example, suppose your PATH looks like this:

```
C:\;C:\DOS;C:\BATCH;C:\WP51\DOCS\PERSONAL;C:\123\BUDGETS
```

The following commands will knock it down to size:

```
subst d: c:\dos
subst e: c:\batch
subst f: c:\wp51\docs\personal
subst g: c:\123\budgets
path c:\;d:\;e:\;f:\;g:\
```

**Guru Tip**

> If you plan to use **SUBST** regularly, be sure you include the appropriate commands in your AUTOEXEC.BAT file, so the substitutions get done automatically whenever you start your computer.

## Your Installation Revenge

Another handy use for SUBST is to fool those annoying installation programs that won't run unless their disks are in drive A:. If the disks are 3.5-inch and your 3.5-inch drive is drive B:, your first instinct is to strangle the genius who wrote the program. Before you do, though, here's a SUBST command that takes care of the problem:

```
subst a: b:\
```

This enables you (and the dumb installation program) to access the B: drive as though it were the A: drive.

Dunce

> While this substitution is in effect, the *real* drive A: is unavailable, so don't forget to cancel the substitution when you've finished installing the program.

# TRUENAME

Don't look in your DOS manual for this one. TRUENAME is an undocumented command that lets you reveal the true identity of a drive letter created with SUBST. This is pretty handy if you use SUBST a lot, because you're bound to forget a substitution or two. To see the true path of the current SUBST drive, enter the TRUENAME command by itself. You also can specify a drive, like so:

```
truename d:
```

# REPLACE

If there was such a thing as a Most Underrated Command award, REPLACE would win it hands down. This command, which you almost never hear about, can do two *very* useful (and very different) things:

- It copies files, but only if their names match those in the target directory.
- It copies files, but only if their names don't exist in the target directory.

Before looking at some examples, Table 16.1 lists the available switches for the REPLACE command.

### Table 16.1. Switches you can use with the *REPLACE* command.

| Use | To |
|---|---|
| /A | Add missing files to the target directory. |
| /P | Get prompted for confirmation before replacing a file. |
| /R | Replace read-only files. |
| /S | Replace matching files in subdirectories. |
| /U | Replace only files that are older. |
| /W | Have REPLACE wait before starting. |

**Dunce**

> Because you could end up with weird (and probably unpleasant) surprises, DOS doesn't let you combine either the /S or /U switch with /A.

A good example where REPLACE comes in handy is when you copy some files to a disk, so you can use them on another machine (such as taking files from your computer at work to use them at home). When you need to copy the files back to the first machine, the following REPLACE command does the job (assuming the disk is in drive A:):

```
replace a:*.* c:\ /s /u
```

For each file on drive A:, REPLACE looks for matching filenames anywhere on drive C: (thanks to the /S switch) and replaces only the ones that have changed (the /U switch).

What if you created some new files on the other computer? To copy those to the first machine, use the /A switch, like so:

```
replace a:*.* c:\123\budgets /a
```

In this case, REPLACE only copies a file from A: if it doesn't exist in the C:\123\BUDGETS directory (you have to specify a destination directory because you can't use the /S switch with /A).

**Guru Tools**

> **COPY**, **XCOPY**, and **REPLACE** are useful in different situations, but why use three tools when one will do the job? A shareware program called PCOPY combines all three DOS commands into a single package and gives you extra features such as prompting you when a disk is full and formatting on the fly.

# FOR

I showed you how to use the FOR command in batch files back in Chapter 7, "Using Variables for Batch File Flexibility," but it can also do double duty at the command line. The only difference is that the parameters use a single percent sign (%) rather than the double one used in batch files. For example, the following FOR command deletes all .TXT and .DOC files from the current directory:

```
for %f in (*.txt *.doc) do del %f
```

## Using *FOR* in DOSKEY Macros

Because FOR commands have a fairly involved syntax, they're perfect candidates for DOSKEY macros. (For DOSKEY details, see Chapter 11, "Customizing the Command Line with DOSKEY.") In particular, you can use DOSKEY's $* replaceable parameter (the one that grabs every parameter from the command line) to create some truly muscular macros. For example, here's a macro that uses FOR and $* to delete any number of file specs:

```
doskey delcity=for %f in ($*) do del %f
```

If you enter the following command:

```
delcity *.tmp *.bak *.$$$
```

DOS takes the three parameters (*.TMP, *.BAK, and *.$$$), substitutes them for $*, and then runs the FOR command.

## Updating File Date and Time Stamps

The date and time stamps on a file reflect the last time the file was modified. Unfortunately, DOS has no easy way to update these stamps to the current date and time. But it is possible, and it only takes a few commands.

To update the date and time stamp on a single file, you can use the `COPY` command's concatenation feature (discussed in Chapter 1, "Guru File Management"). The secret is that you use the concatenation operator (+), but you don't combine the file with anything. For example, the following batch file (called STAMPIT.BAT), after first giving you a chance to adjust the date and time, updates the date and time stamp for whatever file is used as the `%1` parameter (note that this batch file doesn't work if your file spec contains wildcards):

```
@ECHO OFF
TIME
DATE
COPY %1 +,, /B
```

The `+,,` tells DOS to concatenate the file with nothing. When DOS does this, it doesn't change the contents of the file, but it does update the date and time stamp to the current values.

**Guru Trivia**

> DOS assumes that you're concatenating text files, so it normally adds an end-of-file marker to the new concatenated file. If all you're doing is updating the date and time stamp, this can play havoc with the file's structure. For this reason, always use the `/B` switch to tell DOS that it's dealing with a binary file.

This is neat, but if you want to do it to a bunch of files, you need to use a `FOR` command. The following example uses the `CALL` command to update the date and time stamp for every file in the current directory:

```
for %f in (*.*) do call stampit %f
```

# ATTRIB

A file's *attributes* are special codes that indicate the status of the file (see Table 16.2).

**Table 16.2. The DOS file attributes.**

| *Attribute* | *Meaning When Set* |
|---|---|
| Archive | The file has been modified since it was last backed up. |
| Hidden | The file doesn't show up in a `DIR` listing and isn't included in most DOS commands. |
| Read-only | The file can't be modified or erased. |
| System | The file is an operating system file. |

The `ATTRIB` command lets you turn these attributes on or off. For example, if you'd like to hide all the DOC files in the current directory, use the following command:

```
attrib +h *.doc
```

As another example, if you've ever tried to delete or edit a file and got the message `Access denied`, the file is likely read-only. You can turn off the read-only attribute with the following command (assuming the file is named READONLY.TXT):

```
attrib -r readonly.txt
```

**Guru Tip**

> If you want to check out a file's attributes, use the **DIR** command's **/A** switch introduced in DOS 5. Use **/AA** to see files with their archive attribute set, **/AH** for hidden files, **/AR** for read-only, and **/AS** for system files.

For more ways to use `ATTRIB`, see Chapter 20, "Simple System Security."

# SETVER

Most DOS applications require a minimum DOS version number to work properly. For example, a program might say that it needs "at least DOS 2.11" to run. The "at least" normally means that the program will run not only with 2.11, but also with 3.0, 4.0, and so on. In fact, the vast majority of programs written for earlier versions of DOS run just fine on any later version.

However, some older programs are, well, just plain dumb. These dim-witted beasts check for a *specific* version number instead of one that's greater than or equal to one they need. So, for example, if a program requires DOS 2.11, it correctly refuses to run if the version number is 2.0, but it also bails out if it's 3.0 or 5.0! Argh!

If you've upgraded to DOS 5 or 6 and you're getting an `Incorrect DOS version` message (or something similar), you can use the `SETVER` command to fool the goofball program into thinking it's working with the DOS version it needs. Before using `SETVER`, though, you need to load the SETVER.EXE device driver into memory. Add the following line to your CONFIG.SYS file (and reboot when you're done):

```
DEVICE=C:\DOS\SETVER.EXE
```

To use `SETVER`, you just supply it with the name of the file that starts the program and the DOS version number it needs. For example, suppose the program is called IDIOTIC.EXE and it requires DOS 2.11. The following command does the trick:

```
setver idiotic.exe 2.11
```

When you run the program now, DOS waits for it to ask for the version number and then sneakily passes it the version number you specified. DOS, in effect, lies through its teeth.

# Guru Review

This chapter presented you with a six-pack of powerful DOS tools. Here's a recap of the major stories:

- You can use `SUBST` to create virtual drives that are substitutes for a directory path. This saves typing and can cut down the size of your `PATH`.
- To find out the true pathname of a virtual drive, use the `TRUENAME` command.
- The `REPLACE` command does two things: it copies files only if their names match those on the target, and it copies files only if their names don't exist on the target.

- Use `FOR` to create command-line loops. It works just like the batch command of the same name, except that the parameters use only a single percent sign (`%`).
- `ATTRIB` can set and remove the four file attributes: archive, hidden, read-only, and system.
- Use `SETVER` any time a brain-dead DOS application complains that you don't have the correct DOS version.

# The Fun Stuff II: Advanced DOS Techniques

17

CHAPTER

**Guru Stuff In This Chapter ➤**

- *Getting the scoop on redirection, piping, and filters*
- *Controlling your printer from the command line*
- *Controlling your modem from the command line*
- *Changing the number of lines on your display*
- *More batch files, DOSKEY macros, and all-around neat stuff to impress your friends and colleagues*

The last chapter added a few powerful commands to your ever-growing DOS toolkit. With DOS, though, it's not always *what* you use that's important, but *how* you use it. So although you'll be seeing a few new commands in this chapter, the emphasis is on techniques—how to make DOS do what you want it to do.

# Redirecting DOS

As you've seen throughout this book, there are a few DOS commands and concepts that separate the wheat from the chaff, so to speak. Things such as batch files, extended versus expanded memory, and CONFIG.SYS are topics shunned by the average user but embraced wholeheartedly by the guru. If this was the Boy Scouts or Girl Scouts, these things would be merit badges.

*Redirection* (as well as *piping*, its companion technique discussed in the next section) is a merit badge topic, if there ever was one. Few people understand it, but it's the key to some of the most powerful DOS techniques on the planet.

## Redirect What?

DOS is always directing things here and there. This generally falls into two categories:

- Directing data into its commands from a device called *standard input*.
- Directing data out of its commands to a device called *standard output*.

Standard input and standard output are normally handled by a device called CON (console), your keyboard and monitor. (If you have the ANSI.SYS device loaded, all input/output goes through there, instead.) DOS assumes that all command input comes from the keyboard and all command output (such as a `DIR` listing or system message) goes to the screen. *Redirection* is just a way of specifying different input and output devices.

**Guru Trivia**

Standard input and standard output are actually mapped to files in DOS' internal file table. DOS assigns the first file handle in the table (handle 0) to standard input and the second handle (handle 1) to standard output. Redirection actually remaps these file handles so the input or output goes elsewhere.

# Redirecting Command Output

To send command output to somewhere other than the screen, you use the *output redirection operator* (>). One of the most common uses for output redirection is to capture the results of a command in a text file. For example, you might want to use the report produced by the `MEM` command as part of a word processing document. You could use the following command to first capture the report as the file MEM.TXT:

```
mem /c > mem.txt
```

When you run this command, don't be alarmed when the usual `MEM` stuff doesn't appear on-screen. Remember, it has been redirected away from the screen and into the MEM.TXT file. To prove it for yourself, check out MEM.TXT using either `EDIT` or `TYPE`.

You can use this technique to capture `DIR` listings, `CHKDSK` reports, and more. One caveat: if the file you specify as the output destination already exists, DOS overwrites it without any warning. To be safe, you can use the double output redirection symbol (>>). This tells DOS to *append* the output to the file if it exists. For example, if you want to add the results of the `CHKDSK` command to MEM.TXT, use the following command:

```
chkdsk >> mem.txt
```

**Guru Tip**

> If you plan to use output redirection in a DOSKEY macro, remember to use `$G` in place of > (and `$G$G` in place of >>).

You can also redirect output to different devices. Table 17.1 lists the various devices that DOS installs each time you start your system.

### Table 17.1. Devices installed by DOS when you start your system.

| *Device Name* | *Device* |
|---|---|
| AUX | Auxiliary device (usually COM1) |
| CLOCK$ | Real-time clock |

*continues*

**Table 17.1. continued**

| *Device Name* | *Device* |
|---|---|
| COM*n* | Serial port (COM1, COM2, COM3, or COM4) |
| CON | Console (keyboard and screen) |
| LPT*n* | Parallel port (LPT1, LPT2, or LPT3) |
| NUL | NUL device (nothing!) |
| PRN | Printer (usually LPT1) |

For example, you can send a `DIR` listing to the printer with the following command (of course, you need to be sure your printer is on before doing this):

```
dir > prn
```

The *NUL device* usually throws people for a loop when they first see it. This device (affectionately known as the "bit bucket") is, literally, nothing. It's normally used in batch files to suppress the usual messages DOS displays when it completes a command. For example, DOS normally says `1 file(s) copied` when you copy a file. However, the following command sends that message to NUL, so you wouldn't see it on-screen:

```
copy somefile.doc a:\ > nul
```

# Redirecting Input

Getting input to a DOS command from somewhere other than the keyboard is handled by the *input redirection operator* (<). Input redirection is almost always used to send the contents of a text file to a DOS command. The most common example is the `MORE` command, which displays one screen of information at a time. If you have a large text file that scrolls off the screen when you use `TYPE`, the following command, which sends the contents of bigfile.txt to the `MORE` command, solves the problem:

```
more < bigfile.txt
```

Guru Tip

> For DOSKEY macros, use `$L` in place of <.

When you run this command, the first screenful of text and the following line at the bottom of the screen appear:

```
-- More --
```

Just press any key and MORE displays the next screenful. (Whatever you do, don't mix up < and > when using `MORE`. The command `more > bigfile.txt` erases BIGFILE.TXT!) `MORE` is an example of a filter command. Filters process whatever text is sent through them. The other DOS filters are `SORT` and `FIND`, discussed below.

**Guru Tools**

> **MORE** just gives you primitive control over file display. For truly powerful file browsing, check out LIST 7.6. This program lets you view binary and archived files (as well as the usual text files, of course) and you can scroll up or down in a file, select files from a directory listing, and do word searches.

Another handy use for input redirection is to send keystrokes to DOS commands. For example, create a text file called ENTER.TXT that consists of a single press of the Enter key, and then try the following command:

```
date < enter.txt
```

DOS displays the current date, and instead of waiting for you to either type in a new date or press Enter, it just reads ENTER.TXT and uses its single carriage return as input. (For an even easier way to input the Enter key to a command, check out the section titled "Piping Commands," later in this chapter.)

**Guru Tip**

> You can send keystrokes to any DOS command that waits for input. You can even send multiple keystrokes. For example, a typical **FORMAT** command has three prompts: one to insert a disk, one for the volume label, and one to format another. If your normal responses to these prompts are Enter, Enter, N and Enter, include these in a text file called, say, INFORMAT.TXT and run FORMAT with the following command:
>
> ```
> format a: < informat.txt
> ```

One common recipient of redirected input is the `SORT` command. `SORT`, as you may guess from its name, sorts the data sent to it and displays the results on-screen. So, for example, here's how you would sort a file called JUMBLED.TXT:

```
sort < jumbled.txt
```

Instead of merely displaying the results of the sort on-screen, you can, of course, use > to redirect them to another file.

**Guru Tip**

> `SORT` normally starts with the first column and works along. To start with any other column, use the `/+n` switch where `n` is the number of the column you want to use. To sort a file in reverse order use the `/R` switch.

**Dunce**

> `SORT` won't work with files that are larger than 64K.

# Piping Commands

*Piping* is a technique that combines both input and output redirection. Using the *pipe operator* (¦), the output of one command is captured and sent as input to another command. For example, using `MEM` with the `/C` or `/D` switch usually results in more than a screenful of data. DOS 6 has a `/P` switch to pause the output, but DOS 5 users can pipe it to the `MORE` command:

```
mem /c ¦ more
```

The pipe operator captures `MEM`'s output and sends it as input to `MORE`, which then displays everything one screen at a time.

**Dunce**

> Be sure you've defined the `TEMP` system parameter before using pipes (see Chapter 13, "AUTOEXEC.BAT: Your Most Important Batch File"). If you haven't, create a directory called, say, C:\TEMP and include the following line in your AUTOEXEC.BAT file:
>
> ```
> SET TEMP=C:\TEMP
> ```

**Guru Trivia**

> Piping works by first redirecting the output of a command to a temporary file. It then takes this temporary file and redirects it as input to the second command. A command such as `MEM /C ¦ MORE` is approximately equivalent to the following two commands:
>
> ```
> MEM /C > tempfile
>
> tempfile < MORE
> ```

I showed you in the last section how to use input redirection to send keystrokes to a DOS command. But if you only have to send a single key, piping offers a much nicer solution. The secret is to use the `ECHO` command to echo the character you need and then pipe it to the DOS command.

For example, if you use the command `DEL *.*`, DOS always asks if you're sure you want to delete all the files in the current directory. This is a sensible precaution, but you can override it if you do things this way:

```
echo y ¦ del *.*
```

Here, the `y` that would normally be echoed to the screen is, instead, sent to `DEL`, which interprets it as a response to its prompt. For easy access, you should incorporate finger-twisting commands like this in a DOSKEY macro or as part of a batch file.

**Guru Tip**

> You can even use this technique to send an Enter to a command. The command `ECHO.` (that's `ECHO` followed immediately by a period) is equivalent to pressing Enter. So, for example, you could use the following command in a batch file to display the time without user input:
>
> ```
> ECHO. ¦ TIME
> ```

A command that's commonly used in pipe operations is the `FIND` filter. `FIND` searches its input for a specified string and, if it finds a match, it displays the line that contains the string. For example, the last line of a `DIR` listing tells you the number of bytes free on the current drive. Rather than wade through the entire `DIR` output just to get this information, use this command, instead:

```
dir ¦ find "free"
```

You'll see something like the following on your screen:

```
90333184 bytes free
```

`FIND` scours the `DIR` listing that was piped to it and looks for the word *free*. Since this only occurs on the last line, that's the line that gets displayed. You can use this technique to display specific lines from a `MEM` report (to search for, say, *largest* to display the largest executable program size) or `CHKDSK` (*user* finds the number of bytes used on the disk).

To use piping in a DOSKEY macro, replace ¦ with **$B**.

Don't use any of the redirection operators (< > and ¦) on a **REM** line in a batch file. DOS, bizarrely, attempts the redirection *before* it realizes that the line is a **REM** and should be ignored. If you want to comment out a bunch of lines that use these symbols, use **GOTO** to leap over them (as explained in Chapter 7, "Using Variables for Batch File Flexibility").

# Controlling Your Printer

Printing, for the most part, is handled smoothly by your programs. There are times, however, when it's not practical to use your software for printing. For example, if you just want a quick printout of a small text file (such as your AUTOEXEC.BAT file), it's overkill to load, say, WordPerfect to do the job. Similarly, it would be nice to have some quick way to print a hard copy of a `DIR` listing, for example. Fortunately, you can do all these things easily right from the DOS prompt.

# Redirecting DOS Commands to the Printer

The output redirection techniques you learned earlier work just fine if you send the output to your printer. For example, if you've just copied some files to a floppy disk in drive A:, you can get a hard copy list of all the files in drive A:'s root directory by using the following command:

```
dir a:\ > prn
```

`PRN` is the default printing device, usually the LPT1 port. If your printer is attached to a different port, use the appropriate device name from Table 17.1.

Dunce

> If you have a laser printer and your redirected DOS commands aren't printing out, press the Form Feed button to spit out the page. Later in this section, I'll show you how to send a form-feed from a batch file.

# Recording DOS Sessions

From time to time, you may find that you need to write out a series of DOS commands for someone else to follow. Or you may be trying out some of the more complex commands (such as `PROMPT`) and need to keep track of your experiments.

Instead of writing these out by hand, you can tell DOS to record your actions on your printer (this is called *echo printing*). Just press Ctrl+P or Ctrl+PrintScreen and DOS will send everything you see on-screen to the printer. When you're done, press Ctrl+P or Ctrl+PrintScreen to cancel echo printing.

# Printing a Screen

If you only want to print what's on-screen, just press PrintScreen (or, on some keyboards, Shift+PrintScreen). This sends the entire contents of the screen to the printer. If the screen contains any graphics, you first need to run the `GRAPHICS` command. This loads a TSR that intercepts the PrintScreen signal and processes the graphics screen accordingly.

> **Dunce**
>
> If you're having trouble printing graphics, you may need to use one of the GRAPHICS command's printer switches. See your DOS manual for a complete list.

## Using *PRINT*

DOS' PRINT command lets you print text files in the background. This lets you send a bunch of files to PRINT and then move on to bigger and better things while they print out. The general form of the PRINT command looks like this (I only listed a few of PRINT's switches here; see your DOS manual for the others):

```
PRINT [/D:device /Q:size] filespecs [/T /C /P]
```

For filespecs, you can enter multiple filenames or a file specification with wildcards. Table 17.2 explains the listed switches.

### Table 17.2. Some switches for the *PRINT* command.

| *Use* | *To* |
|---|---|
| /D:*device* | Specify a print device. For *device*, use any of the device names from Table 17.1. |
| /Q:*size* | Specify the size of the print queue. The default is 10, but you can use any number between 4 and 32. |
| /T | Terminate all pending print jobs. |
| /C | Cancel a file from the print queue. |
| /P | Add a file to the print queue. |

For example, the following command prints CONFIG.SYS and all the TXT files in the current directory to PRN, as well as increasing the print queue to 20 files:

```
print /d:prn /q:20 c:\config.sys *.txt
```

**Guru Tip**

> If you just need to print a single file, you might not want to load `PRINT`, which takes up nearly 6K in memory (more if you increase the size of the print queue). Instead, you can use the `COPY` command to copy the file to the printer. For example, the following command copies AUTOEXEC.BAT to the PRN device:
>
> ```
> copy autoexec.bat prn
> ```

## Batch File Printing Tricks

Here are a couple of tricks you can use in batch files to make DOS printing a little more palatable:

- To eject a page from your printer (especially if your laser won't print because it hasn't got a full page of data), include the following line in a batch file (call it FF.BAT) to send a form feed to the printer:

  ```
  ECHO ↕ > PRN
  ```

  The ↕ symbol is ASCII 12, the form feed control character. (If you're entering this in `EDIT`, press Ctrl+P and then press Alt+12.)

- To simulate a line feed, use the following redirection command:

  ```
  ECHO. > PRN
  ```

  This is useful if you're sending a couple of things to the printer and you want to create some space in between them. You'll probably want to include four or five of these in a batch file.

# Controlling Your Modem

If you have a modem, you probably use it to connect to information services or bulletin boards. But you can also use it to dial your phone for regular calls. And, what's better, you can do it right from the command line or in a batch file.

In order to use the examples in this section, your modem must be "Hayes-compatible." Although the majority of today's modems do offer Hayes compatibility, you should check the modem's documentation if you're not sure.

# Initializing the Serial Port

Before you can dial with your modem, you need to use the `MODE` command to make sure the serial port is initialized. The `MODE` command has a number of different forms, but here's the one to use in this case

```
MODE COMn baud
```

Here, `COMn` is the device name for the serial port you use (COM1, COM2, and so on), and `baud` is the baud rate for your modem.

# Dialing the Phone

You control your modem by using the standard `AT` command set (`AT` is short for "attention"). The command for dialing a number is `ATDT` (ATtention Dial Tone) and you use it like this:

```
echo atdt 123-4567 > com1
```

This command `ECHO`s both the `ATDT` command and the phone number to COM1. The modem establishes a dial tone and then starts dialing. When entering a number with the `ATDT` command, you can use any of the following forms:

```
987-6543
9876543
1-987-654-3210
1 (987) 654-3210
19876543210
```

You use **ATDT** if you have a touch-tone phone. If your phone doesn't support touch-tone dialing, use **ATDP** (ATtention Dial Pulse).

## Quieting the Modem

One of the problems with using your modem to dial out is that most modems make quite a racket as they try to establish a connection (the modem always assumes that it's going to be talking with another modem). Once you hear the other phone ringing, however, you can pick up the phone's handset and then quiet the modem with the following command:

```
echo ath > com1
```

Here, ATH stands for ATtention Hangup, and it simply shuts off the modem's annoying white noise.

## A Phone Directory Batch File

Here's a batch file (DIAL.BAT) that uses DOS 6's new CHOICE command and these modem techniques to create a combination phone directory and dialer:

```
@ECHO OFF
CLS
MODE COM1 2400 > COM1

ECHO 1. Mom
ECHO 2. Sis
ECHO 3. Cancel
CHOICE Select a number to dial /C:123

IF ERRORLEVEL 3 GOTO END
IF ERRORLEVEL 2 GOTO SIS

REM Dial Mom's number:
ECHO ATDT 123-4567 > COM1
CALL HANGUP
GOTO END

:SIS
ECHO ATDT 987-6543 > COM1
CALL HANGUP

:END
```

DIAL.BAT first initializes the serial port, then it displays a menu of numbers to call (including a Cancel option). Depending on the number entered at the CHOICE prompt, the program branches to the appropriate section and dials the number (or, if Cancel was selected, it just jumps to the end of the batch file). After dialing, the HANGUP.BAT batch file is CALLed:

```
@ECHO OFF
ECHO.
ECHO Pick up the handset when the phone is ringing.
ECHO Press any key to silence the modem...
PAUSE > NUL
ECHO ATH > COM1
```

# Controlling the Number of Lines on Your Screen

The basic DOS screen displays 25 lines of information. If you have an EGA or VGA adapter, you can use the `MODE` command to get even more lines. The first thing you need to do is load the ANSI.SYS device driver. If you haven't done this already, add the following line to your CONFIG.SYS file:

```
DEVICE=C:\DOS\ANSI.SYS
```

When you're done, reboot to put the changes into effect.

To change the number of screen lines, use one of the following techniques:

- If you have an EGA monitor, enter the following command:

  ```
  mode con lines=43
  ```

- If you have a VGA monitor, enter the following:

  ```
  mode con lines=50 (or 43)
  ```

# Guru Review

This chapter added a few cool techniques to your DOS toolkit. Time for a nostalgic look back:

- Use the output redirection operator (>) to send output to a file or device other than the screen.

- If you don't want output redirection to overwrite a file, use the >> operator.
- To input data to a DOS command from somewhere other than the keyboard, use the input redirection operator (<).
- Piping (using the ¦ symbol) combines both input and output redirection in a single command.
- The DOS filter commands (`MORE`, `SORT`, and `FIND`) process text sent through them during redirection operations.
- To control your printer from the DOS prompt, you can use output redirection to send text to the `PRN` (or other) device, echo printing (Ctrl+P), PrintScreen, or the `PRINT` utility.
- You control your modem from the DOS prompt by using two `AT` commands: `ATDT` (to dial) and `ATH` (to hang up).
- To change the number of lines on your screen, use the `MODE CON` command with the appropriate `LINES` parameter.

# Guru Doo-Doo: Troubleshooting DOS

# PART V

# The Guru's Survival Kit

## Guru Stuff In This Chapter ➤

18

CHAPTER

- *Getting a clean boot*
- *Creating a bootable emergency disk*
- *Using* CHKDSK *to diagnose and fix disk problems*
- *Use DOS 6's Microsoft Diagnostics utility*
- *Miscellaneous hints and techniques for surviving the PC jungle*

When they strike out for the wilderness, smart hikers always take along a first-aid package containing assorted ointments, unguents, bandages, and perhaps even a snake bite kit or two. On your daily trek through the PC wilderness, you too, need to be prepared for the worst. Although you won't need to worry about being bitten (even though you never know what a mouse might do when provoked), there are plenty of other things that can go wrong. This chapter collects a few emergency tools and gathers them up into a proper guru survival kit.

# Hard Disks Die

An ad for a popular collection of hard disk utilities says it all: "Hard Disks Die." That's a pretty stark message, but, let's face it, it's an honest one. Just consider everything a modern hard disk has to put up with:

- General wear-and-tear—if your computer is running right now, its hard disk is merrily spinning away at (probably) 3,600 revolutions per minute. That's right, even though you're not doing anything, the hard disk is hard at work. Because of this constant activity, most hard disks simply wear out after a few years.

**Guru Tip**

> This is one of the reasons why hard drives are so much faster than floppy drives. A floppy drive has to crank itself up to speed each time you access it, but the hard disk is ready to go all the time.

- *The old bump-and-grind*—your hard disk includes a number of "read/write heads" that are used to read data from and write data to the disk. These heads float on a cushion of air just above the spinning hard disk platters. However, a bump or jolt of sufficient intensity can send them crashing onto the surface of the disk, which could easily result in trashed data. If the heads happen to hit a particularly sensitive area, the entire hard disk could crash.
- *Power surges*—the current that is supplied to your PC is, under normal conditions, fairly constant. However, it's possible for your computer to be assailed by massive power surges (for example, during a lightning storm). These surges can wreak havoc on a carefully arranged hard disk.

- *Viruses*—computer viruses are a nasty fact of computing life. Although some of these viruses are benign—they display cute messages or cause characters to "fall off" the screen—most are downright vicious and only exist to trash your valuable data.
- *Bad programming*—some not-ready-for-prime-time software programs can end up running amok and destroying large chunks of your hard disk in the process. These rogues are, luckily, fairly rare these days.
- *Operator error*—are hard disk crashes the only way to lose control over your PC? You wish. In fact, any time you can no longer access your hard drive, chances are that the problem is simply an accidentally deleted or improperly edited system file.

## What You Can Do About It

Now that I've got you absolutely convinced that your hard drive is going to burst into flames any second, it's time to prepare for the inevitable. Here are six things you can do right now:

1. Back up your hard disk. Some hard disk problems are treatable and some aren't. If your hard disk crashes permanently, your data goes along with it. Always, always back up your hard disk regularly. (To help you get through this chore, see Chapter 5, "Working with a Net: Backing Up Your Files.")
2. Back up your hard disk.
3. Upgrade to DOS 6, if you haven't already. This release features an improved delete-protection utility, a better backup program, a diagnostics tool (which I'll tell you about later in this chapter), and a couple of antivirus utilities.
4. Back up your hard disk.
5. Create an emergency disk. Having an emergency floppy disk handy is a cheap way to recover from many hard disk problems. The next section shows you how to create this disk and what files to put on it.

# Booting Clean

The typical PC setup is a complex affair with all kinds of TSRs and device drivers crammed into memory. If you're having problems with a program, it may be caused by the software butting heads with one of these memory-resident programs.

The solution, typically, is to do a *clean boot*—to restart your system without loading any TSRs or device drivers. If the program runs fine after the clean boot, add the memory-resident stuff back in one at a time until you isolate the offending program.

## Booting Clean with DOS 6

DOS 6 is chock full of fancy new features, but one of my favorites is the one-key, no muss, no fuss, clean boot option. Although I talked about this in Chapter 14, "Start It Your Way: DOS 6 Boot Options," it's worth a recap here. To bypass your AUTOEXEC.BAT and CONFIG.SYS files at startup, wait until you see the following message:

```
Starting MS-DOS...
```

Then press F5 (or hold down Shift until you see the DOS prompt).

## Creating Clean AUTOEXEC.BAT and CONFIG.SYS Files

If you haven't made the move to DOS 6 yet, you need to create "clean" versions of your AUTOEXEC.BAT and CONFIG.SYS files that don't load any TSRs or device drivers.

Here's a sample of a clean AUTOEXEC.BAT file:

```
@ECHO OFF
PATH=C:\;C:\DOS
SET TEMP=C:\TEMP
```

For CONFIG.SYS, start with the following:

```
FILES=20
```

```
BUFFERS=30
DEVICE=C:\DOS\COMMAND.COM C:\DOS /P
```

Save these files as AUTOEXEC.CLN and CONFIG.CLN (I store mine in my BATCH directory to avoid cluttering my root directory) and keep a copy on a floppy disk. When you need to use them, copy them to the root directory as AUTOEXEC.BAT and CONFIG.SYS (after first making a copy of the original files, of course).

**Dunce**

> Be sure to include in CONFIG.SYS any device drivers that you need to run your system. This would include drivers for your hard disk or DoubleSpace.

## Creating a Bootable Disk

Clean startup files won't do you much good if a software or hardware problem causes you to lose access to your hard disk. In this case, you need to regain control of your system by booting from a floppy disk.

**Guru Trivia**

> The next time you start your computer, keep your eye on drive A:. A few seconds after you throw the switch, the drive light should come on briefly. This means the drive is being set up for use, and once that's done, the light goes out again. A few seconds later, though, the light reappears. In this case, your system is looking to see if there's a floppy disk in the drive. If there is, the computer attempts to load DOS from the floppy disk. If the disk contains the proper files—specifically, the DOS *system files*—DOS loads and you'll see an A> or A:\ prompt instead of the usual C> or C:\.

**Dunce**

> DOS only boots from a floppy in drive A:, so be sure whatever disk you're using is readable in drive A:.

There are two ways to create a bootable disk:

- Use the `FORMAT` command with the `/S` switch. By formatting the disk, you can be sure that you're starting with a "fresh" disk that isn't cluttered with other files or, more importantly, doesn't have any viruses lurking in the weeds.
- If you have a disk that you've already formatted, you can still make it bootable by using the following commands (you only need the second command if you don't store COMMAND.COM in your root directory):

```
sys a:
copy c:\dos\command.com a:
```

**Guru Tip**

> For technical reasons, DOS always tries to place the system files in the same place on every disk. If there are other files already inhabiting that place, DOS abandons the procedure and displays the message `No room for system on destination disk`. If this happens, reformat the disk with the `/S` switch.

**Guru Tip**

> Once you've created your system disk you should immediately try it out to be sure it works. Reboot with the disk still in drive A: and be sure you see the A> prompt.

# The Emergency Disk: Don't Leave Home Without It

Once you've created a system disk, you need to copy a few more files in order to create a true "emergency disk" that you can use to investigate and troubleshoot problems. The number of files you copy depends on the capacity of the disk and what you have in the way of recovery software. Here are some suggestions:

- *A text editor*. This enables you to make changes to your configuration files. You can use `EDLIN` (copy the file EDLIN.EXE from your DOS directory) or, if you have at least DOS 5, `EDIT` (copy both EDIT.COM and QBASIC.EXE from your DOS directory).
- *The partition table.* If you have DOS 5, use MIRROR.COM to save a copy of your hard disk's partition to the disk. See Chapter 19, "An Ounce of Prevention: How to Avoid Trouble," for details.
- *Your computer's setup program*. Some computers come with a setup program on a separate disk (it might be called something like SETUP.EXE). In many cases, you just need to rerun this program to get your hard disk back up and running.
- *Recovery utilities*. If you've accidentally deleted one or more of the system files, or if you've accidentally formatted your hard disk, you can recover with special software. If you have DOS 5 or 6, copy UNDELETE.EXE and UNFORMAT.COM from your DOS directory. If you have any other utility programs, copy the appropriate files.
- *Disk diagnostics*. If you have DOS 6 (or Windows 3.1), copy MSD.EXE, the Microsoft diagnostics program.

**Guru Tools**

> If you don't have DOS 6, check out the Norton Disk Doctor that comes with the Norton Utilities.

- *Virus checker*. Just in case your hard disk goes down for the count because of a virus, you should include an anti-virus program on your emergency disk. Be sure the program can "disinfect" (and not just detect) viruses.

# Using *CHKDSK*

The `CHKDSK` command examines a disk's file allocation table (FAT) and directory structure to look for problems (and, if necessary, fix them). All you do is enter `chkdsk` and, after the program roots around for a while, you'll see a report that looks something like this:

```
Volume Serial Number is 1AB2-C34D

151158784 bytes total disk space
    98304 bytes in 4 hidden files
   147456 bytes in 36 directories
136306688 bytes in 3123 user files
    53248 bytes in bad sectors
 14553088 bytes available on disk

     4096 bytes in each allocation unit
    36904 total allocation units on disk
     3553 available allocation units on disk

   655360 total bytes memory
   624736 bytes free
```

If no problems were found, CHKDSK just reports on disk and memory usage. This is good information (although, if you need memory data, you should use MEM instead), but CHKDSK's real reason for being is to detect FAT and directory errors. Before examining these errors, let's take a quick look at the FAT to get a better idea of how CHKDSK performs its magic.

## How the FAT Works

DOS stores your files in chunks called *clusters*, the size of which depends on the type of disk (clusters are what CHKDSK refers to as "allocation units"). Every cluster on your hard disk is either being used by a file, unused, or marked as bad (these are the "bad sectors" in the CHKDSK report). It's the job of the FAT to keep track of all this.

For every file on your hard disk, DOS maintains an entry in a *file directory*, a sort of table of contents for your files. Table 18.1 outlines the structure of the file directory.

### Table 18.1. The structure of the file directory.

| *Field* | *Size* |
|---|---|
| Filename | 8 bytes |
| Extension | 3 bytes |
| Attributes (archive, hidden, and so on) | 1 byte |

| *Field* | *Size* |
|---|---|
| Reserved (these bytes aren't used) | 10 bytes |
| Time the file was last modified | 2 bytes |
| Date the file was last modified | 2 bytes |
| Starting cluster number in the FAT | 2 bytes |
| File size in bytes | 4 bytes |

When DOS needs to open a file, it first looks it up in the file directory and gets the starting cluster number. It then turns to the FAT to find the rest of the file. The FAT entry that corresponds to the file's starting cluster contains one of two things:

- A pointer to the next cluster used by the file (if there's more of the file in other clusters).
- An end-of-file (EOF) marker if the file ends within the cluster.

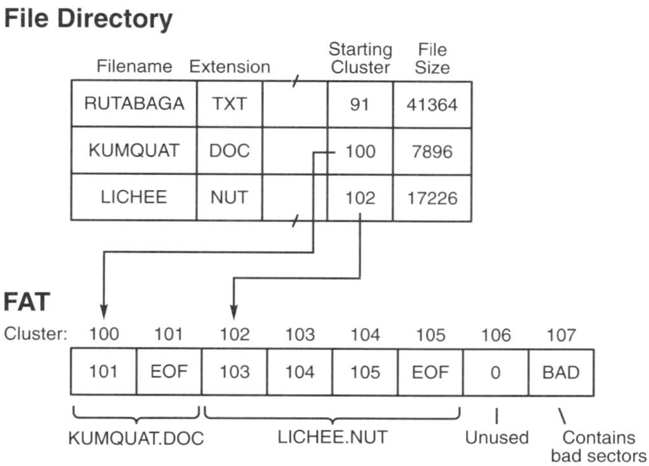


**Figure 18.1.** The relationship between the file directory and the FAT.

The file KUMQUAT.DOC, for example, has a starting cluster number of 100. When I go to the FAT entry for cluster 100, I see that it contains the value 101.

This tells me that I'll find the next portion of the file in cluster 101. So now I move to the entry for cluster 101 and find that it contains EOF. This tells me that the file ends within this cluster, so I know that clusters 100 and 101 contain the entire file (this is called a *cluster chain*).

> That KUMQUAT.DOC is contained in just two sectors is confirmed by the size of the file in the file directory. Assuming a cluster size of 4,096 bytes, KUMQUAT.DOC's size of 7,896 is less than two clusters.

> If you want to see what the FAT looks like on your machine, crank up The Norton Utilities' DiskEdit program.

## Fixing Errors

When you run `CHKDSK`, any problems it finds usually fall into one of these three categories (I'll explain each one as I go along):

- Lost clusters
- Cross-linked clusters
- Invalid clusters

To have `CHKDSK` attempt to fix these problems, run `CHKDSK` again with the `/F` switch.

> Do not, I repeat, *do not* run **`CHKDSK /F`** if you've started the current DOS session from within another program (such as Windows, WordPerfect, or the DOS Shell). **`CHKDSK`** may report (and try to fix) errors that aren't really there, which could trash some valuable data.

**Guru Tip**

If you run **CHKDSK** on a DoubleSpace drive, DoubleSpace checks the compressed drive for errors.

# Dealing with Lost Clusters

A lost cluster (or lost allocation unit, as `CHKDSK` calls it; it's also sometimes called an *orphaned clusters*) is a cluster that, according to the FAT, is associated with a file, but has no link to any entry in the file directory. This is typically caused by rebooting when a program crashes or by power surges.

When you run `CHKDSK /F` to fix these errors, you'll see a prompt that looks something like this:

```
4 lost allocation units found in 2 chains
Convert lost chains to files (Y/N)?
```

If you press `y`, DOS converts the lost clusters into files in your root directory with names like FILE0000.CHK and FILE0001.CHK. You can take a look at these files to see if they contain any useful data and then try to salvage the data. Usually, however, these files are unusable and most people just delete them to save the disk space.

# Dealing with Cross-Linked Clusters

A cross-linked cluster is one that has somehow been assigned to two different files (or twice in the same file), as shown in Figure 18.2.

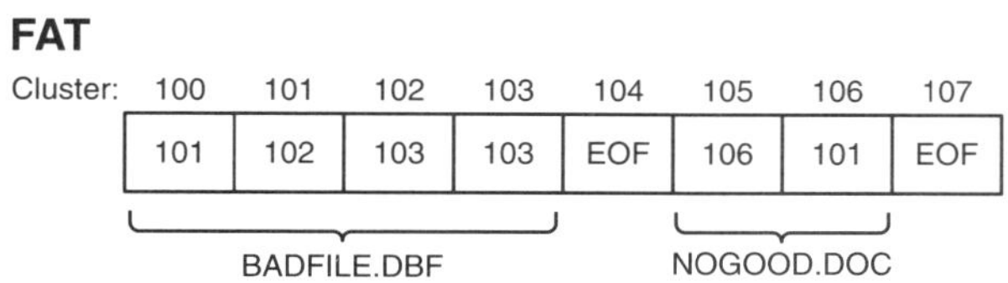


**Figure 18.2.** Files with cross-linked clusters.

In this case, both BADFILE.DBF and NOGOOD.DOC contain FAT entries that refer to cluster 101, so they're cross-linked. BADFILE.DBF also has two FAT entries that refer to the same cluster, which is also a cross-link error.

What can you do about cross-linked files? Well, unfortunately, `CHKDSK` won't fix them, so you're on your own. You basically have two choices:

- Restore the files from backed-up copies.
- Make copies of the files (and then delete the cross-linked originals) and hope that you don't lose too much data.

DOS knows the size of each file, so when you copy a cross-linked file, DOS follows the chain until it has copied the right number of clusters. This has two consequences:

- The copied file contains garbage data from some other file after the point where it was cross-linked. For example, if the file NOGOOD.DOC in Figure 18.2 is three clusters long, the copy contains clusters 105, 106, and 101. You need to delete this junk from the new file.
- The parts of the file that DOS couldn't find thanks to the cross-linkage probably ends up as lost clusters. (This would probably be the fate of cluster 107 in Figure 18.2). Convert these to files with `CHKDSK /F` and try to add them back into the copied file (using the original program that created the file in the first place).

The Norton Utilities' Disk Doctor program or PC Tools' Disk Fix can repair cross-linked files.

## Dealing with Invalid Clusters

An invalid cluster is one that falls under one of the following three categories:

- A FAT entry that refers to cluster 1, because a disk's cluster numbers start at 2.

- ✦ A FAT entry that refers to a cluster number larger than the total number of clusters on the disk.
- ✦ A FAT entry of 0 (which normally denotes an unused cluster) that is part of a cluster chain.

To fix invalid cluster errors, run `CHKDSK /F` and press `y` when you're asked if you want to convert lost allocation units to files. `CHKDSK` truncates the file by replacing the invalid cluster with an EOF marker. The lost clusters are probably the truncated portion of the file, so you can examine them and try to piece everything back together.

Dunce

> If the file with the invalid cluster is an EXE or COM file, don't try to fix it. An improperly repaired executable file could play havoc with the rest of your data when you try to run it.

## Checking for Fragmented Files

If you run `CHKDSK` with a file specification, the program reports whether or not the files are fragmented. See Chapter 3, "Guru Hard Disk Management," for the scoop on file fragmentation and its cure.

# Using the Microsoft Diagnostics Utility

DOS 6 (or Windows 3.1) users get an added bonus: the Microsoft Diagnostics utility (MSD). Just type `msd` and press Enter and you'll see the screen shown in Figure 18.3.

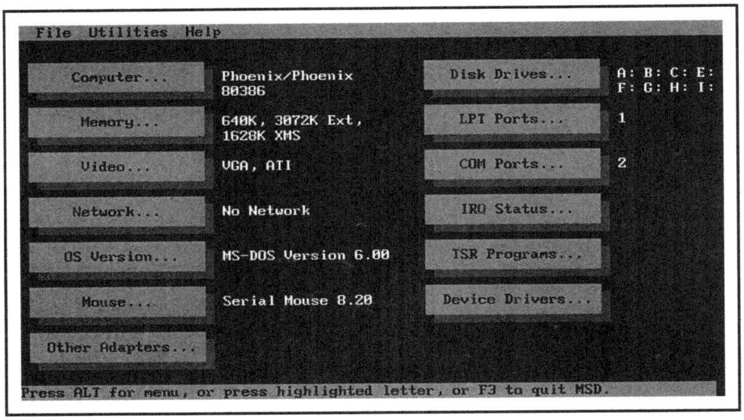


**Figure 18.3.** The Microsoft Diagnostics utility main screen.

Each of the buttons in the MSD screen gives you some inside information about certain aspects of your system. To access a button, press the highlighted key in the button's name or click on it if you have a mouse. Here's a quick rundown of what you'll find:

Computer — Gives you general information about your system: the manufacturer, the BIOS data, and so on.

Memory — Displays a map of the upper memory area. This is useful for determining which blocks are being used in case you want to include more blocks in EMM386.

Video — Gives you general information about your video card and the current video mode.

Network — Displays information about your network configuration.

OS Version — Displays the operating system version, its location in memory, the current environment strings, and more.

Mouse — Gives you mouse information, including the driver version, the IRQ it uses, and its current settings.

Other Adaptors — Shows the status of any game cards installed on your system.

Disk Drives — Tells you the size and bytes free on your system's disk drives.

| | |
|---|---|
| LPT Ports | Shows the address and status of each parallel port on your system. |
| COM Ports | Shows the address and current communications parameters assigned to your system's serial ports. |
| IRQ Status | Displays the deployment of your system's hardware *interrupt request lines* (IRQs). |
| TSR Programs | Lists the name and location of any installed TSRs. |
| Device Drivers | Lists the names of the installed device drivers. |

**Guru Tip**

> If you'd like a report of these system settings, pull down the File menu (press Alt+F) and select the **P**rint Report option. In the window that appears, select which elements to include in the report and where you want it printed (LPT1, a file, and so on).

# Checking Floppy Disk Integrity

I'll conclude this chapter with a simple batch file that takes `CHKDSK` a step further.

The data on your floppy disks is really just a collection of magnetic particles. Over time, these magnetic signals fade and the data may become unreadable. If you have critical backup data loaded on those floppies, you should keep a second backup set just in case, and check the disks from time to time to be sure everything's okay. `CHKDSK` only looks at the disk's FAT and directory structure, but here's a batch file (CHECK.BAT) that checks the integrity of each file:

```
@ECHO OFF
ECHO Checking file integrity of disk in drive %1
COPY %1\*.* NUL > NUL
```

For example, to check a disk in drive A:, enter the following command:

```
check a:
```

CHECK.BAT then copies every file in drive A: to the NUL device (i.e., to nothing). If any of the files have bad sectors, DOS reports `Data error reading drive A:`, and you'll know it's time to replace the disk (which is why you should always have a second backup set for critical data).

# Guru Review

This chapter introduced you to a few programs and utilities to include in your guru survival kit:

- A clean boot is a good way to clear up memory conflicts. If you have DOS 6, you can just press F5 at startup. Otherwise, create stripped down versions of your CONFIG.SYS and AUTOEXEC.BAT files.
- For hard disk problems, you need a bootable disk. You can either format the disk with the `/S` switch, or use the `SYS` command to make an already formatted disk bootable.
- Once you've got a bootable floppy, add things like a text editor, undelete software, and a virus checker to create a true "emergency" disk.
- Use `CHKDSK` regularly to check for disk problems such as lost and cross-linked clusters.
- If you have DOS 6 or Windows 3.1, use the Microsoft Diagnostics utility to sniff out problems in various components.

# An Ounce of Prevention: How to Avoid Trouble

19

CHAPTER

**Guru Stuff In This Chapter➤**

- *Making file copying and deleting safer*
- *Using DOS' deletion protection methods*
- *Guarding your hard disk*
- *Watching out for viruses*
- *Dangerous DOS commands, AUTOEXEC.BAT protection, and more*

Computer problems may be inevitable, but that doesn't mean you just have to sit back and wait for trouble. DOS gurus are proactive—we'd rather do a little extra work now than a lot of extra work later. And therein lies the good news: avoiding trouble really does take only a little extra work. Why, with just a few simple techniques and your newfound knowledge of batch files and DOSKEY macros, you can set up some powerful preventative measures in no time at all. This chapter tells you everything you need to know.

# Guarding Against Accidental Deletions

At some point in your computer career, usually when you least expect it, you'll have the "uh-oh" experience. This occurs anytime you do something you shouldn't have done, such as consign an irreplaceable file to some deletion netherworld.

Just so you're prepared, here are the symptoms: your life inevitably flashes before your eyes (and you remember where you lost that roller skate key in the third grade), you start hallucinating (mostly distorted images of your boss saying "You're fired!"), and your stomach does backflips that would be the envy of any gymnast.

You may not be able to avoid this experience entirely, but you can certainly cut down on its frequency (and maybe delay that ulcer for a few years). The next few sections offer some suggestions.

## Safer Copying

When most people think of accidental deletions, they think of rogue `DEL` or `ERASE` commands blowing away crucial files. But there's another, even more dangerous, way to lose a file: copying over it with another file of the same name. The real problem here is that, unless you have DOS 6, files overwritten with a `COPY` or `XCOPY` command are impossible to recover.

> **Guru Tip**
>
> *DOS 6's new Delete Sentry method can recover files accidentally clobbered with* COPY, XCOPY, *or* MOVE. *See below.*

Forthwith, here are a few suggestions for safer copying:

- Run a DIR listing in the target directory using the same file specification that you'll be using in the copy command.
- Use the REPLACE command instead of COPY or XCOPY. If you include the /A switch, REPLACE will only copy the source files if they *don't* exist in the destination directory.
- Set up your own batch file versions of COPY or XCOPY that check to see if the file exists and give you the option of continuing or canceling.

Creating batch files for safe copying is actually a bit tricky because of the sheer number of ways you can specify the source and destination files (with or without pathnames, with or without wildcards, etc.). The following batch file—SAFECOPY.BAT—uses the most common case: the source files are in the current directory and wildcards may be used:

```
@ECHO OFF
FOR %%F IN (%1) DO CALL CONFIRM %%F %2
```

All SAFECOPY.BAT does is use FOR to cycle through the source files and CALL another batch file named CONFIRM.BAT (I'm assuming that CONFIRM.BAT is somewhere in the current PATH). Here's the listing for CONFIRM.BAT:

```
@ECHO OFF
IF EXIST %2\%1 GOTO FILE_EXISTS
IF EXIST %2%1 GOTO FILE_EXISTS

XCOPY %1 %2
GOTO END

:FILE_EXISTS
ECHO Hey, %1 already exists in %2!
CHOICE Proceed with copy
IF ERRORLEVEL 2 GOTO END

XCOPY %1 %2

:END
```

CONFIRM.BAT checks to see if the destination file exists (the second `IF` is needed when you're copying to the root directory). If it does, the program branches to the FILE_EXISTS label where a warning is displayed and the user is asked to confirm the copy.

# Safer Deleting

Of course, the vast majority of lost files are caused by DEL (and ERASE) commands run amok. The most straightforward way to protect against accidental deletions is to use DEL with its /P switch. This tells DOS that you want to confirm each file before it's deleted. To be extra safe, the following DOSKEY macro actually replaces the DEL command:

```
doskey del=del /p
```

If you have a large number of files to delete, confirming each one can be a pain. Instead, here's a batch file (SAFEDEL.BAT) that first displays a DIR listing of the files you're about to delete and then asks if you want to continue:

```
@ECHO OFF
CLS

ECHO %0 %1
ECHO.
ECHO Here's a list of the files that will be deleted:
DIR %1 /ON /W

ECHO.
ECHO To cancel the deletion, press Ctrl+C. Otherwise,
PAUSE

DEL %1
```

# Using Deletion Tracking

If you have at least DOS 5, you can use a method called *deletion tracking* to protect yourself against accidental deletions. With deletion tracking, every time you erase a file DOS maintains a record of the file's name, its starting cluster, and any other FAT entries for the file. If you subsequently need to recover the file, the `UNDELETE` command uses the deletion tracking information to attempt the rescue.

> When you delete a file, DOS doesn't touch the actual file, it just alters the tables that track it. In particular, the first letter of the filename in the file directory is changed to ASCII 229 ($\sigma$), and the file's FAT entries are set to 0 so those clusters can be used by any other files that get written to disk. The key to using deletion tracking successfully is to run **UNDELETE** before the file's clusters get overwritten. For more details, see Chapter 21, "Common DOS Problems (and How to Fix 'Em").

Just to make life confusing, how you invoke deletion tracking depends on whether you're using DOS 5 or 6. With DOS 5, use the following general form:

```
MIRROR /Tdrive1 [/Tdrive2...]
```

Here's the DOS 6 command:

```
UNDELETE /Tdrive1 [/Tdrive2...]
```

In both cases, `drive1` and `drive2` are the letters of the drives you want to track. For example, to set up deletion tracking on drives C: and D: in DOS 6, use the following command:

```
undelete /tc /td
```

> Don't set up deletion tracking for any virtual drives created with **SUBST** or **ASSIGN**.

Deletion-tracking is actually monitored by a TSR that waits patiently in the background for you to delete a file, and then, once you do, it records the necessary information in a file called PCTRACKR.DEL. You should know, however, that you can only track a finite number of deletions. The default number depends on the size of the drive involved, as shown in Table 19.1.

**Table 19.1. The default number of deletions tracked with the deletion tracking method.**

| *Disk Size* | *Deletions Tracked* | *Size of PCTRACKR.DEL* |
|---|---|---|
| 360K | 25 | 5K |
| 720K | 50 | 9K |
| 1.2M | 75 | 14K |
| 1.44M | 75 | 14K |
| 20M | 101 | 18K |
| 32M | 202 | 36K |
| > 32M | 303 | 55K |

In most cases, the default values will do the job, but, if needed, you can adjust the number with the following commands:

```
MIRROR /Tdrive-number
```

or

```
UNDELETE /Tdrive-number
```

Again, `drive` is the letter of the drive you want to monitor, but `number` is the number of deletions you want to track (you can enter a number between 1 and 999).

Guru Tip

If you've already installed `MIRROR` or `UNDELETE`, you need to uninstall it before you can change the number of deletions being tracked. Just run either command by itself with the `/U` switch.

Why would you want to use a different number? Well, one of the most common ways that files get accidentally deleted is to enter the command `DEL *.*` in the wrong directory (I've done this and, believe me, it's not a pretty sight). To make sure you get all these files back, you should set the number of deletions being tracked to double the size of your largest directory. For example, if the largest directory on your hard drive has 250 files, track 500 files.

**Dunce**

> The more deletions you ask DOS to track, the slower your system runs and the more space the PCTRACKR.DEL file takes up.

## Using Delete Sentry

If you've got some hard disk real estate that you can spare, you should check out DOS 6's new Delete Sentry method. With Delete Sentry, DOS sets up a hidden directory called SENTRY on each drive you're protecting. When you delete a file (either by using `DEL` or `ERASE`, or by overwriting it with `COPY`, `XCOPY`, `MOVE`, or `REPLACE`), DOS just moves it from its current directory to the SENTRY directory. Recovering the file is a simple matter of moving it back to its original location.

To make sure the SENTRY directory doesn't overrun your hard drive, DOS imposes three restrictions on the number of files that get stored there:

- The total size of the directory and its files is limited to a certain percentage of the total disk space. When SENTRY hits this limit, DOS starts purging the oldest files.
- Files are stored in SENTRY for no more than seven days. Anything older than that gets purged.
- Delete Sentry won't save copies of files with certain extensions (such as .TMP or .SWP).

As you'll see later on, it's easy to customize each of these settings to suit your needs. For now though, here's the general format of the command that loads Delete Sentry:

```
UNDELETE /Sdrive1 [/Sdrive2...]
```

The parameters `drive1` and `drive2` are the drive letters that you want to protect with Delete Sentry.

**Dunce**

> If you already have the deletion tracking version of `UNDELETE` loaded, you have to unload it first (with the `/U` switch) and *then* crank up Delete Sentry.

**Guru Tip**

> Delete Sentry takes up a little more than 13K of memory, so, if you can, load `UNDELETE` into upper memory to save some space.

# Customizing Delete Sentry

When you load Delete Sentry, DOS creates a file called UNDELETE.INI that holds various settings. It's just a plain text file, so you can use `EDIT` to view it and make changes. Here's what the default file looks like (yours may appear slightly different):

```
[configuration]
archive=FALSE
days=7
percentage=20
[sentry.drives]
C=
[mirror.drives]
[sentry.files]
sentry.files=*.* -*.TMP -*.VM? -*.WOA -*.SWP -*.SPL -*.RMG -*.IMG -*.THM -*.DOV
[defaults]
d.sentry=TRUE
d.tracker=FALSE
```

The lines in square brackets (such as `[configuration]`) are the section headings.

The `[configuration]` section defines three configuration settings:

- Whether or not files with their archive attribute off will be ignored. If the `archive=` setting is `FALSE`, Delete Sentry protects all files, regardless of the archive attribute setting. If it's `TRUE`, Delete Sentry ignores files with their archive attribute off (presumably because these files have been backed up).
- The number of days that Delete Sentry will save deleted files. Change the `days=` setting to save files for longer or shorter periods.
- The maximum amount of disk space that Delete Sentry absconds for saving the deleted files. The default is a ridiculous 20 percent, but you can change that to a more manageable number (5 percent is probably a good value).

The `[sentry.drives]` and `[mirror.drives]` sections show which drives you've specified for Delete Sentry and deletion tracking, respectively.

The `[sentry.files]` section lists the file extensions you want to include or exclude in Delete Sentry protection. The file specs with a leading hyphen (such as -*.TMP) are the files Delete Sentry *won't* save. The default values are all types of temporary files that certain programs create and delete all the time, so there's no point in having these clutter up the SENTRY directory. You might want to change these settings to include BAK files or any other temporary files used by your applications.

**Guru Tip**

> You can tell if SENTRY is getting clogged with temporary files by running **`UNDELETE`** with the **`/LIST`** switch. This gives you a rundown of the files in SENTRY that were deleted from the current directory.

Finally, the `[defaults]` section specifies whether you're using Delete Sentry or deletion tracking.

# Protecting Your Hard Disk

If your hard disk's system area (its root directory and FAT) gets corrupted (thanks to a virus, power surge, or someone formatting the disk), you can still recover if you've taken some precautions beforehand. All you need is DOS 5's `MIRROR` utility.

**Guru Tip**

> For some unfathomable reason, Microsoft removed MIRROR.COM from DOS 6. However, the file remains in your DOS directory when you upgrade, so you can still use it.

**Guru Tools**

> If you didn't upgrade from DOS 5 and thus don't have MIRROR.COM, you can still protect your hard disk. You can either use the order form in the back of your manual to get a copy of MIRROR.COM, or check out PC Tools (which has the original MIRROR utility) or The Norton Utilities' IMAGE program.

# Using *MIRROR*

`MIRROR` is a real no-brainer. You just type `mirror` and press Enter and the program does the rest. Run a `DIR` listing on your root directory and you'll see a file called MIRROR.FIL that contains all the data needed by `UNFORMAT` to recover the disk. You should run `MIRROR` any time you make changes to your hard disk's directory structure.

**Guru Tip**

> When you format a used floppy disk using either the normal (safe) method or the quick (`/Q`) method, DOS first stores a copy of the disk's system area, much like the **`MIRROR`** command does. If you accidentally format a disk, **`UNFORMAT`** can use this data to recover the disk (see Chapter 21). DOS does *not* save this information if you perform an unconditional (`/U`) format.

# Saving Your Partition Table

`MIRROR` can also save a copy of your hard disk's partition table, which includes such crucial information as the size of your hard disk's sectors and clusters, the location of the FAT, and a small program that loads the operating system into memory every time you boot. If this table gets corrupted, you won't be able to access your hard drive and you'll have to repartition the drive (and lose all your data in the process).

To avoid this nasty fate, use the following command to save a copy of your partition table to a floppy disk:

```
mirror /partn
```

`MIRROR` displays a message and prompts you for the drive you want to use. Type the appropriate letter and press Enter. `MIRROR` writes a file called PARTNSAV.FIL to the disk. (See Chapter 21 to learn how to recover from a corrupted partition table.)

# Guarding Against Viruses

Viruses are nasty little programs that live for the sheer thrill of trashing your valuable data. They're crafted in dark rooms by repressed, pimple-faced, pseudo-human deviants—former gurus who succumbed to the dark side of the Force.

Viruses comes in three basic flavors:

- *File infectors* that attach themselves to executable files and spread among other files when your run the program
- *Boot sector* viruses that replace the hard disk's master boot record (or the boot sector on a floppy disk) with their own and so load themselves into memory whenever you boot your system (the famous "Michelangelo" virus is one of these boot sector beasts)
- *Trojan horse* viruses that appear to be legitimate programs at first glance, but when you load them, they proceed to viciously maul your data

**Guru Trivia**

> The *master boot record* on a hard disk contains code that is loaded by the BIOS during startup. This code reads the disk's partition table in order to locate the *boot sector*—the sector that contains the *bootstrap code* that loads DOS into memory. (Floppy disks don't have a master boot record, just a boot sector.) Boot sector viruses actually copy the bootstrap code to another part of the disk and replace it with their own twisted version.

Viruses are, by now, an unpleasant fact of computing life, and you just have to learn to live with the threat. Fortunately, Microsoft has clued in to this reality and has included a couple of anti-virus programs with DOS 6: Microsoft Anti-Virus (MSAV) and VSafe.

## Using *MSAV* to Check Disks for Viruses

Using Microsoft Anti-Virus is simplicity itself. Just type `msav` and press Enter and you'll see the Main Menu, shown in Figure 19.1.

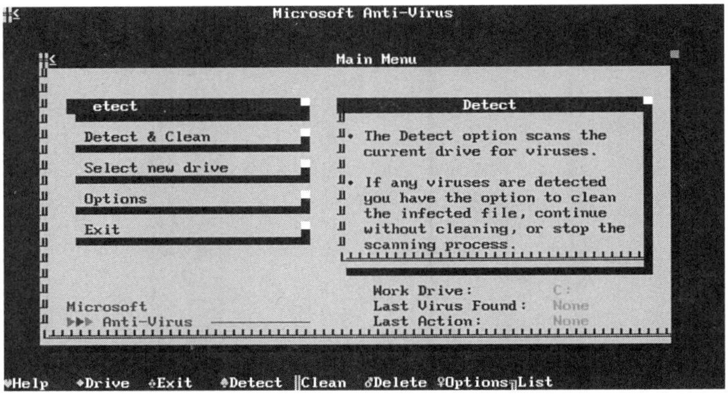


**Figure 19.1.** The Microsoft Anti-Virus main menu.

If you want Anti-Virus to scan the disk and prompt you before cleaning an infected file, select the **D**etect option. To scan the disk and automatically clean infected files, select the Detect & **C**lean option.

**Dunce**

> Anti-Virus creates files called CHKLIST.MS in each directory it scans. It uses these files during subsequent scans, so don't delete them!

# Scanning a Different Drive

By default, Anti-Virus scans whatever drive you were in when you started the program (it's listed as the Work Drive in the main menu). To change the drive, follow these steps:

1. Choose the **S**elect new drive option. Icons for each drive on your system appear in the upper-left corner of the screen.
2. Use the left and right arrow keys to select the drive you want and press Enter. (If you have a mouse, click on the appropriate drive.)

# Anti-Virus Options

Anti-Virus comes with a few options that you can use to control the configuration of the program. Here's a quick look at some of them:

| | |
|---|---|
| Verify Integrity | This option tells Anti-Virus to look for changes in executable files based on the CHKLIST.MS information. Most viruses are detected because they change the size of executables. This option catches these changes. |
| Create New Checksums | This is the option that creates the CHKLIST.MS files. These files contain *checksums*—information that tracks things like the size, attributes, and date and time stamps for each file. |
| Create Checksums on Floppy | This option creates CHKLIST.MS files for each scanned directory on a floppy disk. Turn this option on when you want to protect a floppy. Run MSAV once to create the CHKLIST.MS files and then write-protect the disk. |
| Anti-Stealth | Stealth viruses are particularly sneaky inventions that infect files without changing them outwardly. Turn this option on periodically to check for these types of viruses. (You may not want to use it all the time because it slows down the scan.) |
| Check All Files | If this option is turned off, Anti-Virus only checks executable files for infection. (Most viruses infect executable files.) |

To change these and other Anti-Virus settings, select the **O**ptions button from the Main Menu.

## Using VSafe to Catch Viruses Red-Handed

VSafe is a memory-resident program that constantly monitors your system for any signs of evil, virus-like behavior (such as an attempted hard disk format or disk writes to the boot sector). If it detects anything untoward, you're warned and given a chance to prevent it. To load VSafe, type `vsafe` and press Enter.

**Guru Tip**

> VSafe loads half of itself (a little less than 23K) into conventional memory and the other half into extended or expanded memory, if you have any. If memory is tight, you can load VSafe into upper memory.

If you press Alt+V, VSafe displays a menu of warning options. Here's a brief summary:

| | |
|---|---|
| HD Low-level format | Warns of attempts to format the hard disk. The default is On. |
| Resident | Warns you when programs try to stay in memory. Because so many programs stay in memory, the default here is Off. |
| General write-protect | Warns you when programs try to write to disk. This, of course, happens constantly in most programs, so you should leave it Off. |
| Check executable files | Checks any executable files for discrepancies. The default is On. |
| Boot sector viruses | Checks all disks for boot sector viruses. The default is On. |
| Protect HD boot sector | Warns you any time VSafe detects an attempt to write to the boot sector or partition table on a hard disk. The default is On. |
| Protect FD boot sector | Warns you of any attempts to write to the boot sector of a floppy disk. The default is Off. |
| Protect executable files | Warns you of attempts to modify an executable file. This is fairly common, so the default is Off. |

## Other Anti-Virus Tips

Besides using MSAV and VSafe regularly, here are a few other tips to help keep your system virus-free:

- Most viruses are transmitted from machine to machine via floppy disks, so you should always be careful about which used disks you trust in your computer. If you've inherited some old disks, you can make sure there are no viruses lurking in the weeds by formatting each one before you use them.
- Trust no one when it comes to loading programs on your machine. Whether programs come from family, friends, or a BBS, use MSAV to scan the disks before running anything.
- Keep DOS' virus library up to date. The DOS 6 manual has a coupon in the back that you you can use to send away for virus updates. As you read this, there are probably dozens, maybe even hundreds, of evil scumnerds designing even nastier viruses. Regular updates will help you keep up.

# Miscellaneous Protection

To close, here are a few miscellaneous protection measures that are easy to implement:

- Some system problems are caused by rude programs that make changes to your AUTOEXEC.BAT file without telling you. One way to fool these inconsiderate rogues is by creating a dummy AUTOEXEC.BAT that looks like this:

  ```
  @ECHO OFF
  REALAUTO
  ```

  Your actual startup commands are in the REALAUTO.BAT batch file, but a dumb installation program won't know this. After you've finished installing a program, check AUTOEXEC.BAT to set what havoc was wrought, and then you can decide if you want to incorporate the changes into REALAUTO.BAT.

**Guru Tip**

> If you have DOS 6, you can specify a different startup batch file by including the `/K` switch with the `SHELL` statement in CONFIG.SYS. See Chapter 14, "Start It Your Way: DOS 6 Boot Options," for details.

- Some DOS commands are just plain dangerous and should be avoided at all costs:

  `RECOVER` — This one's a real pooch! The name sounds great, but used incorrectly, it trashes most of your hard disk before you know what hit you. See Chapter 21 for the only safe way to use this mongrel.

  `FASTOPEN` — Another DOS dog. This command gives you slightly faster disk performance, but it just plain doesn't get along with disk optimizers and other utilities.

  `APPEND` — This schizoid command does for data files what `PATH` does for executable files; that is, it lets programs find them even when they're not in the current directory. However, it also lets commands like `DEL` and `ERASE` find them! Yikes!

  `DEBUG.EXE` — Actually, `DEBUG` can be a lot of fun, and if I could've talked my editor into adding another couple of chapters to this book, I would have covered it. Having said that, let me warn you that `DEBUG` is *very* powerful and, so, *very* dangerous. Pick up a good book that covers `DEBUG` before tackling it yourself.

- For important files, you can get an added measure of safety by using `COPY`, `XCOPY`, and `DISKCOPY` with their `/V` switches. This tells DOS that you want it to verify that what is written to disk is a true copy of what is in memory. If you want DOS to verify disk writes all the time, include the following command in your CONFIG.SYS file:

  ```
  VERIFY=ON
  ```

- Don't forget to take advantage of write-protection when you store important data on your floppy disks. The files on a write-protected disk can't be deleted or overwritten, so it's a cheap and easy way to prevent accidents.

# Guru Review

This chapter showed you how to take preventative steps to keep your system trouble-free. Here's a checklist to run through:

- ✦ You can easily lose files by overwriting them with errant `COPY`, `XCOPY`, or `MOVE` commands. To prevent this, use `REPLACE` with its `/A` switch, or construct batch files that warn you when you're going to clobber a file.
- ✦ For safer deleting, tell DOS to wait for confirmation by using `DEL` or `ERASE` with the `/P` switch.
- ✦ DOS' deletion tracking method keeps track of the name and clusters of a deleted file. As long as you get to the file in time, this makes it much easier to recover a deleted file.
- ✦ DOS 6 introduced an even better method of deletion recovery: Delete Sentry. This method moves deleted files to a hidden directory from which they can be quickly and reliably recovered.
- ✦ Use `MIRROR` to create a copy of your hard disk's system area. This provides valuable information if you ever need to recover from a system crash.
- ✦ Use DOS 6's new Anti-Virus and VSafe utilities regularly to check for viruses on your system.

# Simple System Security (Or, It's Not Paranoia When Everyone's Out to Get You)

## 20 CHAPTER

**Guru Stuff In This Chapter ➤**

- *Tips and techniques for protecting files*
- *Disabling dangerous DOS commands*
- *How to protect your directories*
- *Using keyboard remapping to foil evil interlopers*
- *A basic screen blanker*
- *Lots of simple security steps to stop system snoops*

Articles and books on computer security are chock full of references to "intruders," "prying eyes," and "snoops." Read enough of this stuff and you find yourself believing that half the world is out to learn the secrets hidden on your hard drive. This may be true, of course, but most people's security needs are not so grandiose.

In this chapter, the term *security* means protection from two kinds of events:

- Unauthorized use of your computer to run programs and display the contents of files
- Accidental destruction of your data by inexperienced users

This chapter shows you how to thwart the casually curious or novice user who might accidentally wreak havoc on your files. Other DOS gurus may be slowed down somewhat, but if they're determined enough, they'll eventually get past this system. However, if your data is so important that someone would be willing to go to a lot of trouble to take a peek at it, you should probably consider investing in some dedicated security software.

Guru Tools

> There's no shortage of programs that offer a higher level of security than the simple system described in this chapter. For starters, both Norton Utilities and PC Tools offer file encryption and password protection for files. FastLock Plus lets you lock your hard drive and your keyboard to prevent anyone from either using your files or rebooting your system. For high-end security, check out PC/DACS or Data Security Plus.

# Protecting Files

Everyone's computer has at least a few critical files. Besides your precious AUTOEXEC.BAT and CONFIG.SYS files, you might have payroll information, sales figures, or just this year's budgets for the kids' birthdays. In any case, you need to protect these files from being erased or displayed.

- Always keep backup copies of crucial files. Having someone trash your data is bad enough, but not having a backup copy to fall back on is even worse. Don't leave your backup disks by your computer or in a nearby disk case. Keep them locked away in a secure place.

✦ If you give your files names such as PAYROLL.XLS or SECRET.DOC, you're just asking for trouble. Try to use innocuous or cryptic names that won't raise red flags with interlopers.

## Using *ATTRIB* to Protect Files

The ATTRIB command that I told you about back in Chapter 16, "The Fun Stuff: Advanced DOS Commands," can add a couple of levels of protection to your files. ATTRIB can activate (or deactivate) the four file attributes: archive, hidden, read-only, and system. Of these, the hidden and read-only attributes are the most useful for protecting files.

When you hide a file, it doesn't show up in a listing produced by the DIR command. Out of sight is out of mind, so someone taking a casual glance at your files won't see the hidden ones and, therefore, won't be tempted to display or erase them.

Dunce

> You need to have DOS 5 to hide a file. However, if your system has DOS 5, it also means that a savvy snoop can just use **DIR** with the **/AH** switch to see your hidden files.

Although a hidden file is invisible, it's not totally safe. Someone who knows the name of the file can attempt to modify the file with EDIT or EDLIN. As an added measure of safety, you can also set the file's read-only attribute. When you do this, the file can't be modified.

You can set both attributes with a single command:

```
attrib +h +r payroll.xls
```

## A Sneaky Trick for Protecting Files

The ATTRIB command is an easy way to give your files extra protection, but it suffers from two major drawbacks:

✦ It's easily thwarted by anyone who knows how to use ATTRIB.

✦ If someone knows (or can guess) the name of a protected file, it can still be viewed with the `TYPE` command or `EDIT` (if it's a text file), or with a disk editing utility (for all other kinds of files).

You can get around these limitations with the sneaky trick demonstrated in the following steps:

1. Type `copy con cantuse` (don't press Enter yet).
2. Press Alt+255 (be sure you enter the numbers on your keyboard's numeric keypad). When you release the Alt key, a space appears.
3. Finish the filename by typing `.me` and then press Enter.
4. Enter anything you like into the file.
5. Press F6 and then press Enter to copy the file.

To see the effect of adding Alt+255 to the filename, run a `DIR` listing—the file appears perfectly normal. In fact, if you didn't know better, you'd think that the name of the file was CANTUSE.ME. This is the point of the trick. If anyone tries to view the file with, say, the `TYPE` command, a DOS message saying `File not found` appears (go ahead and try it). Combining this trick with the hidden and read-only attributes should keep all but the most knowledgeable user at bay.

**Guru Tip**

You can use this trick to rename the files that execute your programs. For example, the WordPerfect executable file is WP.EXE. Renaming this to WP<Alt+255>.EXE makes it harder for unauthorized users to run the program.

**Dunce**

Many applications won't accept a filename with the Alt+255 character. If you need to work with such a file, you usually need to give it a more conventional name before loading the program.

# Disabling DOS Commands

Nothing puts more of a damper on your day than finding out that someone has accidentally (or maliciously) formatted your hard disk or scrambled your partitions with FDISK. You can make these things a lot harder to do with a few simple precautions:

- You should rename potentially destructive DOS files such as DELTREE.EXE, FDISK.EXE, FORMAT.COM, and RECOVER.EXE. You can simply add an X to the beginning of the name or an Alt+255 to the end. If you're worried about the files being used maliciously (how did you make all these enemies, anyway?), use more obscure names such as ZZZ.COM or YONKERS.EXE.

**Dunce**

> When renaming executable files, always keep the extension the same to avoid running into problems.

- Even with these files renamed, some yahoo may try to run them anyway. For added security, move them out of your DOS directory and use ATTRIB to hide them.

Renaming external DOS commands is fine, but there's no file to rename for the internal DOS commands such as DEL, ERASE, or RD that can also wreak havoc on an unsuspecting hard disk. There is a solution, however: DOSKEY. With DOSKEY, you can create one set of macros that works just like these DOS commands and another that prevents the normal commands from being used. For example, the following macro mimics the DEL command:

```
doskey del<Alt+255>=del $*
```

**Guru Tip**

> Just to be clear about things, the <Alt+255> in this macro (and in the rest of this chapter) means that you hold down Alt and press **255** on your numeric keypad.

To delete a file, you would have to type `del` followed by `Alt+255`. What happens if you just try to run DEL? That's covered by the second macro:

```
doskey del=<Alt+255>
```

If you just type `del` and press Enter, the user gets a `Bad command or file name` message. The other internal commands you should probably safeguard are CD (and CHDIR), COPY, DIR, ERASE, MD (and MKDIR), RD (and RMDIR), REN (and RENAME), SET, and TYPE. (I'd suggest entering them all in a batch file to make life easier.)

> **Guru Tip**
>
> You'll probably get tired of having to press Alt+255 all day long. Instead, you could program a key (F10 is a good choice) to automatically produce Alt+255. Adding the following command to AUTOEXEC.BAT does the trick (be sure ANSI.SYS is loaded in CONFIG.SYS, however; see Chapter 10, "Customizing the Keyboard," for details):
>
> ```
> ECHO █[0;68;255p
> ```

# Protecting Directories

You can prevent someone from working with your files or running your programs by not allowing them to access the appropriate directory. You can do this with techniques similar to those used with filenames:

- Use the `ATTRIB` command to hide a directory. Just use the command `ATTRIB +h` *`pathname`* where *`pathname`* is the name of the directory you want to hide.
- Add Alt+255 to the end of your directory names to make it harder for someone to change to the directory. To make things really hard, you can also use Alt+255 as the directory's *extension* (DATA<Alt+255>.<Alt+255>). Directories rarely have extensions, so this will really throw those snoops for a loop.
- This one's a little drastic, but it's diabolically effective: create a directory called just <Alt+255>, hide it, and then set up your hard disk so that every other directory is a subdirectory of <Alt+255>. Snoops running a `DIR` listing see only the files in your root directory and nothing else.

# Modifying the Keyboard

The Achilles' heel of any system intruder is that they have to use the keyboard to do their dirty work. In this section, I'll show you a couple of ways to modify the keyboard and foil those nasty people.

**Guru Tip**

> Both techniques in this section can be circumvented by simply rebooting the computer. If you're serious about your security, include a `CALL` command in your AUTOEXEC.BAT file that runs either of the batch files. If you use DOS 6, an interloper could just press F5 or F8 to bypass AUTOEXEC.BAT. To prevent this, include the following line in your CONFIG.SYS file:
>
> ```
> SWITCHES=/N
> ```

# Using Alt+255 to Disable the Enter Key

The best way to thwart unauthorized users is to make sure they can't actually *do* anything. This is surprisingly easy to do. To see how, enter the following command:

```
dir<Alt+255>
```

When you press Enter, you receive the following error:

```
Bad command or file name
```

What happened here? Well, instead of running the `DIR` command, you actually ran something called DIR<ALT+255>. DOS doesn't know what this is, so it produced an error message. You get the same result if you try this with any DOS command and any program name.

The idea then is to add an Alt+255 to the end of every command. How do you do that? Simple: you just use the `PROMPT` or `ECHO` commands to redefine the Enter key (see Chapter 10, "Customizing the Keyboard," for a complete discussion on using `PROMPT` and `ECHO` to reconfigure your keyboard). Here's a batch file called NOENTER.BAT that does precisely that:

**Guru Tip**

> To use the batch files in this section, you need to include the following line in your CONFIG.SYS file (be sure to reboot when you're done):
>
> ```
> DEVICE=C:\DOS\ANSI.SYS
> ```

```
@ECHO OFF
ECHO █[13;255;13p
ECHO █[0;94;13p
CLS
```

The first ECHO command reconfigures the Enter key (keyboard code 13) so that when anyone presses Enter, they actually get the ASCII 255 character first and *then* Enter. ASCII 255 is effectively added to the command line, and so DOS always produces an error message.

To enter your own commands, however, you need some way of circumventing this. This is the task of the second ECHO command, which reconfigures Ctrl+F1 (keyboard code 0;94) to produce Enter. To run your own commands and programs, type the command or program name and then press Ctrl+F1. (You don't have to use Ctrl+F1; check out Appendix D, "Keyboard Codes," for a list of the appropriate codes for other key combinations.)

To reset the keys, use YESENTER.BAT:

```
@ECHO OFF
ECHO █[13;13p
ECHO █[0;94;0;94;13p
CLS
```

# Disabling the Whole Keyboard

If your goal is to make system snoops apoplectic, here's a batch file (called NOKEY.BAT) that'll do it (thanks to DOS guru extraordinaire Paul Somerson for the inspiration behind this work of batch file art):

```
@ECHO OFF
SET N=0 1 2 3 4 5 6 7 8 9
FOR %%C IN (%N%) DO ECHO █[3%%C;219p
FOR %%C IN (%N%) DO ECHO █[4%%C;219p
FOR %%C IN (%N%) DO ECHO █[5%%C;219p
FOR %%C IN (%N%) DO ECHO █[6%%C;219p
FOR %%C IN (%N%) DO ECHO █[7%%C;219p
FOR %%C IN (%N%) DO ECHO █[8%%C;219p
FOR %%C IN (%N%) DO ECHO █[9%%C;219p
FOR %%C IN (%N%) DO ECHO █[10%%C;219p
FOR %%C IN (%N%) DO ECHO █[11%%C;219p
FOR %%C IN (%N%) DO ECHO █[12%%C;219p
ECHO █[0;94;"YESKEY";13p
SET N=
```

The keyboard codes for the standard keys run from 32 to 127 (see the ASCII chart in Appendix C). NOKEY.BAT just runs through these codes (technically, it goes from 30 to 129) and remaps them all to ASCII 219, which is the block character (ÿ). This magic is accomplished first by setting an environment variable named `N` to "0 1 2 3 4 5 6 7 8 9" and then having the `FOR` commands cycle through these values. For example, the first `FOR` translates into ten separate commands:

```
FOR %%C IN (%N%) DO ECHO ÿ[30;219p
FOR %%C IN (%N%) DO ECHO ÿ[31;219p
.
.
FOR %%C IN (%N%) DO ECHO ÿ[39;219p
```

**Guru Tip**

> For extra safety, you might also want to disable the function keys and arrow keys (especially if you have DOSKEY loaded). See Appendix D for the appropriate keyboard codes.

Each `ECHO` statement remaps the appropriate key to ASCII 219, which means that no matter which key the snoops press, they'll just get a bunch of blocks. Ah, to see their faces when this happens! The last `ECHO` command remaps Ctrl+F1 to run YESKEY.BAT, which resets everything:

```
@ECHO OFF
SET N=0 1 2 3 4 5 6 7 8 9
FOR %%C IN (%N%) DO ECHO ÿ[3%%C;3%%Cp
FOR %%C IN (%N%) DO ECHO ÿ[4%%C;4%%Cp
FOR %%C IN (%N%) DO ECHO ÿ[5%%C;5%%Cp
FOR %%C IN (%N%) DO ECHO ÿ[6%%C;6%%Cp
FOR %%C IN (%N%) DO ECHO ÿ[7%%C;7%%Cp
FOR %%C IN (%N%) DO ECHO ÿ[8%%C;8%%Cp
FOR %%C IN (%N%) DO ECHO ÿ[9%%C;9%%Cp
FOR %%C IN (%N%) DO ECHO ÿ[10%%C;10%%Cp
FOR %%C IN (%N%) DO ECHO ÿ[11%%C;11%%Cp
FOR %%C IN (%N%) DO ECHO ÿ[12%%C;12%%Cp
ECHO ÿ[0;94;0;94p
SET N=
```

# Blanking the Screen

If you're going to leave your computer for a while, you should reconfigure your screen so that snoops can't see anything. If you read Chapter 9, "Customizing the Prompt," you know that you can use the PROMPT command to change the attributes of screen text. One of those attributes actually hides text, so this accomplishes your goal perfectly. Here's the command to use:

```
prompt $e[8m
```

Run CLS after entering this command to get a pristine, blank screen. Any characters you type don't appear, and even though you can run commands, output doesn't show either. To restore the screen, type the following command:

```
prompt $e[0m$p$g
```

(If you don't feel like typing this complicated command blindly, add it to a batch file—you could call it UNBLANK.BAT—and then run the batch file, instead.)

# Guru Review

This chapter showed you a number of methods for adding some simple security precautions to your system. Although none of the techniques discussed are powerful enough to stop sophisticated users, it should serve to prevent the casually curious from wreaking havoc on your files. Here's a rehash of the main events:

- ✦ Always keep backup copies of your important files. If anything disastrous should happen, at least you'll know your data isn't gone for good.
- ✦ Use ATTRIB to protect crucial files by setting their hidden and read-only attributes. You can use ATTRIB to hide important directories, too.
- ✦ The Alt+255 character is great for thwarting snoops who aren't too knowledgeable. You can use it in file or directory names to prevent anyone from displaying or deleting the file or directory; you can use it to rename dangerous external DOS commands; and you can use it in DOSKEY macros to prevent users from accessing internal DOS commands.

- With ANSI.SYS loaded, you can remap your keyboard to prevent intruders from doing anything.
- Take advantage of the DOS' text attributes to hide your screen. A simple `PROMPT` command can set the hidden attribute for all characters, which prevents an interloper from seeing anything on-screen.

# Common DOS Problems (and How To Fix 'Em)

21

CHAPTER

## Guru Stuff in This Chapter ➤

- *Using* UNDELETE *to recover accidentally deleted files*
- *Using* UNFORMAT *to recover accidentally formatted disks*
- *Rebuilding a corrupted partition table*
- *Recovering files marred by bad sectors*
- *Dealing with EMM386 problems*
- *Tips and tricks for dealing with the DOS doldrums*

Although I've spent the last three chapters showing you ways to avoid trouble, I'd be living in a dream world if I told you that you're now immune to DOS problems. No, unfortunately, they *will* happen, and as a guru it's your task to suck it up and deal with it. This chapter tackles a few of the most common DOS dilemmas and their solutions.

**Guru Tip**

> The proverbial "space limitations" prevent me from talking about DOS difficulties in great depth. If you have a problem that isn't covered here, you have two choices:
>
> ✦ Pick up a good troubleshooting book such as *Oops! What To Do When Things Go Wrong*, by Mike Miller.
>
> ✦ Call Microsoft's DOS tech support line at (206) 646-5104.

# Recovering Accidentally Deleted Files

It's an old saw that there are two types of computer users: those who have accidentally deleted files and those who will accidentally delete files. If it's happened to you, you know only too well that sinking feeling you get in the pit of your stomach when you realize you've just consigned your life's work to nothingness.

When this happened to the world's programmers once too often, they decided to do something about it. The result was software that could actually undelete a trashed file. With DOS 5, Microsoft decided to license this technology from Central Point Software, the makers of PC Tools. Thus the `UNDELETE` command was born.

## How Can You Undelete a File?

To understand how it's possible to undelete a file, you need to know a bit more about what happens when you delete the thing in the first place. Basically, DOS does two things:

✦ In the file directory (the table that stores information on every file on the disk), DOS changes the first letter of the file's name to the lowercase Greek sigma character ($\sigma$ or ASCII 229).

✦ In the FAT (the table that tracks which clusters are used by the file), DOS replaces every entry used by the file with a 0 (which indicates that the cluster can be used by another file).

Here's what DOS *doesn't* do:

✦ It doesn't touch the actual contents of the file. Remember, only the FAT entries that *point* to the clusters have been zeroed, not the clusters themselves. Sure, they'll eventually get overwritten by another file, but they're still intact immediately after the deletion.

✦ It doesn't change anything else in the file directory entry including, crucially, the starting cluster number and the size of the file.

Thanks to DOS' laziness when deleting a file, the UNDELETE command can take advantage of all this untouched information to try to recover the file. The key (unless you use DOS 6's Delete Sentry method) is speed—because another file may overwrite the deleted file's clusters at any time, the faster you attempt the recovery, the greater the chance of success.

Dunce

> Another thing that hampers recovery operations is file fragmentation. The more fragmented a file is, the harder it is to recover. See Chapter 3, "Guru Hard Disk Management," for details on how to defragment files with DOS 6.

## Recovering Files: The DOS Directory Method

If you haven't been using any of DOS' deletion protection methods (deletion tracking or Delete Sentry), you can still recover files, but it takes a bit more work, and you may have trouble recovering the entire file. Just switch to the directory where the file used to reside and enter the following command (assuming the file was named CRUCIAL.TXT):

```
undelete crucial.txt /dos
```

Instead of a single filename, you can also use wildcard characters to undelete multiple files. If you don't include a file spec, `UNDELETE` just looks for all deleted files.

`UNDELETE` looks through the file directory for deleted entries (the ones with sigma as the first letter) and tries to find the entry for your file. If it does, it looks up the starting cluster number and one of two things will happen:

✦ If the starting cluster is being used by another file, the following message appears on-screen:

```
Starting cluster is unavailable. This file cannot be recovered with
the UNDELETE command. Press any key to continue.
```

You're out of luck in this case, so just press a key to return to DOS (or to move on to the next file if you're trying to recover multiple files).

✦ If the starting cluster is not being used, something like the following appears on-screen:

```
MS-DOS directory contains
5 deleted files.
Of those,
4 files may be recovered.

Using the MS-DOS directory method.

?RUCIAL  TXT     2301  4-17-93 10:38a  ...A Undelete (Y/N)?
```

Press `y` and `UNDELETE` prompts you for the first letter of the file. Enter the appropriate letter and `UNDELETE` recovers the file.

If the recovered file already exists, DOS warns you and gives you two options: enter a different filename or press F5 to cancel the recovery.

When it recovers the file, UNDELETE looks at the file's size and grabs as many adjacent clusters as it needs. If there aren't enough unused clusters available, you'll see a message telling you that the entire file could not be recovered. This is why it's important to keep your files defragmented.

# Recovering Files: The Deletion Tracking Method

The deletion tracking method stores any deleted file's directory entry and FAT cluster chain. This makes it easy to recover a file (again, provided you do it right away) because UNDELETE has all the information it needs to reconstruct the file. To recover a file named CRUCIAL.TXT with deletion tracking, switch to the appropriate directory and enter the following command:

```
undelete crucial.txt /dt
```

Depending on the state of the deleted file's clusters, one of three things happens:

- If all the file's clusters are available, UNDELETE asks if you want to undelete the file. Press y to recover it.
- If only some of the file's clusters are still intact, UNDELETE warns you and asks if you want to recover just the available clusters. Again, press y to proceed.
- If none of the clusters are available, UNDELETE tells you so and asks you to press any key to continue.

# Recovering Files: The Delete Sentry Method

DOS 6's Delete Sentry method brings idiot-proof file recovery to the DOS world. With Delete Sentry, you don't have to worry about a file's clusters being overwritten, because DOS just moves the file to a hidden directory. Recovery becomes a simple matter of moving the file back to its original location.

To recover the CRUCIAL.TXT file, change to its original directory and enter the following command:

```
undelete crucial.txt
```

You'll see a screenful of information, including the following at the bottom of the screen:

```
Using the Delete Sentry method.
 ?RUCIAL  TXT   2301 4-17-93 10:38a   ...A Deleted: 4-20-93  3:52p
This file can be 100% undeleted. Undelete (Y/N)?
```

Press `y` to undelete the file.

## *UNDELETE* Options

`UNDELETE` features a number of switches you can use to gain more control over the recovery process (see Table 21.1 for a partial listing).

**Table 21.1. Some *UNDELETE* switches.**

| Use | To |
|---|---|
| `/LIST` | Displays a list of all files deleted from the current directory that are available for recovery. |
| `/ALL` | Undeletes all files without asking for confirmation. |
| `/PURGE` | Purges all files stored in Delete Sentry's directory. |

# Recovering Accidentally Formatted Disks

Unless you unconditionally format a disk (using `FORMAT`'s `/U` switch), DOS versions 5 and 6 only reset the disk's root directory and FAT. The data on the disk is left untouched, so it's possible to recover the entire disk using the `UNFORMAT` command.

How is this possible if there's no directory structure or FAT information? Well, the `FORMAT` command first saves a copy of this data in a file called MIRROR.FIL. `UNFORMAT` just uses this copy to reconstruct the disk.

> As with deleted files, you stand your best chance of recovering a disk if you run **UNFORMAT** as soon as possible. Adding new files and directories to the disk may overwrite the old data and make a complete recovery impossible.

> Don't bother looking for MIRROR.FIL after formatting a disk—the **FORMAT** command deletes it. **UNFORMAT**, however, being the smart fellow that it is, can find it by examining the disk's physical sectors.

# Recovering a Disk Using MIRROR.FIL

Recovering a disk that has had its unformat information saved is a breeze (provided you haven't written any other files to the disk, of course). For a disk in drive A:, enter the following command:

```
unformat a:
```

`UNFORMAT` prompts you to insert the disk and then displays a warning about the destructiveness of `UNFORMAT` if used improperly. To proceed with the recovery, press `y` (or press `n` to cancel). In a few minutes, your disk will be as good as new.

# Recovering a Disk Without MIRROR.FIL

If you need to recover a disk without MIRROR.FIL (a disk that was formatted unconditionally), it's possible, although it takes forever. You should wait until you won't be needing your machine for a while. If the disk is in drive A:, enter the following command:

```
unformat a:
```

You'll be prompted to insert the disk, and then you'll see a message cautioning you about the limitations of this method. To start the search phase (this is where UNFORMAT just looks for the disk's deleted subdirectories and files; nothing actually gets recovered), press y (or any other key to cancel).

At this point, you may as well go get some coffee, because DOS painstakingly searches every cluster on the disk for subdirectories. It then searches all the found subdirectories for files and displays the names of the files it finds.

When it's finally done, UNFORMAT warns you that it's about to write the changes to the disk and asks if you want to continue. Again, press y to proceed or anything else to bail out. If you continue, UNFORMAT starts restoring the subdirectories and files. If it can't recover an entire file, you'll see a message to that effect on-screen, and UNFORMAT will ask if you want to truncate (press t) or delete (press d) the file.

# Recovering a Corrupted Partition Table

You should suspect a corrupted partition table if you see the following message when you try to access your hard drive:

```
Invalid drive specification
```

Scary! However, if you read Chapter 19, "An Ounce of Prevention: How to Avoid Trouble," you saw how to save a copy of the partition table to a floppy disk (in a file called PARTNSAV.FIL). To restore the partition table, enter the following command:

```
unformat /partn
```

UNFORMAT prompts you to insert the disk and enter the appropriate drive letter. When you've done this, UNFORMAT attempts to restore the partition table.

# Deleting Stubborn Files

Some files seem to cling to life with an admirable tenacity. You can DEL and ERASE till you're blue in the face, and still they hang on. Before getting your shotgun, here are two things to check:

✦ The file might have its read-only attribute set, which means the file can't be deleted or even modified. Try running the `ATTRIB` command with the `-R` parameter:

```
attrib -r cantkill.me
```

Try deleting the file now.

> Most read-only files are read-only for a good reason. Be sure none of your programs (or DOS) need the file before you try deleting it.

✦ If the file is still scoffing at your efforts, it may have the blank ASCII 255 character at the end of its name—as explained in Chapter 20, "Simple System Security (Or, It's Not Paranoia When Everyone's Out to Get You)." If the file is called (or appears to be called), say, TOUGH.TXT, try the following command:

```
del tough*.txt
```

> The TOUGH*.TXT file spec also applies to files named TOUGHER.TXT and TOUGHIE.TXT. Be sure there are no files with names like these before running this **DEL** command.

# Recovering a File That Has Bad Sectors

If a hard disk sector poops out in the middle of a file, DOS refuses to read the file and a message like this appears on-screen:

```
Sector not found error reading drive C
Abort, Retry, Ignore, Fail?
```

The first thing you should do when this happens is to try finishing the operation by pressing `r` (for retry) a few times. Every now and then you get lucky and DOS kicks in after 5 or 6 tries.

Your next task is to try and salvage as much of the file as you can. You have two choices:

- Restore a backed up copy of the file. For now, restore the file to a different name.
- Use the `COPY` command to copy the file to a different name. You will, of course, see the same error, but this time press `i` (for Ignore). The new copy contains all the data before and after the bad sector and a bunch of garbage characters at the location of the defect. Use the original application to get rid of this junk and try to restore the original data.

> If the file is an executable file, you may as well just junk it because you have no way of fixing it. You should be able to restore the file from one of the original program disks.

With the file salvaged, you now need to tell DOS to mark the cluster containing the sector as bad in the FAT (so DOS knows not to use it for any other file). To do this, you need to use the infamous `RECOVER` command. `RECOVER` is one of those commands that proves the old adage that a little knowledge is a dangerous thing. Most people see the name and figure that it'll do all kinds of miraculous things. So they just type `recover` and are dismayed (to say the least!) when their entire hard drive is turned into gibberish. Don't let this happen to you—always, always, *always*, use `RECOVER` with a filename.

> You want to know how dangerous **RECOVER** is? There are utilities packages (such as the Norton Utilities) that have programs to help you recover from **RECOVER**!

If the file that contains the bad sector is called HURTIN.DOC, use the following command to mark the defective cluster:

```
recover hurtin.doc
```

DOS prompts you to press any key to start the recovery process (press Ctrl+C if you want to bail out).

**Guru Tools**

> Instead of using **RECOVER**, here's a better idea: get yourself a copy of the Norton Utilities and run the Norton Disk Doctor program. It not only marks the bad clusters, it also salvages any affected files at the same time.

# Problems with EMM386

DOS's 386 memory manager (EMM386.EXE) is great for freeing up gobs of conventional memory real estate (see Chapter 15, "Memory Management Made Easy," for the scoop on memory machinations), but it's a complex beast that has been known to cause a problem or two.

## DOS Won't Load EMM386

If DOS refuses to load EMM386, it's usually for one of two reasons:

- If DOS reports **EMM386 not installed—other expanded memory manager present**, it means that CONFIG.SYS is first loading a different memory manager (such as QEMM or 386MAX). EMM386 jealously wants your system all to itself, so it refuses to run and you have to choose between them.
- If DOS reports **EMM386 not installed—XMS manager not present**, it means that you either forgot to include HIMEM.SYS in CONFIG.SYS or you're not loading HIMEM *before* EMM386.

## Your Computer Locks Up When You Load a TSR or Device Driver into Upper Memory

The upper memory area (the area between 640K and 1M) was originally reserved for ROM or video adapter RAM. EMM386 works by scooping out empty pockets (called upper memory blocks, or UMBs) of upper memory not used by this code. If your PC hangs when you load something high, it means that EMM386 has tried to load the TSR or driver into a reserved area.

If you have DOS 6, use the Microsoft Diagnostics utility (MSD) to see where the ROM and adapter RAM are stored. Then use EMM386's `X=` parameter to exclude these areas from the UMBs. For example, to exclude the area from C000 to CBFF, use the following EMM386 command in CONFIG.SYS:

```
DEVICE=C:\DOS\EMM386.EXE X=C000-CBFF
```

If you're using DOS 5, try excluding the area from C000 to DFFF. If this fixes the problem, try reducing the upper end of this area to provide your system with more UMBs. (I'd try DBFF, then D7FF, D3FF, CFFF, and finally CBFF).

## EMM386 Doesn't Create Enough UMBs

This is the opposite problem from the last one. If you can't load all your device drivers and TSRs into upper memory, you have four choices:

- You may simply be out of luck. The upper memory area is only so big, and there's only a finite amount of stuff you can cram in there.
- Upgrade to DOS 6. The latest version of EMM386 is much better at digging up space for UMBs than the DOS 5 version.
- If none of your programs require expanded memory, you can get back another 64K in the upper memory area by using EMM386's `NOEMS` parameter. The 64K is the amount of space that EMM386 would otherwise reserve for the expanded memory page frame.
- Use EMM386's `I=` parameter to force it to use sections of upper memory as UMBs. Again, MSD can show you some prospective areas. Here are some potential areas to consider: B000-B7FF (if you have VGA and a color monitor), C000-C5FF, and E000-EFFF (if your computer isn't an IBM PS/2).

Dunce

> Including some of these areas may cause your system to lock up. If you don't have DOS 6, be sure you have a bootable disk nearby so you can regain control of your machine (see Chapter 18, "The Guru's Survival Kit," for bootable disk basics).

## A Program Reports That EMM386 Has an "Invalid Path"

Some programs (such as Windows) expect EMM386.EXE to be in a specific place. They can usually find it in the DOS directory, but sometimes you just have to spell things out explicitly. You do this with EMM386's `/Y` parameter, like so:

```
DEVICE=EMM386.EXE /Y=C:\DOS\EMM386.EXE
```

# DOS Doesn't Recognize a New Drive

If you add a new drive to your system (for example, if you upgrade an old drive or add a tape drive), DOS may not recognize it, or it may format the drive's disks improperly. One solution is to use the `DRIVPARM` command to configure the drive properly.

`DRIVPARM` goes in your CONFIG.SYS file and it has the following general form:

```
DRIVPARM=/D:n [switches]
```

Table 21.2 lists some of the available switches for DRIVPARM.

**Table 21.2. Some switches for the *DRIVPARM* command.**

| *Switch* | *Description* | |
|---|---|---|
| `/D:`*n* | Specifies the physical drive number (*n*) of the physical floppy drive. The first drive (drive A:) is 0, the second (usually drive B:) is 1, and so on. | |
| `/F:`*n* | Specifies the type of disk drive. *n* can take the following values: | |
| | 0 | 160K/180K or 320K/360K, 5.25-inch |
| | 1 | 1.2M, 5.25-inch |

*continues*

**Table 21.2. continued**

| *Switch* | *Description* | |
|---|---|---|
| | 2 | 720K, 3.5-inch |
| | 3 | 8-inch single-density |
| | 4 | 8-inch double-density |
| | 5 | Hard disk |
| | 6 | Tape drive |
| | 7 | 1.44M, 3.5-inch |
| | 8 | Read/write optical disk |
| | 9 | 2.88M, 3.5-inch |
| `/I` | Specifies that the drive is an electronically compatible 3.5-inch drive. | |

So, for example, if DOS formats disks in your 1.44M drive B: as 720K, include the following command in CONFIG.SYS:

```
DRIVPARM=/D:2 /F:7
```

If this still doesn't work, try adding the `/I` switch, as well.

**Guru Tip**

> If **DRIVPARM** won't do the job, you might want to give DRIVER.SYS a try. See Chapter 12, "CONFIG.SYS: What Every Guru Should Know," for details.

# Guru Review

This chapter went through a few common DOS problems and showed you how to get back up and running. Here's what happened:

- When you delete a file, DOS preserves most of the file's information, thus making it possible for you to undelete the file (and for some utilities makers to become rich).

- You can use `UNDELETE` with three different methods: DOS directory (use the `/DOS` switch), deletion tracking (`/DT`), and Delete Sentry (this is DOS 6's default method).
- Formatting a disk is similar to deleting a file in that DOS doesn't touch the file data. This makes it possible to recover an accidentally formatted disk.
- `UNFORMAT` stands a better (and faster) chance of recovering a disk if the MIRROR.FIL file exists. For this reason, you should always format your disks using either the safe or quick formats (unless the disk has bad sectors, in which case an unconditional format is called for).
- Use `UNFORMAT` with the `/PARTN` switch to rebuild a corrupted partition table.
- If you're having trouble deleting a file, look for the read-only attribute or an ASCII 255 character.
- The `RECOVER` command can mark bad sectors, but it should be used with extreme caution. Always include a file spec when using this command.
- You can use EMM386's `X=` and `I=` parameters to exclude and include, respectively, sections of the upper memory area for use as UMBs.
- Use `DRIVPARM` (or DRIVER.SYS) if DOS doesn't properly recognize a new disk or tape drive.

# Huh? Those Mysterious DOS Error Messages

22

CHAPTER

**Guru Stuff In This Chapter ➤**

- *An alphabetical listing of 50, count 'em, 50 DOS error messages*
- *What DOS is really trying to tell you*
- *What you should do about it*

DOS' error messages—from the notorious `Abort, Retry, Fail?` to `Write protect error writing drive A`—have been the bane of users from day one. The common complaint heard throughout the land is that, well, they're just so darned vague! I mean, c'mon, `Bad command or file name`? Which is it?

The problem, of course, is that DOS (or even the hardware it runs on) just isn't smart enough to know exactly what just blew up its face. Heck, it started life as a simple program loader; it didn't ask for all this responsibility. This chapter takes you through the most common error messages and explains what they mean and what you should do next.

# Abort, Retry, Fail?

Ah yes, the big Kahuna, the top dog, the head honcho of DOS error messages (a.k.a., `Abort, Retry, Ignore, Fail?` and, in earlier versions, `Abort, Retry, Ignore?`). Technically speaking, this isn't an error, but a symptom of something else that's gone askew. For example, if you attempt to access a floppy drive with no disk in it, the following messages appears on-screen:

```
Not ready reading drive A
Abort, Retry, Fail?
```

DOS has tried its level best to do as you asked, but it just couldn't pull it off, and now it needs to know what you want to do next. Here's a summary of your options:

| | |
|---|---|
| Abort | Select this option (by pressing `a`) to bail out of the operation altogether. Don't Abort if the error appears within an application, because DOS aborts not only the operation, but the program as well! Fail is usually the better choice. |
| Retry | Press `r` to have DOS try again. Unless you see what the problem is right away (like the lack of a disk in a disk drive), retry the operation a few times to try and get DOS unstuck. |
| Ignore | Heading down the Ignore path (by pressing `i`) tells DOS not to bother you with its incessant complaining and just get the job done. The only problem is that DOS may incorporate whatever errors it found in the results of the operation, which means some of your data may get |

trashed. There are times when Ignore is necessary, though. See my explanation of the RECOVER command in Chapter 21, "Common DOS Problems (and How To Fix 'Em)."

Fail — Fail is the saddest of the options, but it's probably the one you'll use the most. DOS just shuts down the current operation and returns to whatever program it originated from.

**Guru Tip**

> If you're sick of this error message, there's a trick you can use that enables you to avoid it altogether. Just include the following line in your CONFIG.SYS file:
>
> ```
> SHELL=C:\DOS\COMMAND.COM C:\DOS /P /F
> ```
>
> The undocumented /F switch tells DOS to always default to Fail.

# Access denied

This one always makes me feel like some little kid: "Sorry, Sonny, unless you have a note from your mother, I'm going to have deny you access to that file."

DOS denies you access to a file if its read-only attribute is set. This means you can't delete it, rename it, overwrite it with another file, or make changes to it. Take a look at the file (which is about the only thing you can do to a read-only file) to see why it has been protected. If you still want to work with it, use the ATTRIB command's -R parameter to remove the read-only attribute.

# Allocation error, size adjusted

As explained oh so carefully in Chapter 18, "The Guru's Survival Kit," there's a direct correspondence between the size of a file as listed in the directory table and the number of clusters allocated to it in the FAT. This error means that CHKDSK has detected a discrepancy between the size of the file and the cluster allocation. Run CHKDSK /F to fix the problem and then do one of two things:

- Restore the file from a backed-up copy.
- Repair the file. Depending on the situation, CHKDSK either adds garbage to the end of the file or truncates some usable data. In the former case, you just need to edit out the junk. For the latter, save any lost allocation units, because they may contain the truncated bits. Then use the original application to try and salvage what you need from the CHK files that CHKDSK creates.

> If the error occurs with an executable file (EXE or COM), just delete it and reinstall the program. Running a truncated executable can do untold damage to your system.

# ANSI.SYS must be installed to perform requested function

You'll see this error if you try to use the MODE command to change the number of screen lines that DOS displays (as explained in Chapter 17, "The Fun Stuff II: Advanced DOS Techniques"). You need to include the following command in CONFIG.SYS:

```
DEVICE=C:\DOS\ANSI.SYS
```

# Bad command or file name

I've seen this error more times than I've had hot dinners. It just means that you're trying to run a command that DOS either doesn't recognize or can't find. If you made a typing error, try the command again (slowly, this time!). If the command looks okay, you may need to add the program's directory to the PATH statement so DOS can find it.

If you have a long PATH, it can be a real pain to type the whole thing out just to add a directory. Instead, here's a batch file called ADD2PATH.BAT that enables you to easily tack on a directory to your current PATH:

```
@ECHO OFF
PATH > C:\BATCH\OLDPATH.BAT
SET PATH=%PATH%;%1
PATH
```

To add, say, the directory C:\GRUMPY to your PATH, enter the following command:

```
add2path c:\grumpy
```

ADD2PATH works by first saving your old PATH to a file called OLDPATH.BAT in your BATCH directory. (Use whatever directory you normally store your batch files in.) It then appends the directory to PATH and finishes by showing you the new PATH. To restore your old PATH, just run the OLDPATH batch file.

> This batch file only works properly if your **PATH** isn't near the 127-character limit. If it is, use **SUBST** to try and shorten it, as explained in Chapter 16, "The Fun Stuff: Advanced DOS Commands."

# Bad or missing command interpreter

This error means that DOS can't find COMMAND.COM and misses it terribly. You need to place a bootable disk in drive A: and reboot (see Chapter 18 for the scoop on creating a bootable disk). With control restored, you need to add the following line to your CONFIG.SYS file:

```
SHELL=C:\DOS\COMMAND.COM C:\DOS /P
```

I'm assuming here that COMMAND.COM is in your DOS directory. If it's not, change the SHELL command accordingly. If this still doesn't solve the problem, COMMAND.COM may have been accidentally deleted, and you need to copy it from your original DOS disks.

# Bad or missing file name

If you add a device driver to CONFIG.SYS and DOS can't find the file, you'll see this message during startup. Check the appropriate CONFIG.SYS line for three things:

- That you spelled out the complete pathname for the file
- That there are no typing errors
- That the file really does exist where you said it does

# Cannot CHKDSK a network drive

`CHKDSK` is for local drives only. Trying to run it on a drive assigned to a network is a definite no-no, and you'll get this message. Also, if you try to check a virtual drive created with `SUBST` or `ASSIGN`, you'll see this message:

```
Cannot CHKDSK a SUBSTed or ASSIGNed drive
```

# Current drive is no longer valid

This one's not as scary as it sounds. It shows up when you select Fail after trying to access a drive with no disk. It means that DOS is lost in some wilderness of its own creation and needs you to point the way home. Just log on to a valid drive (such as C:) to regain control.

# Data error reading drive x

You'll see this error anytime DOS encounters a bad sector in a file on drive `x` (A:, B:, C:, or whatever). I covered this pain in the you-know-what in Chapter 21, "Common DOS Problems (and How To Fix 'Em)."

# Disk boot failure

Yikes! This is an ugly one. It means that the files normally loaded by the bootstrap programs (IO.SYS and MSDOS.SYS) are either missing or corrupted. Try soft booting (pressing Ctrl+Alt+Delete) a couple of times. If the problem persists, you need to follow these steps:

1. Dig out your DOS disks, insert Disk 1 in drive A:, and reboot.
2. When you see the `A>` prompt, type `sys c:` to send fresh copies of IO.SYS and MSDOS.SYS to the hard drive.
3. To be safe, also copy COMMAND.COM from the disk to your DOS directory.

# Duplicate file name or file not found

You tried to rename a file that doesn't exist or the new name is already being used by another file. *Bad* guru!

# File cannot be copied onto itself

Your source and destination files in a `COPY`, `XCOPY`, or `REPLACE` command are the same. This usually happens if you leave off the destination file spec.

# File not found

DOS either couldn't find the file you entered in a command, or you mistyped the file spec.

# General failure reading drive x

This error (and its better half, `General failure writing drive x`) means that DOS, after trying every trick it knows, just can't read anything on whatever disk is in drive x. This is DOS' way of shrugging its shoulders and saying, "Heck, I don't know what's wrong with it."

The disk may simply be unformatted, or, if it's an old disk, its magnetic coating may have just faded with age. If that's the case, you'll probably have to toss it.

**Guru Tools**

> All may not be lost if you have Norton Utilities or PC Tools. The DiskTools program (Norton) or Disk Fix (PC Tools) can sometimes recondition old disks.

# HMA not available; loading DOS low

This means that you included the line `DOS=HIGH` in your CONFIG.SYS file, but DOS won't load itself high because the high memory area (HMA) is not available. Bummer. The most likely cause is that you didn't load HIMEM.SYS at the beginning of CONFIG.SYS. Alternatively, you may be using an old XT-compatible computer that has no HMA.

# Insufficient disk space

This one's a no-brainer: you don't have enough space on whatever disk you were using to hold the file that DOS was trying to write. If it's a floppy disk, either delete some files or try a different disk. If it's your hard disk, either delete files or check out a hard disk compression program such as DOS 6's DoubleSpace (see Chapter 3, "Guru Hard Disk Management").

## Insufficient file handles

When a program barks out this message and refuses to run, it means you need to up the FILES parameter in your CONFIG.SYS file. Most considerate programs suggest an appropriate number. If not, try 30 or 40 to start.

## Insufficient memory

Ah, yes, the bane of computer users everywhere. Low memory has been a problem since the first PC shipped. Before you run out and spend your hard-earned money on extra memory chips, check out Chapter 15, "Memory Management Made Easy," for some free DOS stuff you can try.

## Insufficient memory to store macro

If you use lots of DOSKEY macros, it won't take long before you bump your head on DOSKEY's default buffer size of 512 bytes. A buffer of 1,024 bytes is probably a good size, although if you think you'll be defining a lot of macros, 2,048 bytes gives you all the room you need. To redefine the DOSKEY buffer with 1,024 bytes, enter the following command:

```
doskey /bufsize=1024 /reinstall
```

## Internal stack overflow

This is telling you that DOS' reserved stack space just isn't cutting it, and you need to increase it by using the STACKS system parameter. See Chapter 12, "CONFIG.SYS: What Every Guru Should Know," for the stack scoop.

## Invalid drive in search path

One of your PATH directories is messed up, either because you mistyped the sucker or because the directory doesn't exist.

# Invalid drive specification

You tried to access a drive that doesn't exist, you silly person! This can happen if you use a lot of SUBST commands (or, of course, if you pull a typing boner). Remember that you can remind yourself of the current SUBSTed drives by entering the SUBST command by itself.

# Invalid environment size specified

So, you took my advice back in Chapter 12 and decided to increase the size of your environment space. That's *very* guru of you. The problem is that you used a number that DOS didn't like. The valid values are between 160 and 32,768.

# Invalid file name or file not found

You usually see this message when you try to run the TYPE command with a file spec that includes wildcards. Tsk, tsk. If you like, you can create your own version of the TYPE command that will accept wildcards. Here's a DOSKEY macro that does the job:

```
doskey suprtype=for %f in ($*) do type %f
```

# Invalid media or Track 0 bad—disk unusable

This objection occurs when you try to format a disk in a capacity it can't handle, or if the disk is trashed (which is where it belongs).

**Guru Trivia**

Track 0 is the first track on a disk, and this is where DOS stores crucial disk information such as the boot record, file directory, and FAT. If this track is bad, the whole disk is shot.

# Invalid parameter

You entered an incorrect parameter in that last DOS command. Check your typing and be sure the parameter is valid for the command you're using.

# Invalid path

This one means that you entered an incorrect directory name in a DOS command. Be sure the directory exists and that you didn't mistype the pathname.

# Invalid path, not directory, or directory not empty

Don't you love it when DOS speak with forked tongue? This little ditty almost always shows up when you try to `RD` a directory that still has files or subdirectories. Clean out the directory and try again, or use DOS 6's new `DELTREE` command to blow that sucker right out of the water.

# Invalid switch—/s

The command you're trying to run doesn't accept the displayed switch (`s`). Check your typing or run the command with the `/?` switch to check the syntax.

# Memory allocation error

This one sounds more serious than it really is. It just means that some ill-conceived program has run amok and has stuck its nose into an area of memory where it doesn't belong. Just reboot your system and start again. If the problem persists, complain long and loud to the company that developed the software.

# No free file handles

See "*Insufficient file handles.*"

# No room for system on destination disk

You get this complaint when you try to run SYS to transfer the DOS system files (IO.SYS and MSDOS.SYS) to a floppy. It's a little misleading, though, because you can still get it even if you have acres of free space on the disk. The problem is that the system files have to be stored in a certain spot on the disk. If some other files have usurped that area, DOS shouts "No room!" Your best bet is to format the disk with the /S switch.

**Guru Trivia**

> The IO.SYS system file contains DOS' default device drivers (such as CON and PRN). It's always stored on the disk immediately after the last sector of the file directory. MSDOS.SYS is the *kernel* of DOS; it handles all function requests (such as reading and writing files) and sends device requests to IO.SYS. It's stored immediately after the last sector of IO.SYS.

# Non-System disk or disk error

You started or rebooted your system with a non-bootable disk in drive A:. Just remove the disk (or simply open the drive latch if it's a 5.25-inch drive) and press any key. See Chapter 18 for the details on creating a disk that is bootable.

# Not enough memory

See "*Insufficient memory.*"

# Not ready reading drive x:

Another `Abort, Retry, Fail` error. This missive occurs most often when you try to access a drive that has no disk (or the drive latch is not closed on a 5.25-inch drive). Insert a disk (or close the latch) and select Retry.

# Out of environment space

Your current environment space isn't large enough to handle all the junk you're trying to cram in there. Chapter 12 tells you everything you need to know to get yourself out of this one.

# Packed file corrupt

Sounds pretty nasty, doesn't it? Nah. It just means that the software you're trying to load isn't quite with the program (no pun intended—I think).

You see, in the pre-DOS 5 days, DOS usurped the first 64K of conventional memory for its own greedy purposes, so it set up a sort of Berlin Wall at the 64K mark that regular programs couldn't cross. However, the capability to load DOS into the HMA has opened up the first 64K to any and all comers. And, just like confused East Germans crossing over to the West for the first time, some programs just can't handle this new freedom and they generate this error. Thoughtfully, DOS includes a utility called `LOADFIX` to make everything okay. If a program named CONFUSED.EXE is causing the problem, start it like this:

```
loadfix confused
```

# Path not found

See "*Invalid path.*"

# Printer out of paper error writing device

This one doesn't take a genius to figure out. Your printer is out of paper, so load it up and select Retry.

# Program too big to fit in memory

See "*Insufficient memory*."

# Sector not found

Hmm. This lament is usually the first sign that a disk is heading south. You can Retry a few times to see if you can finish your operation or just choose Fail. Then copy whatever files are salvageable to a safe location, and reformat the disk with the `/U` parameter, which resets the sector layout and marks the disk's bad sectors. If `FORMAT` only reports a few bad sectors, you can probably still use the disk for nonessential files. If the disk is riddled with defects, toss it.

# SOURCE diskette bad or incompatible

DOS is reproaching you for `DISKCOPY`ing with disks of different formats, or the source disk is unformatted or just plain defective.

# TARGET diskette bad or incompatible

This is similar to the last message. In this case, though, it's the target disk that's causing DOS to choke.

# Unable to create directory

DOS lodges this protest under any of the following conditions:

- Another directory of the same name already exists.
- The name you're using has illegal characters.
- The current directory includes a file with the same name as the one you're trying to use for the new directory.
- The root directory is full.

# Unable to write BOOT

When you format a disk, DOS places a copy of the boot record in the first sector of the first track. If this track is defective, DOS can't write the boot record and the disk is useless. All you can do is throw it in the garbage and try another.

> The *boot record* consists of the bootstrap code (needed in case you ever make the disk bootable) and a table that holds key disk information such as the number of bytes per sector and the total number of sectors.

# Unrecognized command in CONFIG.SYS

One of your fingers slipped when you were entering a command in CONFIG.SYS. Edit the file to fix the offending characters.

# Write failure, diskette unusable

DOS is telling you that it can't do a thing with this disk (or that you should be buying higher quality disks).

# Write fault error writing drive x

DOS is trying to write a file to the disk in drive x, but it's a no go. First check to see if the disk is inserted properly. If it is, select Retry a few times to try to coax DOS into completing the operation. If nothing works, select Fail and trash the disk.

# Write protect error writing drive x

DOS is objecting to you trying to write some information on a write-protected disk. You'll need to remove the write-protection if you want to get anywhere with this one.

# Guru Review

This chapter gave you a quick tour of 50 of the most common DOS error messages. You learned not only what the darned things mean, but how to repair the damage and get on with your life.

APPENDIX

A

# 20 Tips and Tricks Every DOS Guru Should Know

DOS gurus know that the real way to win friends and influence people is to dazzle them with cool DOS tricks. As a public service, here are 20 of my favorite DOS tips and tricks, in no particular order.

## 1. Traveling from Dot to Dot

DOS uses the dot symbol (.) to represent the current directory, and the double-dot (..) to represent its parent directory. Here are a few tips that take advantage of this notation:

- Use `CD..` to jump quickly to the parent directory. Similarly, use `CD..\..` to jump up two directory levels.

- To move to a directory on the same level with the same parent, use `CD..\directory`. For example, if you're in C:\ANIMAL\MAMMAL\DOLPHIN and you want to switch to C:\ANIMAL\MAMMAL\BABOON, you can do it with this command:

```
cd..\baboon
```

- You can often use the dot or double dots in place of the `*.*` notation. For example, to copy all the files in the current directory to drive A:, you normally use the command COPY `*.* A:`. However, `COPY . A:` does the same thing.

# 2. A Quick Check Before Deleting

Here's the situation: you want to use wildcards to delete a bunch of files, but you're paranoid that you might blow away some files you want to keep (throwing out the baby with the bath water, so to speak).

Elsewhere in the book, I showed you some batch files that'll help, but here's a quick trick that also works. First, check the files you'll be deleting by running the `DIR` command on the file spec. If everything looks okay, type `del` and then press F3 to redisplay the file specification. Now you can press Enter knowing that your deletion will proceed safely.

# 3. Locating a Lost File

Have you lost a file somewhere on your hard disk? Don't go searching through all your directories. Just create the following DOSKEY macro that'll find a file anywhere in the current drive:

```
doskey ?=dir \$1 /s /b
```

This macro searches for the file you specify, starting from the root and working through every subdirectory (thanks to `DIR`'s `/S` switch). For example, to find a file called LOSTFILE.DOC, use the following command:

```
? lostfile.doc
```

# 4. Giving DOS a Break

Remember that pressing Ctrl+C or Ctrl+Break cancels any batch file or DOSKEY macro, and just about any command. To activate DOS' extended Ctrl+Break checking, include the following command in CONFIG.SYS:

```
BREAK=ON
```

# 5. NUL: Something for Nothing

NUL, the DOS device that maps to absolutely nothing, is useful in all kinds of situations:

- Redirecting output to NUL suppresses most DOS messages (error messages are the exception).
- To check to see if a directory exists, use a command such as the following:

  ```
  IF EXIST A:\BACKUP\NUL
  ```

  Since NUL "exists" in every directory (it gets mapped to a file handle normally used by CON), this condition is only true if A:\BACKUP exists.
- To check the integrity of files on a disk, use the following command:

  ```
  COPY A:\*.* NUL > NUL
  ```

  This just copies every file to NUL (nothing), but if DOS finds a bad sector, you'll get a `Data error reading drive A` message. You can include this command in a batch file or DOSKEY macro with an input parameter to check any disk.

# 6. Adding Control Characters in Edit

If you use `EDIT`, press Ctrl+P before trying to enter a control character (any of the first 32 ASCII characters). This tells `EDIT` not to treat the character literally.

# 7. Bypassing Startup Files in DOS 6

If you have DOS 6, you can bypass your CONFIG.SYS and AUTOEXEC.BAT files and so get a "clean boot" by pressing F5 (or by holding down Shift) when you see `Starting MS-DOS...` during bootup. To bypass individual commands, press F8.

# 8. The *PATH* Less Traveled

If your `PATH` is getting cramped by DOS' 127-character command restriction, use `SUBST` to give yourself more room. Just take each `PATH` directory and use `SUBST` to assign a drive letter to each one. Then re-enter the `PATH` command using just the drive letters. The command looks something like this:

```
path c:\;d:\;e:\;f:\;g:\;h:\
```

Remember to add a `LASTDRIVE` statement to CONFIG.SYS to give DOS more drive letters to work with.

# 9. Answer DOS Automatically

Many DOS commands prompt you for input or confirmation. You can bypass these annoying prompts with a couple of simple tricks:

- If DOS just requires a single keystroke, you can use `ECHO` to pipe the appropriate key. For example, to automatically answer Yes when you try to `DEL *.*`, use the following pipe command:

  ```
  ECHO Y ¦ DEL *.*
  ```

  To pipe the Enter key, use `ECHO.` (`ECHO` followed by a period).

- To send multiple characters, create a text file that includes only those characters and use input redirection. For example, you can avoid the three

FORMAT prompts by including Enter, Enter, N, and Enter in a text file (called, say, INENTER.TXT) and using the following command:

```
format b: < inenter.txt
```

# 10. Avoid *FORMAT's* Incessant Prompts

A better way to avoid FORMAT's prompts (provided you don't want to perform a Quick Format), is to use the undocumented /AUTOTEST switch. This switch tells DOS that the disk is already in the drive (be sure this is true!), that you don't want to add a volume label, and that you don't want to format another. The only problem is that you can't use /AUTOTEST with the /Q switch.

# 11. How to Fail All the Time

To automatically default to Fail in an Abort, Retry, Fail error message, use the SHELL command's undocumented /F switch:

```
SHELL=C:\DOS\COMMAND.COM C:\DOS /P /F
```

# 12. Adding to Your *PATH*

One of DOS' biggest pains is having to retype your entire PATH just to add another directory (the longer the PATH, the bigger the pain). Forget that. Instead, here's a batch file called ADD2PATH.BAT that lets you easily tack on a directory to your current PATH:

```
@ECHO OFF
PATH > C:\BATCH\OLDPATH.BAT
SET PATH=%PATH%;%1
PATH
```

To add, say, the directory C:\GRUMPY to your PATH, enter the following command:

```
add2path c:\grumpy
```

# 13. Protect Files and Directories with Alt+255

If you have files or directories that you don't want any snoops to view or delete, one easy way to protect them is to add Alt+255 to the end of their names. They look normal enough in a DIR listing, but they can't be accessed without adding the special character.

# 14. Installing on Drive B:

Some incredibly dumb installation programs refuse to install on any drive other than A:. This is bad news if you have 3.5-inch disks and your 3.5-inch drive is drive B:. To get around this aggravation, use the following SUBST command to fool the program into thinking it's dealing with drive A:.

```
subst a: b:\
```

# 15. Automatic *DIR* Switches

Starting with DOS 5, the DIR command was beefed up with all kinds of great new switches. However, it's a hassle trying to remember the appropriate letters and then typing them in. Pass. Instead, use the DIRCMD environment variable to preset your DIR switches. For example, suppose you always want DIR to display directories first, sort everything in alphabetical order by filename, and pause after each screenful. You can accomplish all this by adding the following line to your AUTOEXEC.BAT file:

```
SET DIRCMD=/OGN /P
```

# 16. Updating a File's Date and Time Stamp

Use the following variation of the `COPY` command to update a file's date and time stamp to the current date and time:

```
COPY filename +,, /B
```

# 17. The Hot Rod Keyboard

Give your keyboard a massive speed boost by including the following line in your CONFIG.SYS file:

```
MODE CON RATE=32 DELAY=1
```

This sets your keyboard's repeat rate to its fastest speed and also minimizes the normal delay you get when you press and hold down a key (such as a cursor key).

# 18. Lines, Lines, and More Lines

If you have an EGA or VGA monitor and DOS' normal 25-line screen just doesn't cut it anymore, enter the following command to bump yourself up to a spacious 43-line screen:

```
mode con lines=43
```

VGA owners get an extra bonus: or they can use the `MODE` command to double their screen lines to 50.

# 19. A Macro for Macro Mavens

If you love DOSKEY macros as much as I do, you should store them in a macro library (a batch file that just runs the appropriate DOSKEY commands to define the macros). You'll probably need to edit your macro library quite often to remove macros you never use and add new ones. To make this chore easier, here's a macro that loads the macro library into EDIT and runs the batch file when you're done:

```
doskey editlib=edit c:\batch\macros.bat $t macros
```

# 20. Batch File Subroutines

Here's a bonus tip that wasn't covered in the book. You can use environment variables to easily set up batch file subroutines. (A *subroutine*, in case you don't know, is a collection of commands that a program needs to execute several times. Instead of cluttering the program with multiple instances of the code, you just "call" the subroutine each time you need it.) Here's the general format:

```
@ECHO OFF
.               [Main program commands]
.
SET RETURN=MAIN1
GOTO SUBROUTINE
:MAIN1
.
.               [More main program commands]
.
SET RETURN=MAIN2
GOTO SUBROUTINE
:MAIN2
.
.               [etc.]

:SUBROUTINE
.
.               [Subroutine commands]
.
GOTO %RETURN%
```

Whenever the program needs to run the subroutine code, the RETURN environment variable is set to a label name (first MAIN1, then MAIN2, and so on). Then a GOTO jumps to the :SUBROUTINE label, the subroutine commands are executed, and another GOTO sends control back to the label given by %RETURN%.

APPENDIX B

# Glossary of Guru Words

DOS has its own, often arcane, terminology. As a DOS guru, you need to know what these terms mean so you can show off to your friends and impress the heck out of your colleagues.

**Address space**—The total memory area that can be addressed by a microprocessor. It's equal to 2 to the power of the number of address lines contained in the microprocessor.

**Alignment hole**—The hole on the *central hub* of a 3.5-inch disk that the drive's spindle uses to align the disk properly.

**ANSI.SYS**—DOS file that enables you to customize your screen and keyboard by using special codes within the `PROMPT` or `ECHO` command.

**ASCII**—The acronym for American Standard Code for Information Interchange. A common numeric code for expressing letters, numbers, and other symbols. See also *extended ASCII character set*.

**Attributes**—The settings (archive, directory, hidden, read-only, and system) that indicate the status of a file.

**AUTOEXEC.BAT**—A text file containing commands run by DOS each time you turn on your computer.

**Batch file**—A special text file that performs a number of instructions with a single command.

**BIOS**—Your computer's Basic Input-Output System. It's a collection of programs hard-wired into *read-only memory* that handles all the interactions between your computer and its peripheral hardware.

**Boot**—The process that occurs when you start your computer. The computer performs several internal checks and then DOS loads itself into memory. Functions within the AUTOEXEC.BAT and CONFIG.SYS files are run at this time. See also *boot sector* and *clean boot*.

**Boot record**—The area on a floppy disk that contains the *bootstrap code* and a table of the disk's characteristics (bytes per sector, number of sectors, and so on). See also *boot sector*.

**Boot sector**—The sector on a disk that contains the *boot record*.

**Bootstrap code**—The program that loads DOS (specifically, IO.SYS and MSDOS.SYS) into memory during system startup.

**Buffers**—See *disk buffers*.

**Byte**—The equivalent of a single character of information.

**Central hub**—The hole in a floppy disk that the disk drive's spindle uses to grab and turn the disk.

**Child directory**—The subdirectory one level below the current directory. See also *parent directory*.

**Clean boot**—A startup where no device drivers or TSRs are loaded into memory. With DOS 6, you can get a clean boot by pressing F5 or holding down Shift when you see the `Starting MS-DOS...` message.

**Cluster**—The minimum amount of storage space that DOS devotes to a file, usually equal to one or more *sectors*. The size of a cluster depends on the size and type of the disk. Most hard disks use 2,048-byte clusters.

**Cluster chain**—A collection of clusters that make up a file.

**Command aliasing**—Replacing a DOS command with a DOSKEY macro of the same name.

**COMMAND.COM**—The DOS program that interprets everything you type at the prompt.

**Compression ratio**—The ratio of the size of a compressed file to its uncompressed size. For example, a file that is 5,000 bytes compressed and 10,000 bytes uncompressed has a compression ration of 2 to 1. You can check out the compression ratio of any file or group of files by using `DIR` with the `/C` switch. See also *disk compression*.

**Concatenate**—To combine two or more files into a single file. You can use the `COPY` command and the plus sign (+) to concatenate text files.

**CONFIG.SYS**—The text file used by DOS to set your system configuration each time you start your computer.

**Control characters**—The first 32 characters in the ASCII character set (see Appendix C). They're used to control hardware such as printers, modems, and the like.

**Conventional memory**—The first 640K of memory that DOS uses to run programs.

**Cross-linked files**—Files that have FAT entries that point to the same cluster.

**Defragment**—To rearrange files on your hard disk so they occupy contiguous clusters and speed up disk access. DOS 6's `DEFRAG` command will do this for you. See also *file fragmentation*.

**Delay**—When you press and hold down a key, the amount of time it takes before the second character appears. See also *repeat rate*.

**Delete Sentry**—New with DOS 6, this is the highest level of deletion protection. DOS creates a hidden directory called SENTRY that it uses to store copies of deleted files. See also *deletion tracking*.

**Deletion tracking**—A method available in DOS 5 and 6 where, each time you delete a file, DOS keeps a record of the file's name and cluster locations. The UNDELETE program can use this information to recover the file. See also *Delete Sentry*.

**Device driver**—A small program that controls the way a device (such as a mouse) works with your system.

**Directory**—A hard disk organizational structure that contains a number of related files. This is equivalent to a room in a house.

**Disk buffers**—Small chunks of memory set aside by DOS to hold recently used data or program code. The number of disk buffers is controlled by the `BUFFERS` system parameter.

**Disk compression**—To reduce the size of a file by replacing redundant characters with smaller tokens. DOS 6's DoubleSpace utility can reduce the size of your files by an average of 2 to 1, thus effectively doubling your hard disk space. See also *compression ratio*.

**DOS prompt**—Your link to DOS. The prompt is DOS' way of saying "What is your next command?"

**EDLIN**—A line-oriented text editor available in all versions of DOS except 6.0.

**Environment**—A small memory buffer that stores *environment variables* used by DOS, batch files, and some programs.

**Environment variable**—String values held in memory that control certain aspects of DOS and other programs. Examples of DOS environment variables are `PATH`, `PROMPT`, and `DIRCMD`.

**Exit code**—A number reported by some commands that tells DOS how the operation went (if it was completed successfully or, if it wasn't, what went wrong). You can use ERRORLEVEL conditions in batch files to check exit codes.

**Expanded memory**—Memory, usually in the form of an add-on circuit board, outside of the normal memory installed on your computer's main circuit board. See also *extended memory*.

**Extended ASCII character set**—A set of special characters not found on your keyboard. Many of these characters are useful for creating boxes and displaying foreign symbols. See also *ASCII*.

**Extended memory**—Memory, in the form of extra chips on your computer's main circuit board, over and above one megabyte. See also *expanded memory*.

**External commands**—DOS commands such as `FORMAT`, `UNDELETE`, and `BACKUP` that exist as files separate from COMMAND.COM. See also *internal commands*.

**FAT**—See *file allocation table*.

**File**—An organized unit of information inside your computer. Files can be either programs (such as a word processor) or data (information used by you or by a program).

**File allocation table**—A table on a disk that keeps track of which *clusters* on the disk have been allocated to which files.

**File directory**—A table that DOS uses to keep track of each file on a disk. Each entry contains, among other things, the file's name and extension, the date and time it was last modified, its size, and its starting *cluster* number.

**File fragmentation**—The allocation of files in noncontiguous *clusters*. Fragmentation slows down hard disk performance because DOS must search in several locations for each piece of a file. If you have DOS 6, you can use the `DEFRAG` command to *defragment* your hard disk. See also *defragment*.

**Floppy disk**—A portable storage medium that consists of a flexible disk protected by a plastic case. Floppy disks are available in a variety of sizes and capacities.

**Formatting**—The process of preparing a disk so DOS can use it to store information.

**Gigabyte (G)**—1,024M or 1,073,741,824 bytes.

**Head slot**—The exposed area on a floppy disk's case where the *read/write heads* do their reading and writing. On a 5.25-inch disk, the head slot is an oval at the bottom of the disk; on a 3.5-inch disk, the head slot is covered by the *metal shutter*. The drive's spindle turns the disk so that the appropriate area is visible through this head slot.

**High-density indicator hole**—An extra hole on a 3.5-inch disk that tells you the disk is high-density.

**High memory area (HMA)**—A 64K segment of memory available on all 286 or better computers with at least one megabyte of memory. If you have at least DOS 5, you can load most of DOS into this area.

**Index hole**—A small hole in a 5.25-inch floppy disk that the disk drive uses to position the disk at the "beginning" (where DOS stores the disk's *FAT*).

**Internal commands**—DOS commands such as `COPY`, `DIR`, and `DEL` built into COMMAND.COM. See also *external commands*.

**Kilobyte (K)**—1,024 bytes.

**Label**—A line in a batch file used as a destination for a `GOTO` command.

**Lost cluster**—A FAT entry that isn't linked to any entry in the *file directory*.

**Master boot record**—The section of a hard disk that contains the code that reads the *partition table* during startup in order to locate the disk's *boot sector*.

**Megabyte (M)**—1,024K or 1,048,576 bytes.

**Memory manager**—A software program that controls the use of expanded or extended memory.

**Memory-resident program**—A program that stays in memory once it is loaded and works "behind the scenes." The program normally responds only to a specific event (such as the deletion of a file) or a key combination. See also *terminate-and-stay-resident*.

**Metal shutter**—The slidable metal door that protects the *head slot* on a 3.5-inch disk. The drive opens this shutter automatically whenever the disk is accessed.

**Metastrings**—Codes used to control the way the `PROMPT` command works.

**Parameter**—A variable element in a command that controls the way the command works.

**Parent directory**—The directory one level above the current directory. See also *child directory*.

**Partition table**—A section of a hard disk that contains information on things like the number of sectors in the disk and the location of the *boot sector*.

**Pathname**—A list of names of the parents and grandparents of the current directory.

**Peripheral**—A device, such as a modem or printer, that is separate from the main computer.

**Random access memory (RAM)**—The memory in your computer that DOS uses to run your programs.

**Read-only memory (ROM)**—Memory that retains its data when you turn off your computer. Your system's ROM is located in the *upper memory area*, and it contains, usually, the *BIOS* programs (especially those needed during booting).

**Read/write head**—The device inside a disk drive that stores and retrieves information on the disk as it travels across the surface of a disk.

**Redirection**—Rerouting data to or from devices other than standard input (usually the keyboard) or standard output (usually the screen).

**Repeat rate**—The rate at which characters appear when you press and hold down a key. See also *delay*.

**Replaceable parameters**—The symbols `%1` through `%9` that you can use in batch files (or `$1` through `$9` in DOSKEY macros) as placeholders for parameters entered as you run a batch file.

**ROM**—See *read-only memory*.

**Root directory**—The primary directory on any formatted disk. The root directory always has a physical limitation on the number of files it can contain.

**Sector**—A disk storage location created by formatting the disk. Most sectors hold 512 bytes. See also *cluster*.

**Slack**—For a small file (or part of a large one), the difference between the file's size and the disk's *cluster* size.

**Spindle**—A part inside a disk drive that grabs and turns a floppy disk.

**Switch**—Characters added to a DOS command to modify the way the command works. A switch usually consists of a forward slash (`/`) followed by one or more letters or numbers.

**System files**—Operating system files used by DOS to interpret your commands and to work with your system's hardware. The three DOS system files are IO.SYS, MSDOS.SYS, and COMMAND.COM.

**System parameters**—Variables that configure DOS stuff such as the command processor and how it interacts with your programs. You use the CONFIG.SYS file to add or change the system parameters.

**Terminate-and-stay-resident (TSR)**—A program that loads itself into memory and remains available if you or one of your programs needs to use it. Examples are mouse drivers, network software, and productivity enhancers such as Borland's SideKick.

**Upper memory**—The area between the first 640K (conventional memory) and one megabyte. If you have DOS 5 or 6, you can use the EMM386 utility to load TSRs and device drivers into this area.

**Upper memory block (UMB)**—An unused portion of *upper memory*. 80386 and higher computers with special software can take advantage of UMBs by moving *TSRs* and *device drivers* out of *conventional memory* and into the UMB areas.

**Virtual drive**—A drive that doesn't exist physically, but can be used in DOS commands. You create virtual drives using the DRIVER.SYS device driver or the `SUBST` command.

**Write-protect**—To modify a disk physically so that no information can be written to or erased from a floppy disk. See *write-protect notch* and *write-protect tab*.

**Write-protect notch**—A small cutout on the side of a 5.25-inch disk that controls the *write-protect* status of the disk. If the notch is covered with tape (or if, in some cases, it's not there at all), the disk is write-protected. See also *write-protect*.

**Write-protect tab**—A slidable tab on a 3.5-inch disk that controls the *write-protect* status of the disk. If you slide the tab towards the edge of the disk, the disk is write-protected. See also *write-protect*.

APPENDIX C

# Guru ASCII Chart

| *Dec* $X_{10}$ | *Hex* $X_{16}$ | *Binary* $X_2$ | *ASCII Character* |
|---|---|---|---|
| 000 | 00 | 0000 0000 | null |
| 001 | 01 | 0000 0001 | ☺ |
| 002 | 02 | 0000 0010 | ☻ |
| 003 | 03 | 0000 0011 | ♥ |
| 004 | 04 | 0000 0100 | ◆ |
| 005 | 05 | 0000 0101 | ♣ |
| 006 | 06 | 0000 0110 | ♠ |
| 007 | 07 | 0000 0111 | ● |
| 008 | 08 | 0000 1000 | ◘ |
| 009 | 09 | 0000 1001 | ○ |
| 010 | 0A | 0000 1010 | ◙ |
| 011 | 0B | 0000 1011 | ♂ |
| 012 | 0C | 0000 1100 | ♀ |
| 013 | 0D | 0000 1101 | ♪ |
| 014 | 0E | 0000 1110 | ♫ |
| 015 | 0F | 0000 1111 | ☼ |
| 016 | 10 | 0001 0000 | ► |

| Dec $X_{10}$ | Hex $X_{16}$ | Binary $X_2$ | ASCII Character |
|---|---|---|---|
| 017 | 11 | 0001 0001 | ◄ |
| 018 | 12 | 0001 0010 | ↕ |
| 019 | 13 | 0001 0011 | !! |
| 020 | 14 | 0001 0100 | ¶ |
| 021 | 15 | 0001 0101 | § |
| 022 | 16 | 0001 0110 | – |
| 023 | 17 | 0001 0111 | ↨ |
| 024 | 18 | 0001 1000 | ↑ |
| 025 | 19 | 0001 1001 | ↓ |
| 026 | 1A | 0001 1010 | → |
| 027 | 1B | 0001 1011 | ← |
| 028 | 1C | 0001 1100 | FS |
| 029 | 1D | 0001 1101 | GS |
| 030 | 1E | 0001 1110 | RS |
| 031 | 1F | 0001 1111 | US |
| 032 | 20 | 0010 0000 | SP |
| 033 | 21 | 0010 0001 | ! |
| 034 | 22 | 0010 0010 | " |
| 035 | 23 | 0010 0011 | # |
| 036 | 24 | 0010 0100 | $ |
| 037 | 25 | 0010 0101 | % |
| 038 | 26 | 0010 0110 | & |
| 039 | 27 | 0010 0111 | ' |
| 040 | 28 | 0010 1000 | ( |
| 041 | 29 | 0010 1001 | ) |
| 042 | 2A | 0010 1010 | * |
| 043 | 2B | 0010 1011 | + |
| 044 | 2C | 0010 1100 | , |
| 045 | 2D | 0010 1101 | - |
| 046 | 2E | 0010 1110 | . |
| 047 | 2F | 0010 1111 | / |

| *Dec* $X_{10}$ | *Hex* $X_{16}$ | *Binary* $X_2$ | *ASCII Character* |
|---|---|---|---|
| 048 | 30 | 0011 0000 | 0 |
| 049 | 31 | 0011 0001 | 1 |
| 050 | 32 | 0011 0010 | 2 |
| 051 | 33 | 0011 0011 | 3 |
| 052 | 34 | 0011 0100 | 4 |
| 053 | 35 | 0011 0101 | 5 |
| 054 | 36 | 0011 0110 | 6 |
| 055 | 37 | 0011 0111 | 7 |
| 056 | 38 | 0011 1000 | 8 |
| 057 | 39 | 0011 1001 | 9 |
| 058 | 3A | 0011 1010 | : |
| 059 | 3B | 0011 1011 | ; |
| 060 | 3C | 0011 1100 | < |
| 061 | 3D | 0011 1101 | = |
| 062 | 3E | 0011 1110 | > |
| 063 | 3F | 0011 1111 | ? |
| 064 | 40 | 0100 0000 | @ |
| 065 | 41 | 0100 0001 | A |
| 066 | 42 | 0100 0010 | B |
| 067 | 43 | 0100 0011 | C |
| 068 | 44 | 0100 0100 | D |
| 069 | 45 | 0100 0101 | E |
| 070 | 46 | 0100 0110 | F |
| 071 | 47 | 0100 0111 | G |
| 072 | 48 | 0100 1000 | H |
| 073 | 49 | 0100 1001 | I |
| 074 | 4A | 0100 1010 | J |
| 075 | 4B | 0100 1011 | K |
| 076 | 4C | 0100 1100 | L |
| 077 | 4D | 0100 1101 | M |
| 078 | 4E | 0100 1110 | N |

| Dec $X_{10}$ | Hex $X_{16}$ | Binary $X_2$ | ASCII Character |
|---|---|---|---|
| 079 | 4F | 0100 1111 | O |
| 080 | 50 | 0101 0000 | P |
| 081 | 51 | 0101 0001 | Q |
| 082 | 52 | 0101 0010 | R |
| 083 | 53 | 0101 0011 | S |
| 084 | 54 | 0101 0100 | T |
| 085 | 55 | 0101 0101 | U |
| 086 | 56 | 0101 0110 | V |
| 087 | 57 | 0101 0111 | W |
| 088 | 58 | 0101 1000 | X |
| 089 | 59 | 0101 1001 | Y |
| 090 | 5A | 0101 1010 | Z |
| 091 | 5B | 0101 1011 | [ |
| 092 | 5C | 0101 1100 | \ |
| 093 | 5D | 0101 1101 | ] |
| 094 | 5E | 0101 1110 | ^ |
| 095 | 5F | 0101 1111 | – |
| 096 | 60 | 0110 0000 | ` |
| 097 | 61 | 0110 0001 | a |
| 098 | 62 | 0110 0010 | b |
| 099 | 63 | 0110 0011 | c |
| 100 | 64 | 0110 0100 | d |
| 101 | 65 | 0110 0101 | e |
| 102 | 66 | 0110 0110 | f |
| 103 | 67 | 0110 0111 | g |
| 104 | 68 | 0110 1000 | h |
| 105 | 69 | 0110 1001 | i |
| 106 | 6A | 0110 1010 | j |
| 107 | 6B | 0110 1011 | k |
| 108 | 6C | 0110 1100 | l |
| 109 | 6D | 0110 1101 | m |

| Dec $X_{10}$ | Hex $X_{16}$ | Binary $X_2$ | ASCII Character |
|---|---|---|---|
| 110 | 6E | 0110 1110 | n |
| 111 | 6F | 0110 1111 | o |
| 112 | 70 | 0111 0000 | p |
| 113 | 71 | 0111 0001 | q |
| 114 | 72 | 0111 0010 | r |
| 115 | 73 | 0111 0011 | s |
| 116 | 74 | 0111 0100 | t |
| 117 | 75 | 0111 0101 | u |
| 118 | 76 | 0111 0110 | v |
| 119 | 77 | 0111 0111 | w |
| 120 | 78 | 0111 1000 | x |
| 121 | 79 | 0111 1001 | y |
| 122 | 7A | 0111 1010 | z |
| 123 | 7B | 0111 1011 | { |
| 124 | 7C | 0111 1100 | ¦ |
| 125 | 7D | 0111 1101 | } |
| 126 | 7E | 0111 1110 | ~ |
| 127 | 7F | 0111 1111 | DEL |
| 128 | 80 | 1000 0000 | Ç |
| 129 | 81 | 1000 0001 | ü |
| 130 | 82 | 1000 0010 | é |
| 131 | 83 | 1000 0011 | â |
| 132 | 84 | 1000 0100 | ä |
| 133 | 85 | 1000 0101 | à |
| 134 | 86 | 1000 0110 | å |
| 135 | 87 | 1000 0111 | ç |
| 136 | 88 | 1000 1000 | ê |
| 137 | 89 | 1000 1001 | ë |
| 138 | 8A | 1000 1010 | è |
| 139 | 8B | 1000 1011 | ï |
| 140 | 8C | 1000 1100 | î |

| *Dec* $X_{10}$ | *Hex* $X_{16}$ | *Binary* $X_2$ | *ASCII Character* |
|---|---|---|---|
| 141 | 8D | 1000 1101 | ì |
| 142 | 8E | 1000 1110 | Ä |
| 143 | 8F | 1000 1111 | Å |
| 144 | 90 | 1001 0000 | É |
| 145 | 91 | 1001 0001 | æ |
| 146 | 92 | 1001 0010 | Æ |
| 147 | 93 | 1001 0011 | ô |
| 148 | 94 | 1001 0100 | ö |
| 149 | 95 | 1001 0101 | ò |
| 150 | 96 | 1001 0110 | û |
| 151 | 97 | 1001 0111 | ù |
| 152 | 98 | 1001 1000 | ÿ |
| 153 | 99 | 1001 1001 | Ö |
| 154 | 9A | 1001 1010 | Ü |
| 155 | 9B | 1001 1011 | ¢ |
| 156 | 9C | 1001 1100 | £ |
| 157 | 9D | 1001 1101 | ¥ |
| 158 | 9E | 1001 1110 | ₧ |
| 159 | 9F | 1001 1111 | ƒ |
| 160 | A0 | 1010 0000 | á |
| 161 | A1 | 1010 0001 | í |
| 162 | A2 | 1010 0010 | ó |
| 163 | A3 | 1010 0011 | ú |
| 164 | A4 | 1010 0100 | ñ |
| 165 | A5 | 1010 0101 | Ñ |
| 166 | A6 | 1010 0110 | ª |
| 167 | A7 | 1010 0111 | º |
| 168 | A8 | 1010 1000 | ¿ |
| 169 | A9 | 1010 1001 | ⌐ |
| 170 | AA | 1010 1010 | ¬ |
| 171 | AB | 1010 1011 | ½ |

| *Dec* $X_{10}$ | *Hex* $X_{16}$ | *Binary* $X_{2}$ | *ASCII Character* |
|---|---|---|---|
| 172 | AC | 1010 1100 | ¼ |
| 173 | AD | 1010 1101 | ¡ |
| 174 | AE | 1010 1110 | « |
| 175 | AF | 1010 1111 | » |
| 176 | B0 | 1011 0000 | ░ |
| 177 | B1 | 1011 0001 | ▒ |
| 178 | B2 | 1011 0010 | ▓ |
| 179 | B3 | 1011 0011 | │ |
| 180 | B4 | 1011 0100 | ┤ |
| 181 | B5 | 1011 0101 | ╡ |
| 182 | B6 | 1011 0110 | ╢ |
| 183 | B7 | 1011 0111 | ╖ |
| 184 | B8 | 1011 1000 | ╕ |
| 185 | B9 | 1011 1001 | ╣ |
| 186 | BA | 1011 1010 | ║ |
| 187 | BB | 1011 1011 | ╗ |
| 188 | BC | 1011 1100 | ╝ |
| 189 | BD | 1011 1101 | ╜ |
| 190 | BE | 1011 1110 | ╛ |
| 191 | BF | 1011 1111 | ┐ |
| 192 | C0 | 1100 0000 | └ |
| 193 | C1 | 1100 0001 | ┴ |
| 194 | C2 | 1100 0010 | ┬ |
| 195 | C3 | 1100 0011 | ├ |
| 196 | C4 | 1100 0100 | ─ |
| 197 | C5 | 1100 0101 | ┼ |
| 198 | C6 | 1100 0110 | ╞ |
| 199 | C7 | 1100 0111 | ╟ |
| 200 | C8 | 1100 1000 | ╚ |
| 201 | C9 | 1100 1001 | ╔ |
| 202 | CA | 1100 1010 | ╩ |

| Dec $X_{10}$ | Hex $X_{16}$ | Binary $X_2$ | ASCII Character |
|---|---|---|---|
| 203 | CB | 1100 1011 | ╦ |
| 204 | CC | 1100 1100 | ╠ |
| 205 | CD | 1100 1101 | ═ |
| 206 | CE | 1100 1110 | ╬ |
| 207 | CF | 1100 1111 | ╧ |
| 208 | D0 | 1101 0000 | ╨ |
| 209 | D1 | 1101 0001 | ╤ |
| 210 | D2 | 1101 0010 | ╥ |
| 211 | D3 | 1101 0011 | ╙ |
| 212 | D4 | 1101 0100 | ╘ |
| 213 | D5 | 1101 0101 | ╒ |
| 214 | D6 | 1101 0110 | ╓ |
| 215 | D7 | 1101 0111 | ╫ |
| 216 | D8 | 1101 1000 | ╪ |
| 217 | D9 | 1101 1001 | ┘ |
| 218 | DA | 1101 1010 | ┌ |
| 219 | DB | 1101 1011 | █ |
| 220 | DC | 1101 1100 | ▄ |
| 221 | DD | 1101 1101 | ▌ |
| 222 | DE | 1101 1110 | ▐ |
| 223 | DF | 1101 1111 | ▀ |
| 224 | E0 | 1110 0000 | α |
| 225 | E1 | 1110 0001 | β |
| 226 | E2 | 1110 0010 | Γ |
| 227 | E3 | 1110 0011 | π |
| 228 | E4 | 1110 0100 | Σ |
| 229 | E5 | 1110 0101 | σ |
| 230 | E6 | 1110 0110 | μ |
| 231 | E7 | 1110 0111 | τ |
| 232 | E8 | 1110 1000 | Φ |
| 233 | E9 | 1110 1001 | θ |

| *Dec* $X_{10}$ | *Hex* $X_{16}$ | *Binary* $X_2$ | *ASCII Character* |
|---|---|---|---|
| 234 | EA | 1110 1010 | Ω |
| 235 | EB | 1110 1011 | δ |
| 236 | EC | 1110 1100 | ∞ |
| 237 | ED | 1110 1101 | ø |
| 238 | EE | 1110 1110 | ∈ |
| 239 | EF | 1110 1111 | ∩ |
| 240 | F0 | 1111 0000 | ≡ |
| 241 | F1 | 1111 0001 | ± |
| 242 | F2 | 1111 0010 | ≥ |
| 243 | F3 | 1111 0011 | ≤ |
| 244 | F4 | 1111 0100 | ⌠ |
| 245 | F5 | 1111 0101 | ⌡ |
| 246 | F6 | 1111 0110 | ÷ |
| 247 | F7 | 1111 0111 | ≈ |
| 248 | F8 | 1111 1000 | ° |
| 249 | F9 | 1111 1001 | • |
| 250 | FA | 1111 1010 | · |
| 251 | FB | 1111 1011 | √ |
| 252 | FC | 1111 1100 | η |
| 253 | FD | 1111 1101 | ² |
| 254 | FE | 1111 1110 | ■ |
| 255 | FF | 1111 1111 | |

# Keyboard Codes

D

APPENDIX

Chapter 10, "Customizing the Keyboard," showed you how to get all kinds of cheap thrills by using the `PROMPT` and `ECHO` commands to reconfigure your keyboard. Here's a table of keyboard codes you can use with these commands, including the appropriate codes for using the keys with Shift, Ctrl, and Alt.

Guru Tip

When using this table, keep an eye on the codes in parentheses. Your exterded keyboard may not accept these codes unless you load ANSI.SYS with the /X switch. If you can't get these codes to work at all, check your computer documentation (if you dare). It ought to let you in on whatever keyboard quirks the company's engineers came up with.

| Key | Code | Shift+Key | Ctrl+Key | Alt+Key |
|---|---|---|---|---|
| | | Function Keys: | | |
| F1 | 0;59 | 0;84 | 0;94 | 0;104 |
| F2 | 0;60 | 0;85 | 0;95 | 0;105 |
| F3 | 0;61 | 0;86 | 0;96 | 0;106 |
| F4 | 0;62 | 0;87 | 0;97 | 0;107 |
| F5 | 0;63 | 0;88 | 0;98 | 0;108 |
| F6 | 0;64 | 0;89 | 0;99 | 0;109 |
| F7 | 0;65 | 0;90 | 0;100 | 0;110 |
| F8 | 0;66 | 0;91 | 0;101 | 0;111 |
| F9 | 0;67 | 0;92 | 0;102 | 0;112 |
| F10 | 0;68 | 0;93 | 0;103 | 0;113 |
| F11 | 0;133 | 0;135 | 0;137 | 0;139 |
| F12 | 0;134 | 0;136 | 0;138 | 0;140 |
| | | Numeric Keypad: | | |
| Home | 0;71 | 55 | 0;119 | - |
| Up arrow | 0;72 | 56 | (0;141) | - |
| Page Up | 0;73 | 57 | 0;132 | - |

| Key | Code | Shift+Key | Ctrl+Key | Alt+Key |
|---|---|---|---|---|
| Left arrow | 0;75 | 52 | 0;115 | - |
| 5 | (0;76) | 53 | (0;143) | - |
| Right arrow | 0;77 | 54 | 0;116 | - |
| End | 0;79 | 49 | 0;117 | - |
| Down arrow | 0;80 | 50 | (0;145) | - |
| Page Down | 0;81 | 51 | 0;118 | - |
| Insert | 0;82 | 48 | (0;146) | - |
| Delete | 0;83 | 46 | (0;147) | - |
| Enter | 13 | - | 10 | (0;166) |
| * | 42 | (0;144) | (0;78) | - |
| + | 43 | 43 | (0;150) | (0;55) |
| - | 45 | 45 | (0;149) | (0;164) |
| / | 47 | 47 | (0;142) | (0;74) |
| | | Cursor Keypad: | | |
| Home | (224;71) | (224;71) | (224;119) | (224;151) |
| Up arrow | (224;72) | (224;72) | (224;141) | (224;152) |
| Page Up | (224;73) | (224;73) | (224;132) | (224;153) |
| Left arrow | (224;75) | (224;75) | (224;115) | (224;155) |
| Right arrow | (224;77) | (224;77) | (224;116) | (224;157) |
| End | (224;79) | (224;79) | (224;117) | (224;159) |
| Down arrow | (224;80) | (224;80) | (224;145) | (224;154) |
| Page Down | (224;81) | (224;81) | (224;118) | (224;161) |
| Insert | (224;82) | (224;82) | (224;146) | (224;162) |
| Delete | (224;83) | (224;83) | (224;147) | (224;163) |

| Key | Code | Shift+Key | Ctrl+Key | Alt+Key |
|---|---|---|---|---|
| | | Alphanumeric Keypad: | | |
| A | 97 | 65 | 1 | 0;30 |
| B | 98 | 66 | 2 | 0;48 |
| C | 99 | 67 | 3 | 0;46 |
| D | 100 | 68 | 4 | 0;32 |
| E | 101 | 69 | 5 | 0;18 |
| F | 102 | 70 | 6 | 0;33 |
| G | 103 | 71 | 7 | 0;34 |
| H | 104 | 72 | 8 | 0;35 |
| I | 105 | 73 | 9 | 0;23 |
| J | 106 | 74 | 10 | 0;36 |
| K | 107 | 75 | 11 | 0;37 |
| L | 108 | 76 | 12 | 0;38 |
| M | 109 | 77 | 13 | 0;50 |
| N | 110 | 78 | 14 | 0;49 |
| O | 111 | 79 | 15 | 0;24 |
| P | 112 | 80 | 16 | 0;25 |
| Q | 113 | 81 | 17 | 0;16 |
| R | 114 | 82 | 18 | 0;19 |
| S | 115 | 83 | 19 | 0;31 |
| T | 116 | 84 | 20 | 0;20 |
| U | 117 | 85 | 21 | 0;22 |
| V | 118 | 86 | 22 | 0;47 |
| W | 119 | 87 | 23 | 0;17 |

| Key | Code | Shift+Key | Ctrl+Key | Alt+Key |
|---|---|---|---|---|
| X | 120 | 88 | 24 | 0;45 |
| Y | 121 | 89 | 25 | 0;21 |
| Z | 122 | 90 | 26 | 0;44 |
| 0 | 48 | 41 | - | 0;129 |
| 1 | 49 | 33 | - | 0;120 |
| 2 | 50 | 64 | 0 | 0;121 |
| 3 | 51 | 35 | - | 0;122 |
| 4 | 52 | 36 | - | 0;123 |
| 5 | 53 | 37 | - | 0;124 |
| 6 | 54 | 94 | 30 | 0;125 |
| 7 | 55 | 38 | - | 0;126 |
| 8 | 56 | 42 | - | 0;127 |
| 9 | 57 | 40 | - | 0;128 |
| ' (apostrophe) | 39 | 34 | - | 0;40 |
| , (comma) | 44 | 60 | - | 0;51 |
| - | 45 | 95 | 31 | 0;130 |
| . | 46 | 62 | - | 0;52 |
| / | 47 | 63 | - | 0;53 |
| ; | 59 | 58 | - | 0;39 |
| = | 61 | 43 | - | 0;131 |
| [ | 91 | 123 | 27 | 0;26 |
| \ | 92 | 124 | 28 | 0;43 |
| ] | 93 | 125 | 29 | 0;27 |
| ' (single quote) | 96 | 126 | - | (0;41) |

| Key | Code | Shift+Key | Ctrl+Key | Alt+Key |
|---|---|---|---|---|
| | | Miscellaneous: | | |
| Enter | 13 | - | 10 | (0;28) |
| Tab | 9 | 0;15 | (0;148) | (0;165) |
| Backspace | 8 | 8 | 127 | (0) |
| Print Screen | - | - | 0;114 | - |
| Pause | - | - | 0;0 | - |

E

APPENDIX

# Guru Tools Directory

Here are the names, addresses, and phone numbers of the vendors mentioned in the Guru Tools sections of this book.

**386MAX**
Qualitas
7101 Wisconsin Ave., Ste 1386
Bethesda, MD 20814
(800) 733-1377

**4DOS**
JP Software Inc.
P.O. Box 1470
East Arlington, MA 02174
(800) 368-8777

**America Online**
8619 Westwood Center Dr.
Vienna, VA 22182
(800) 827-6364

**BootSys**
Public Software Library
P.O. Box 35705
Houston, TX 77235
(713) 524-6394

**CompuServe**
5000 Arlington Center Blvd.
Columbus, OH 43220
(800) 848-8199
San Rafael, CA 94901

**Data Security Plus**
PC Guardian
(800) 288-8126

**Fastback Plus**
Fifth Generation Systems, Inc.
10049 North Reiger Road
Baton Rouge, LA 70809
(800) 873-4384

**FastLock Plus**
Rupp Software
(800) 852-7877

**FormatQM**
SYDEX
P.O. Box 5700
Eugene, OR 97405
(503) 683-6033

**GEnie**
401 North Washington Street
Rockville, MD 20850
(800) 638-9636

**List 7.6**
Buerg Software
850 Petaluma Blvd. N. Ste F
Petaluma, CA 94952
(707) 769-5478

**Norton Utilities**
**The Norton Backup**
Symantec Corp.
10210 Torre Road
Cupertino, CA 95014
(800) 441-7234

**PC/DACS**
Pyramid Development
70 Inwood Rd.
Rocky Hill, CT 06067
(203) 257-4223

**PCOPY**
Norm Patriquin
P.O. Box 8308
San Bernadino, CA 92412

**PC Tools**
**Central Point Backup**
Central Point Software
15220 NW Greenbrier Pkwy.
Beaverton, OR 97006
(800) 445-4208

**Prodigy**
445 Hamilton Avenue
White Plains, NY 10601
(800) 776-3449

**Public Brand Software**
P.O. Box 51315
Indianapolis, IN 46251
(800) 426-3475

**QEMM-386**
Quarterdeck Office Systems
150 Pico Boulevard
Santa Monica, CA 90405
(800) 354-3222

**Stacker**
Stac Electronics
5993 Avenida Encinas
Carlsbad, CA 92008
(800) 522-7822

**SuperStor**
AddStor Inc.
3905 Bohannon Drive
Menlo Park, CA 94025
(415) 688-0470

# Index

## Symbols

## C

## D

## E

## G

## K



## L

## M

## N

## Q

## T

## W



## X-Z

Book ISBN 0-672-30349-3